JOURNALS OF THE PRIEST
IOANN VENIAMINOV
IN ALASKA, 1823 TO 1836

The Rasmuson Library
Historical Translation Series
Volume VII
Marvin W. Falk, Editor

Additional titles in the Series:

THE GREAT RUSSIAN NAVIGATOR, A. I. CHIRIKOV. By Vasilii A. Divin. Translated and annotated by Raymond H. Fisher. RLHTS Volume VI, 1993.

THE KHLEBNIKOV ARCHIVE. UNPUBLISHED JOURNAL (1800-1837) AND TRAVEL NOTES (1820, 1822, and 1824). Edited with introduction and notes by Leonid Shur. Translated by John Bisk. RLHTS Volume V, 1990.

RUSSIAN EXPLORATION IN SOUTHWEST ALASKA: THE TRAVEL JOURNALS OF PETR KORSAKOVSKIY (1818) AND IVAN YA. VASILEV (1829). Edited with introduction by James W. VanStone. Translated by David H. Kraus. RLHTS Volume IV, 1988.

BERING'S VOYAGES: THE REPORTS FROM RUSSIA. By Gerhard Friedrich Müller. Translated, with commentary by Carol Urness. RLHTS Volume III, 1986.

TLINGIT INDIANS OF ALASKA. By Archimandrite Anatolii Kamenskii. Translated, with an Introduction and Supplementary Material by Sergei Kan. RLHTS Volume II, 1985.

HOLMBERG'S ETHNOGRAPHIC SKETCHES. By Heinrich Johan Holmberg. Edited by Marvin W. Falk. Translated from the original German of 1855-1863 by Fritz Jaensch. RLHTS Volume I, 1985.

NOTES ON THE ISLANDS OF THE UNALASKHA DISTRICT. By Ivan Veniaminov. Translated by Lydia T. Black and R. H. Geoghegan. Edited with an introduction by Richard A. Pierce. Published jointly by the Elmer E. Rasmuson Library Translation Program and the Limestone Press, 1984.

All titles listed are available from the University of Alaska Press.

JOURNALS OF THE PRIEST
IOANN VENIAMINOV
IN ALASKA, 1823 TO 1836

Translated by Jerome Kisslinger

Introduction and commentary
by S. A. Mousalimas

University of Alaska Press
Fairbanks, 1993

Library of Congress Cataloging-in-Publication Data

Innokentiĭ, Saint, Metropolitan of Moscow and Kolomna, 1797-1879.
    Journals of the priest Ioann Veniaminov in Alaska, 1823 to 1836 /
translated by Jerome Kisslinger ; introduction and commentary by
S. A. Mousalimas.
    p. cm. -- (The Rasmuson Library historical translation series
; v. 7)
    Includes bibliographical references and index.
    ISBN 0-912006-64-2
    1. Innokentiĭ, Saint, Metropolitan of Moscow and Kolomna,
1797-111879--Diaries. 2. Orthodox Eastern Church--Alaska--Bishops-
-Diaries. 3. Russkaia pravoslavnaia tserkov'--Alaska--Bishops-
-Diaries. 4. Alaska--Church history. 5. Alaska--Description and
travel--To 1867. I. Mousalimas, S. A. II. Title. III. Series.
BX597.I55A3 1993
281.9'092--dc20   92-44542
[B]   CIP

International Standard Series Number: 0890-7935
International Standard Book Number: 0-912006-64-1
Library of Congress Catalog Card Number: 92-44542
English Translation © 1993 by The University of Alaska Press.
All rights reserved. Published 1993.

"A story about Father Veniaminov" by Ismail Gromoff,
page 211, reprinted with permission.
The story originally appeared in Aleut for Beginners,
Aleut Language Instruction, Unalaska City School, 1975, pp. 33-34.

Printed in the United States of America
by McNaughton & Gunn, Inc. on recycled and acid-free paper.

This publication was printed on acid-free paper that meets the minimum
requirements of American National Standard for Information Sciences-
Permanence for Paper for Printed Library Materials, ANSI Z39.48-1984.

Publication coordination and production by Deborah Van Stone,
with assistance from Katherine L. Arndt and Pamela Odom.

Cover graphic: Pectoral cross reproduced from
Zakon Bozhii Rukovodstvo dlia sem'i i shkoly,
by Priest Serafim Slobodskoi.
Published by Holy Trinity Monastery, Jordanville, New York, 1957.

CONTENTS

Foreword by Alice Petrivelli   vii

Foreword by Bishop Kallistos of Diokleia   ix

Introduction by S. A. Mousalimas   xiii

Journals of the Priest Ioann Veniaminov

Journal No. 1, October 20, 1823, to May 1, 1824,
Island of Sitka   3

Journal No. 2, July 29, 1824, to July 1, 1825,
Unalaska   17

Journal No. 3, July 1, 1825, to July 1, 1826,
Unalaska   37

Jouranl No. 4, April 17, 1827, to July 15, 1827,
Unalaska   49

Journal No. 5, July 1, 1827, to July 1, 1828,
Unalaska   57

Journal No. 6, July 1, 1828, to June 21, 1829,
Unalaska   85

Journal No. 7, June 21, 1829, to July 1, 1830,
Unalaska   107

Journal No. 8, July 1, 1830, to July 1, 1831,
Unalaska   129

Journal No. 9, July 1, 1831, to September 1, 1832,
Unalaska   149

Journal No. 10, September 1, 1832, to September 1, 1833,
Unalaska   167

Journal No. 11, September 1, 1833, to August 15, 1834,
Unalaska   185

Excerpt from the Journal of the Priest Ioann Veniaminov,
   August 23, 1834, to May 1836, Sitka   197

Travel Journal of the Priest Ioann Veniaminov,
   July 1, 1836, to October 13, 1836, to California and back
   to Sitka   201

Afterword by Father Ismail Gromoff   211

Index   213

FOREWORD
by Alice Petrivelli

With these journals, we now have a work through which we may read Aleut history as it was taking place at the time. We may read, for instance, an account of a man of one origin, the Aleut toion Ivan Pan'kov, coming together with a man of another origin, the Russian priest Ivan (Ioann) Veniaminov, to produce through their cooperation the first literature published in the Aleut language. The process is chronicled. Other people who contributed are mentioned by name. We may read of bilingual elders gathering to perfect the syntax, and we may read of whole villages gathering to hear the work recited. May their intellectual and spiritual aspirations be our inspiration.

This history pertains particularly to the Aleut religion, and it is their religion that has sustained our people. "The fruits of the Word of God are evident," Veniaminov wrote about our ancestors, "even quite evident." May their achievements be ours.

Many people might be unaware of all that Fr. Veniaminov accomplished. Now, through these journals, they may become familiar with his dedication, his achievements in strengthening the Aleuts spiritually, and indeed his own spiritual and physical strengths, for he endured many hardships to achieve his goals.

A man of such genius and such innate gifts chose to come to the Aleutians, where he gave much more than he received. In return, he knew our ancestors' gratitude and respect. We feel the same about him today.

Alice Petrivelli
President, the Aleut Foundation

FOREWORD
by Bishop Kallistos of Diokleia

The author of these journals, the priest Ivan (Ioann) Veniaminov (1797-1879)—he subsequently took the monastic name Innokentii—was a person of exceptionally varied gifts. What strikes us first of all, as we read these pages, is his physical stamina. Strong and athletic—'standing in his boots about six feet three inches: quite herculean,' states a British visitor to Sitka in 1837—Fr. Ivan undertook exhausting journeys of many months' duration throughout his vast parish. Sometimes he travelled overland on foot, but more often by sea along a notoriously treacherous coast, usually in a kayak, 'with not a single plank to save you from death—just skins,' as he remarked on one occasion.

Energetic and versatile, Fr. Ivan seems never to be idle. He was gifted with his hands and practical, supervising the construction of church buildings, and himself making a clock for the church tower at Sitka, as well as furniture for his own home and even musical instruments. At the same time he was intellectually gifted; although he made no claim to be a trained scholar, he was full of scientific curiosity, observant, tireless and exact in collecting data.

From the start, one of his overriding concerns was to communicate with the native people in their own language. As he records in the first pages of these journals, long before he had even reached his assigned post in Unalaska he had commenced learning Aleut. Soon he was busy compiling a grammar and a dictionary, as well as translating parts of the New Testament. He worked quickly and for long hours each day: beginning his version of St. Matthew's Gospel on 10 September 1829, he had already completed the first draft two weeks later on 24 September. Yet he was at the same time highly conscientious, checking and rechecking his renderings with the help of native Aleut experts. He also wrote in Aleut a vivid account of the Christian faith that he had himself composed, *An Indication of the Path to the Heavenly Kingdom*. Himself an intrepid traveller, he saw the Christian life as a way or journey.

Besides this, he found time to study and record the traditions of the native peoples, and his imaginative research in this field forms today a vital first-hand source. His interest extended to the flora and fauna of the region, and we find him busy compiling meteorological records. Long before the word 'ecology' had become fashionable, he was a true ecologist, protecting threatened species and caring for the natural environment.

It has to be remembered that in addition to all this he was performing the normal duties of an Orthodox parish priest, celebrating the daily services, preaching, teaching, baptizing, hearing confessions, visiting the sick. He was moreover a married man with responsibility for a growing family (his wife died in 1839, shortly after the period covered by these journals). He even managed to keep up with his own personal reading, as the notes in his journals testify. The range is impressive: 'a detailed guide to the raising of children,' 'a glossary of technical words,' and such Western authors as Thomas à Kempis, Voltaire and Chateaubriand. He could make good use of what he read: Sir George Simpson, who met him in 1842, remarks that 'his conversation teems with amusement and instruction.'

Despite the factual and formal character of the journals—they were reports to the diocesan office in Irkutsk—and despite their author's modesty, the extraordinary amount that he achieved in the thirteen years that they describe (1823-1836) is plainly apparent. It is an astonishing record.

Along with his energy, at least three other qualities impress us as we read this narrative: his love for the people to whom he ministered, his openness, and his humility. The love was returned, as can be seen from the warm and at times enthusiastic reception that he received on his pastoral journeys. The openness is evident particularly in the account of his visit to California during July-September 1836: he took a keen interest in the work of the Spanish missionaries, and there is no sign of any defensive hostility towards them because of their Roman Catholicism. The humility is clear not least when on rare occasions he quietly commends his own work: 'It is not boasting for me to say that this translation was carried out through unremitting labour' (24 September 1829: of the Aleut version of St. Matthew); 'We checked our translations of the Catechism...They found no errors' (22 August 1830).

The same humility is reflected in the words quoted by Aleksei Khomiakov, which Bishop Innokentii (as he had now become) later used to describe his episcopal ministry: 'The bishop is at the same time both the teacher and the disciple of his flock.' If he proved so influential as teacher and pastor, it was because he was willing to listen to the native Alaskans and to learn from them. That influence continues up to the present. Honoured today in the Orthodox Church as a saint, he is still remembered with sincere gratitude in Alaska—and far beyond.

Bishop Kallistos of Diokleia
Pembroke College, Oxford University

INTRODUCTION
by S. A. Mousalimas

These twelve journals comprise formal reports by Ivan (Ioann) Veniaminov to his diocesan office at Irkutsk, written by him while he was the first priest assigned to the Unalashka (Unalaska) parish, and the second assigned to the Novo-Arkhangel'sk (Sitka) parish. They encompass a period of time from September 1823 to September 1836. The original manuscripts are located at the Alaska State Historical Library in Juneau, Alaska, with microfilm copies in other repositories such as the Library of Congress and the University of Alaska Fairbanks.

The following introduction consists of:

> (1) an indication of the journals' general content;
> (2) an explanation of some technical terms and concepts;
> (3) a description of the formation of the Unalaska parish
>   by the laity beginning in 1761, three generations
>   before Veniaminov's arrival;
> (4) an example of the journals' usefulness as a source for
>   Aleut history;
> (5) an example of the journals' usefulness as a source for
>   Veniaminov's ministry and character.

(1) The Journals' General Content

The initial journal records Veniaminov's stay at Sitka, on arrival from Irkutsk by way of Okhotsk, from 20 October 1823 to 30 April 1824, before assuming his assignment at Unalaska. The last journal from 23 August 1834 to September 1836 records a portion of his ministry as priest of the Sitka parish, following Unalaska. The last journal also includes the account of a trip to Fort Ross and into the newly independent Republic of California. The ten journals for the intervening years, comprising the majority of the text, provide reports of his decade in the Unalaska parish.

The majority of the text thus refers to the Unalaska parish, and its journal entries locate villages, provide insights into village leadership, describe travel routes and travel conditions, and specify modes of transportation throughout this vast parish. Indeed the parish was vast: it extended from Unalaska Island eastward to Unga Island and the tip of the Alaska Peninsula to encompass the villages of Grekodeliarovskii, Morzhovoi, Belkofski, and Pavlof; westward along the Aleutians to Umnak Island to encompass the village of Recheshnoe (Nikolski); then northward to the Pribilof Islands in the Bering Sea. Veniaminov made pastoral visits to various locations through this enormous parish during the summer and spring months of that decade. During autumns and winters, he remained mostly in Unalaska's harbor village (Iliuliuk; present-day Unalaska).

In addition to references such as these for the Aleuts, the journals contain significant accounts regarding the Nushagak region Yupiit, when Veniaminov visited Nushagak on two occasions. One of these entries constitutes an extended report, and both contribute essential information for Yup'ik history.[1] Some references to the Tlingits are contained in the journal from the Sitka years.[2] And references to Californian Indians (Pomo, probably) can be found in entries from the journey south to Fort Ross.[3]

Fort Ross itself is described.[4] The entries for the subsequent journey farther south across "the boundaries of Russia," as Veniaminov expressed it, into California describe some of the Roman Catholic missions of the San Francisco Bay area, soon after that republic's newly gained independence. The description of Mission San Jose is the most detailed.[5]

Beyond details such as these, complete themes can be extracted from the journals, but these themes exist under the surface of the entries. They come to light when the journals' technicalities become transparent, and when Veniaminov's ministry is placed within the Unalaska region's prior history.

(2) An Explanation of Terms and Concepts

Comprising a formal report to a diocesan office, the journals contain some technical terms and presuppose certain concepts that will be explained below, as follows:

(2.1) "church" and "communion cloth";
(2.2) "tent" and the concept of sacred space;

xiv

(2.3) the use of a sacred language in worship;
(2.4) the numbering of Sundays, and the annual cycles of
liturgics;
(2.5) the conduct of ritual by the laity.

(2.1) The vast parish is referred to as the "Unalaska church." A church contains an altar where the Divine Liturgy can be celebrated for Holy Communion. Upon the altar, a smaller cloth is placed. Embroidered with symbols of Christ and containing relics of His saints, the cloth is known as an antimins.[6] And upon the antimins, the gifts of wine in the chalice and bread on the paten are placed when brought to the altar in procession. This symbolic cloth is a prerequisite for the celebration of the Liturgy, and is entrusted to the parish priest by his bishop.

Veniaminov was the first priest to have brought an antimins to the Aleutians, and was therefore the first to celebrate the Divine Liturgy there. This explains his statement in the journal on 1 August 1824, soon after his arrival at Unalaska, when he declared: "I celebrated the Liturgy in the chapel sanctuary on the portable communion cloth [the antimins] for the first time since the birth of Christ and even since the creation of the world."

(2.2) Where a chapel had not yet been built, Veniaminov most often pitched a tent for liturgical services. When he visited that village again, he pitched a tent anew at the same site.[7] Especially sacred space was thus defined. The same dynamic is found in the ministry of Iakov Netsvetov as priest of the neighboring Atka parish (1828-1844) and as missionary in the Yukon and Kuskokwim River regions (1845-1863).[8] At the site where the liturgy had been celebrated, a village chapel would probably be built.

(2.3) Related to the concept of sacred space is the use of a sacred language. The apparent dichotomy of sacred and profane is mitigated in both instances: in the first case, by rituals within nature proper[9] and at home; in the second case, by the inclusion of the vernacular language in worship. Instead of a strict dichotomy the interpretation, therefore, may involve either the permeability of categories or alternatively the coinherence of the sacred with the profane.

Among the Aleuts as among other Alaskans, the primary sacred language was, and largely remains, Slavonic. The liturgical language of the Slavs and of the native peoples of northern Eurasia, it derives from translations from the original Greek during the ministry of Sts. Cyril and

Methodius in the 9th century. Interestingly, the translations into formal Aleut accomplished at the millenium, in the l9th century, have become a sacred language along with Slavonic for present Aleut generations.

To what extent was the Aleut language incorporated into worship during Veniaminov's ministry? The question must remain open. Yet a fact is certain: that neither language displaced the other. This is evident in the journals where both languages are reported in worship, and it is clearly evident in subsequent history when Slavonic and Aleut were both taught by multilingual elders to the community youth, well into the mid-20th century. The two languages were complementary. No precedent for a monolingual policy will be found in these journals during Veniaminov's constructive ministry, nor in subsequent Aleut history.

(2.4) Many Sundays are numbered throughout the journals. Their numbering is based on the date of Easter for that year. Pentecost follows Easter by fifty days, and the Sundays begin to be numbered after Pentecost. The numbering progresses towards Great Lent, then ceases as preparations commence for the following Easter.

This yearly rotation constitutes the Paschal cycle. It involves Great Lent, Palm Sunday and Holy Week prior to Easter; and then Ascension as well as Pentecost afterwards. While the intervals between these events remain constant, the calendar dates vary with the exact date of Easter within each year.

There is another annual cycle, but its calendar dates do not vary: they are fixed. For example, the Nativity, Epiphany, Annunciation, Transfiguration, and Dormition always take place respectively on 25 December, 6 January, 25 March, 6 August, and 15 August.

Like a wheel within a wheel, the two yearly cycles—the Paschal and the fixed—will coincide slightly differently with each rotation, that is to say, with each year. Variety thus occurs, as the meanings for coinciding commemorations come together in hymns, icons, scripture readings, and sermons. This coinciding of cycles is reflected in the journals on 7 January 1824 when Veniaminov teaches from the Gospel readings for "the 29th Sunday of Pentecost" (on the Paschal cycle) and for "the week before Epiphany" (on the fixed cycle). It was the coordination of these liturgical movements, or cycles, that Veniaminov was imparting at Unalaska on 30 October 1832.

(2.5) Laity will conduct rituals modified according to ability and circumstance. Rubrics will be abbreviated to the minimum when the expertise is minimal or when texts are unavailable. (Conversely, rubrics may be observed with detail.) Noncontingent on expert knowledge, noncontingent also on a complete set of liturgical texts, corporate worship as well as the basic life-crisis sacraments (baptism and funeral) are always possible whether in a village or a hunting camp, in a chapel or a iurt.[10]

Throughout Veniaminov's ministry, village laity were conducting the basic life-crisis sacraments (baptisms, funerals). This vital fact is evident in the journals in the records of the sacraments he ministered. Rarely did he baptize: he would chrismate the newly baptized. Very rarely did he bury: he would sometimes lead a memorial service. Only at the harbor village, Unalaska Island, where he himself remained most of the year, did he conduct baptisms and funerals regularly. Elsewhere the villagers were ministering these sacraments themselves. When he visited villages, he conducted those sacraments that require an ordained minister: chrismation, confession, and communion. For a marriage, he "sacramentally blessed" the couple (a phrase from the journals): in other words, he performed the complete marriage ceremony for a couple who had already been bonded through local customs.

(3) The Formation of the Unalaska Parish Prior to Veniaminov's Arrival.

Orthodox services were being conducted by the Aleut laity throughout the region when Veniaminov arrived. Yet he was the first priest of the parish. How had this parish come into being? The formation of the Unalaska parish was a movement and development by the laity beginning three generations prior to Veniaminov's arrival. This can be explained with reference to:

(3.1) a chronology of the clergy prior to him;
(3.2) social dynamics that brought forth Eastern Orthodox
      leadership: (.i) intermarriage, and earlier
      (.ii) alliances;
(3.3) a native social process in the upbringing of baptized
      men who succeeded their elder kinsmen as toions;

(3. 4) the merging of faith and polity:
        (.i) the successful exercise of leadership by Aleut
        Orthodox on behalf of their people, in the 1780s
        and 1790s;
        (.ii) the continuity of leadership from the 1760s;
        (.iii) examples of this merging from the 1760s into the time
        of these journals.

(3.1) *Chronology of clergy prior to Veniaminov.* No clergyman had been assigned as a missionary to the Aleutian Islands before Fr. Ivan Veniaminov arrived as the parish priest in 1824, except one who served a year, from summer 1795 to summer 1796: the hieromonk (priest-monk) Makarii whose ministry was located mainly on Unalaska Island.[11]

Other clergy in transit had made brief landfalls at Unalaska Island, the port-of-call for east-west voyages between Okhotsk-Kamchatka and Kodiak-Sitka, and for north-south voyages between the north Pacific and the Bering Sea. Their combined total of time amounted to less than a year. A chronology is provided below:

   (a) Briefly in 1790: Fr. Vasilii Sivtsov, chaplain to the
       Slava Rossii, Billings/Sarychev expedition, per-
       formed baptisms and marriages.[12]
   (b) Two days in September 1794: missionaries in transit
       from Okhotsk to Kodiak Island stopped at
       'Unalaska. They also harbored through inclement
       weather at a remote bay on the same island. They
       performed baptisms.[13]
   (c) A week in July 1807: hieromonk Gideon in transit from
       Kodiak to Okhotsk performed baptisms,
       chrismations, and marriages at Unalaska.[14]
   (d) During a period in June 1820, at the end of August
       1820, and mid-June 1821: Fr. Mikhail Ivanov,
       chaplain to the Vasil'ev/Shishmarev
       circumnavigatory expedition on the
       Blagonamerennyi, may have landed while that
       vessel was anchored in the Unalaska harbor.[15]
   (e) August 1824: Veniaminov arrived as the parish priest

and recorded nearly the same list of clergy in the
region before him, but without the chronological
details.[16]

In summary, prior to Veniaminov's arrival a single missionary had been
assigned who had served for a year. Otherwise, chaplains and missionaries
in transit had made landfalls at Unalaska Island alone, for a combined total
of less than a year. The total combined time of all clergymen before
Veniaminov's arrival thus amounted to less than two years.

(3.2) *Social dynamics that brought forth Native Eastern Orthodox leaders
on the Aleutian Islands.* The interval between the first baptism in the
Unalaska region in 1762 and Veniaminov's arrival as the first parish priest
in 1824, three generations later—a sixty-two year interval—had been
punctuated sporadically by clergy for two years or less, mainly on a single
island, Unalaska. Yet when Veniaminov arrived sacraments were already
being performed by laity throughout the region,[17]and he was assigned as
the priest of an existing parish—a parish made up of Aleut villages, or
polities.

The history in the neighboring Atkha (Atka) parish is even more
impressive in this respect. Encompassing the central and western Aleutian
Islands, this region knew its first baptism by 1747. Four generations later
in 1828 the first clergyman Fr. Iakov Netsvetov arrived, likewise assigned
as the parish priest. Yet never had a clergyman been in these regions prior
to him; and he himself had roots here: his mother, Maria, was an Atkan
Aleut.

How had such Orthodox leadership developed prior to the arrival of
parish priests? (i) Intermarriage was one social dynamic that brought it
forth. An example is provided by the parents of Fr. Iakov Netsvetov. His
mother Maria Alekseeva from Atka married his father Egor Vasil'evich
from Tobol'sk, a man of particular piety.[18] He had arrived in 1794 within
the second generation following the first baptisms on the central and
eastern Aleutians. The couple was married according to local customs; and
their first child Iakov was born in 1804. In July 1807, they had their
marriage blessed sacramentally by hieromonk Gideon; the only priest in
this region since 1796, he had landed at Unalaska for a week while
journeying from Kodiak to Okhotsk. It is significant that the couple

sought him. They received an anointing with blessed oil from him, as well. At that date, Egor was 34 years old and Maria was in her 20s, according to Gideon's records.[19] They raised a family of six children on St. George, Pribilof Islands, a location that eventually became part of the Unalaska parish. All their children distinguished themselves: one son as a master shipwright; another as a navigator; one daughter as the wife of a company manager at Sitka; another as the wife of a Russian-Aleut educated at Petersburg; and the eldest son Iakov as a graduate of the Irkutsk seminary, then as the first priest of the Atka parish (1828-1844). Later, Iakov became the first clergy missionary to the Yukon and Kuskokwim River regions (1845-1863).

The leadership this marriage brought forth was bilingual. Netsvetov translated into Atkan Aleut and cooperated with Veniaminov in creating an alphabet based on the Cyrillic for the Aleut languages. Netsvetov instructed the next generation of parish priests for both the Atka and Unalaska parishes: Fr. Lavrentii Salamatov and Fr. Innokentii Shaiashnikov. These men, who also derived from intermarriages, were fluently bilingual: they translated scriptures and authored original work in Atkan and Unalaskan Aleut, respectively.

A fact has been indicated that deserves attention. From the beginning the priests had kinship ties within the parishes. Netsvetov, Salamatov, and Shaiashnikov were raised and were kindred on islands where they served. A foreigner intervened between Shaiashnikov and Veniaminov: Fr. Golovin, who may have been a Kamchadal. As for Veniaminov, who had come from Irkutsk, he became competently bilingual and he developed kinship ties through the marriage of a brother to an Aleut woman and the marriage of a daughter to a Russian-Aleut man. The combination of dual kinship and dual language (Russian-Aleut) must have been instrumental to the communication and indigenization of this faith, instrumental to its implanting from Asia and engrafting in the Aleutians.[20]

(.ii) While intermarriage was thus a vital social dynamic for the development of proficient native Orthodox leadership, this dynamic occurred rather later. An earlier social dynamic began with the initial contacts. It occurred within the alliances formed between hunters across the Aleutian Islands.[21]

In 1762, Shashuk, a toion of Umnak, entered into alliance with S. Glotov, a Russian Orthodox hunter who had come from northeastern Asia and who remained in the Umnak region from 1758 to 1762. Shashuk entrusted a nephew to him, and the ally baptized the youth. This was the first baptism, or among the first, in the Unalaska region. Names were given and shared: the godson received the baptismal name Ivan and he assumed his godfather's names as his own patronymic and surname; thus the youth Mushkal (Mushkalyax) became the Aleut Ivan Stepanovich Glotov.[22] He remained beside his godfather for the next three years. Together they departed Umnak aboard the *Sv. Iulian* and traveled to Kamchatka where they stayed from August until October 1762. They then journeyed aboard the *Sv. Andreian i Natalia* to Kodiak Island where they spent the winter of 1762-63, before returning along the eastern Aleutian Islands to Umnak, Ivan's home island, in spring of 1764.

Eventually succeeding his uncle Shashuk as the primary toion of Umnak, the Aleut Ivan Stepanovich Glotov exercised mature political and spiritual leadership into the next century, including the conducting of Russian Orthodox services in a chapel he himself had had constructed, as reported in 1808.[23]

Another example of this social dynamic is evident concurrently at the other side of the island chain, on the western Aleutians. On Attu in 1761 a toion named Makuzhan had his young kinsman baptized by men who had come there from northeast Asia for the hunt. The toion's young kinsman received the baptismal name Leontii and also assumed his godfather's names as his own patronymic and surname, becoming the Aleut Leontii Vasil'evich Popov.[24]

Entrusted thus to his godfather, he journeyed beside him, departing that same year on the *Sv. Ioann Ustiuzhskii*, sailing east to the islands of Buldir, Kiska, Segula, Awadax, Little Sitkin, and Amchitka, then turning westward to hunt on Shemya (one of the Near Islands) in summer 1763, before continuing to Kamchatka. In September of the following year, the merchant Popov funded the same vessel for a voyage that spent nearly a year on Bering Island before returning to the Near Islands in summer 1765. This would be the voyage that brought Leontii home.[25] By then, he would have had four years in his godfather's company, hunting, exploring, and learning the ways of these men who had come from northeastern Asia. The Aleut Leontii Vasil'evich Popov may then have succeeded his elder kinsman Makuzhan as toion.

(3.3) *A native social process.* A process occurred in these parallel, concurrent examples that corresponded to a native social process guiding the successions of toions. Three key elements were involved. Firstly, succession occurred among "customary lineage chiefs" on the eastern Aleutians, and within a "hereditary kin group" on the central and western Aleutians.[26] Hence in the examples, on the eastern islands the Aleut Ivan Stepanovich Glotov succeeded his own uncle Shashuk as toion of Umnak, and on the western islands the Aleut Leontii Vasil'evich Popov probably succeeded his elder kinsman Makuzhan. A further example derives before 1786 when the Aleut Sergei Dmitrievich Pan'kov succeeded his own brother as toion.[27] The successor's names clearly indicate baptism, for Sergei is a baptismal name, and also indicate an alliance with the Russian Dmitrii Pan'kov, who had made a number of voyages into this region and had evidently entered into a number of lasting alliances.[28]

The second component in the social process was the fostering of children. Parents permitted their children to be raised by kinsmen or even by non-consanguine affines:[29] the latter would be friends and allies. Hence the young men were entrusted to their godfathers by elder kinsmen. The Aleut Ivan Stepanovich Glotov's godfather and the Aleut Leontii Vasil'evich Popov's godfather clearly honored the trust by returning the youngsters to their elders after years of traveling, exploring, and hunting.

Succession depended also on skill and on valor. A successor was expected to have distinguished himself by mastering techniques of seafaring and of hunting. He was expected also to have completed expeditions to foreign lands and thus to have gained experience of wider geography and of other peoples.[30] This was the third component. Hence the successor journeyed beside his godfather for a series of years in each example: exploring, hunting, and learning the ways of these men who had come from northeast Asia.

In each example the godson went to Kamchatka. What would he have seen? By the early 1740s, the Kamchadals were Eastern Orthodox; churches (with priests) or chapels (without priests) existed in the major settlements where Kamchadal men exercised leadership.[31] The first clergy had been assigned in 1705, from Tobol'sk.[32] A priest was described at Petropavlovsk in 1779, an embarkation site for the Aleutians since 1741: the "benevolent and hospitable pastor" was "native on his mother's side."[33]

The Kamchadals themselves comprised up to 50 percent of the men who came to the Aleutians for the sea hunts during the initial contact period, between 1745 and the 1760s. Later during the 1770s when the purpose of enterprises and the nature of contacts changed, the percentage of Kamchadals involved decreased.[34]

(3.4) *The merging of faith and polity*: (.i) The exercise of leadership by the Aleut Orthodox, 1780s-1790s. The following is a chronological summary of protests against an influx of enterprises and imperial interests into the Unalaska region during the later 1700s. Before June 1787, a toion's kinsman named Izosim Polutov dispatched a written protest from the central Aleutian Islands to the Okhotsk district commander.[35] At the same time, toion Tukulan Aiugnin dispatched a report from the "third Fox Island" (an eastern island: Akutan, possibly Akun, or even Unalaska) also to the Okhotsk office.[36] Before 1791, a toion Algamalinag named Mikhail and bilingual Saguakh named Ivan Chuloshnikov spoke out in person to the naval captain G. Sarychev who had anchored at Unalaska, whose expedition for the government had been charged in part to collect such testimony.[37] In 1796, toion Ivan Stepanovich Glotov of Umnak led twenty-two other toions of his region in a protest directed to the imperial capital Petersburg.[38] In 1797, a toion Yelisei Popachev traveled with the Aleuts Nikolai Lukanin and Nikifor Svin'in and with the missionary hieromonk Makarii toward Petersburg.[39]

The key to the chronology consists in the men's names. Only one lacked a baptismal name. Eastern Orthodox leaders were in place, stood firmly, and acted on behalf of their people through the influx.

An extended example is found in the toion Sergei Dmitrievich Pan'kov. By 1791, he had visited Kamchatka and had made at least two journeys to Okhotsk,[40] whence in response to protests received, offical communications had been dispatched that clearly articulated the Aleutian Island peoples' civil rights as Russian subjects.[41] In that year of 1791, this toion had traveled to Unimak Island (in the Unalaska region) where he consulted with kinsmen. Then he journeyed to Unalaska to meet with naval captain Sarychev, whose governmental expedition was charged, in part, to investigate. Pan'kov came with twenty-five Aleut men: fourteen with him in a baidara (an umiak), another eleven alongside in single-hatch baidarkas (kayaks).[42] At the meeting, other toions were present as well, among whom Pan'kov presided. Addressing Sarychev in Russian, this primary toion wore a headcovering and an over-garment of light red cloth and of velvet with gold or golden trim, presented to him by a government office in northeastern Asia. Outstanding in color, unusual in texture, they distinguished him from the other toions in the council and from Sarychev, for the clothing was unlike a European uniform. Dressed as an Aleut of high status, the primary toion stood and spoke.

Through leadership such as this, the Aleuts maintained remarkable autonomy on the Aleutian Islands and achieved an unusual degree of independence. As observed by Veniaminov in the 1830s, they were more independent than the Kamchadals and were freer even than some Asians: "in their own locale, the Aleuty are more independent and free than the people of Kamchatka and even baptized Asians."[43] Autonomy was reflected in the moral qualities described for them consistently by Veniaminov;[44] it was reflected as well in their intellectual pursuits in their own language, evident in these journals and also in the work of subsequent generations on the islands. With autonomy and with the language, the culture prevailed.[45] The leadership was successful.

(.ii) These leaders were empowered legally and morally: legally through information received from northeast Asia where an articulated prerequisite for trade on the islands was humane conduct; and morally through the ethics intrinsic in Orthodox Christianity. Especially those leaders who had succeeded their kinsmen as toions through native social processes of upbringing and succession,[46] would have known themselves to be empowered in these ways, by having traveled to Kamchatka and moreover having had Christianity imparted to them through alliances with hearty men, men like themselves. They exercised this power.

Their leadership on behalf of polity was a continuation of leadership in the previous generation. Earlier in the mid-1760s, toions in the Unalaska region had created a militant alliance to counter the escalating influx. The alliance was formed by polities on major islands in the Unalaska region (later the parish): it was led by the polities of the islands of Tigalda and Akun and included Unimak, Unalaska, and Umnak.[47] The successors continued, employing new tactics now, including reports directly to Petersburg and petitions for the governmental enforcement of legality.

When one reads of the Russian Orthodox Church defending native people during this time of trouble, one should therefore recognize the Aleut Orthodox toions in the Unalaska region. They were already leading when they were joined by the missionary hieromonk Makarii. While thus widened, the perception would also be refined, for Makarii was reprimanded by authorities in the imperial city for his unauthorized activity.

Who was Makarii? A hieromonk (monastic-priest) from the Konevskii monastery in Karelia, he was a member of the spiritual mission to Kodiak Island, that initially consisted of ten monastics. Arriving at Kodiak in September 1794, and serving particularly in the villages on the southern coast of that island, he was dispatched with an interpreter the following summer to the Unalaska region where he traveled to a few of the eastern islands including Unga and Akun, then came to Unalaska Island. Here he joined Aleut toions in action against the Shelikhov-Golikov Company which was escalating commercial and imperialist enterprises in this region. With six Aleut men, he journeyed from Unalaska through northeast Asia towards Petersburg carrying a petition signed by the region's toions to present it to the imperial Throne in person.

The dimensions of the task become clear when one considers the purpose and circumstances of the journey: they were traveling to protest against a commercial power which had representatives in the towns of Okhotsk and Irkutsk and which was gaining economic and administrative control in Russia's Pacific regions. The men had to arrange transportation through those regions and had to travel through those towns which were coming increasingly under company control. Makarii himself was a monastic without title, and he would have had few if any sources of financial support. Furthermore he lacked authority to travel: he had departed without authorization. He journeyed resourcefully and (one may well imagine) cleverly. Of the original group of seven men, three survived to arrive at Petersburg in spring 1798: hieromonk Makarii, Nikolai Lukanin and Nikifor Svin'in were granted their audience with the Emperor. Makarii was reprimanded for unauthorized activity. Intercessions by the Aleut men spared him from punishment.[48] All three were sent back. All three died while returning. This was the Russian missionary to the eastern Aleutians: the conscientious and resourceful Makarii who gave his life with these Aleut leaders.

(.iii) Russian Orthodoxy thus merged with the people's own leadership, with their own struggle, with their destiny. This merging of faith and polity is reflected particularly in a person who recurs in Veniaminov's journals: Ivan Pan'kov, the toion of the islands of Tigalda and Akun. The same islands had provided the leadership for the Aleut wars in Pan'kov's grandparents' generation during the mid-1760s; and in his parents' generation in 1791, the toion Sergei Dmitrievich who presided at the council at Unalaska had had the same surname.[49] Yet, prior to Veniaminov's arrival, Ivan Pan'kov was providing religious instruction within his polity himself.[50] When Veniaminov arrived, Pan'kov donated money for the reception and settlement of the priest and family: indeed he donated more than the average sum.[51] Elder in age to the priest, Pan'kov accompanied

Veniaminov on pastoral visits to Tigalda and Akun where the priest was warmly received.[52] This toion co-translated the catechism and the Gospel; and after Veniaminov's transfer, Pan'kov had chapels constructed in 1842 and 1843 on both those islands for his own people.[53]

An earlier example of the merging of faith and polity is provided by Ivan Stepanovich Glotov the Aleut toion of Umnak. It was he who had led twenty-two men of the Unalaska region in a protest written directly to the imperial capital in 1796. Yet when hieromonk Gideon landed briefly at Unalaska in 1807, the same toion came to receive an anointing from him.[54] This same toion constructed a chapel for his polity (Recheshnoe in the journals; today's Nikolski). Baptized in 1762 through his uncle's alliance, journeying to northeast Asia, having become literate and bilingual, he also became proficient in Orthodox rubrics: in his mature years this same toion was conducting daily services in that chapel himself.[55] Indeed, "he may have substantially assisted in spreading Christianity among the Aleuts."[56]

Section conclusion. How had the Unalaska parish come into being? It was a development by the people beginning three generations prior to Veniaminov's arrival through social dynamics such as alliances and later intermarriages with northeast Asians and northern Eurasians. Eastern Orthodoxy was thus engrafted from like to like within social and material cultures indigenous to the Arctic.

Thus when Veniaminov arrived, the Aleuts were already Russian Orthodox, and he had been assigned as their parish priest. He ministered within an existing parish with people whom he described as "exemplary Christians."[57]

In this context, Veniaminov's ministry can be described as cooperative leadership. It is recorded in these journals, and the journals are therefore a source both for this man and for these people.

A question. While clarifying the journals, the context also stimulates a question. Aleut faith and polity had merged during the preceding generations when Russian Orthodox toions led their people against and through an influx that was tantamount to a tacit invasion. What was Veniaminov's own retrospective view of the influx?

He was ministering and writing in the aftermath of assaults on the eastern Aleutian and Kodiak Island archipelagos by the Shelikhov enterprises. On the eastern Aleutian Islands, a Shelikhov enterprise had been either named or implicated in each of the protests by the Russian Orthodox toions during the 1780s and 1790s.[58] However in 1799 by imperial decree, the major interests in those enterprises were granted a renewable charter for monopoly rights in the region. Within a year, they had erected a monument lauding the company's progenitor Grigorii Shelikhov, who had died in 1795, and by extension thus lauding the company themselves, for, among other achievements, "emplanting the Orthodox faith" in (what came to be known as) Alaska.[59] The Russian-American Company continued to usurp this credit for themselves while seeking periodic renewals of their charter from the government; an example is a history they commissioned.[60]

Veniaminov had been raised and schooled in the shadow of such a monument erected in 1800 by imperial decree on cathedral grounds at Irkutsk.[61] He attended the Irkutsk Theological Seminary (seminaries and ecclesiarchy in the Petersburg Empire were supervised by the imperial government),[62] where it seems he assimilated the euphemisms that had rendered the invasion a "colonization," the advance an "advancement."

He criticized the methods of change, or the lack of methods. In this sense he was very insightful.[63] But was he insightful with regard to the euphemisms? Did he criticize the undercurrents that were causing the change?

The question is partly rhetorical, for when he arrived in 1824, a social equilibrium had settled. Aleutian Island hegemony and Aleut culture had proved resilient. Veniaminov was not confronted with the crisis which had faced Makarii in 1795-1796. And if he erred in his theoretical outlook in this respect, the error pales in the brilliance of his practice: for in practice, he never entirely acquiesced to the status quo, as he became proficient in Aleut intellectual culture (traditions as well as language), proficient as well in material culture (e.g. , kayaking). He learned Aleut, he created in that language. Veniaminov the priest of Unalaska rose above the question.

Yet the question persists. When crises threaten the hegemony and culture of a people, it asks: Are the presuppositions of colonization being accepted by foreign (non-native) clergy and by ecclesiarchy in the political capital; if so, then whose interests are being served?

(4) The Journals as a Source for Aleut History.

Among the themes contained in these journals, one is the creation of Aleut literature. The process was chronicled as it was occurring, and it can be gleaned from the journal entries. A portion will be developed here to indicate the value of this source for history.

Veniaminov began to study the Aleut language as soon as he arrived at Sitka, before reaching Unalaska. By 24 October 1823, he had sought a bilingual tutor, one who knew "Russian grammar as well"; and within two months while performing various other duties, he had taken notes for over 200 vocabulary items. He could have chosen not to embark on this course, because he was aware that many Aleuts knew Russian. Yet he did so straightaway. Once he reached Unalaska, he added this task of learning to his many parish activities, and by January 1826, he had progressed to his first work of translation, a catechism.

In March of that year, Ivan Pan'kov, the toion of Tigalda and Akun, arrived at Veniaminov's "invitation and request." Bilingual, literate, and knowledgeable in the faith,[64] he "corrected the portion of the catechism" that Veniaminov had translated, "up to the Nicene Creed." On 14 May, the priest read their translation at a gathering in another toion's iurt in the village of Pavlof on the Alaska Peninsula: "In the evening (we gathered) in the iurt of the toion, and those who knew Russian heard me read from the Catechism that I had translated into their language. They heard with pleasure and showed a desire to have copies for themselves."

By 13 January 1828, Veniaminov was teaching the Lord's Prayer in Aleut as well as in Russian to the pupils at school at Unalaska. The students were Russians, Creoles, and Aleuts. A year later, 28 January 1829, he was teaching them the Aleut alphabet, in addition to their Russian lessons.

He embarked on a translation of the Gospel according to Matthew later that same year, during September 1829. Rather than setting to the work alone, however, the priest Ivan Veniaminov traveled to Akun to accomplish the task with the toion Ivan Pan'kov. Both men's names eventually appeared on the published title page as co-translators. Arriving on the 7th after a difficult and eventful sea crossing by baidarka (kayak), Veniaminov began the very next day, and by nightfall the two Ivans had translated the first two chapters. The priest and the toion continued diligently, interrupting their work to celebrate liturgical services daily and once to make a pastoral visit to a lone, ailing parishioner, 15 versts away, about 10 miles, going by baidarka over water and by foot over land, then returning to their task straightaway. They finished the first draft of the translation with remarkable diligence on 24 September 1829, and on that day, Veniaminov described their process in retrospect:

> We translated in the following fashion: we would work on
> the translation from morning until evening, and then in the
> evening we would read that which we had translated that
> day to an assembly of the most learned Aleuts and many
> others who wished to be there. Then we made corrections.

Two verses had been omitted: *Matthew* 7:17 and 9:17. "The first was not done because the local language has no words for a single thing mentioned therein." The second verse was "incomprehensible to many people." Instead, "we supplemented the account of the Passion of Christ with passages from other Gospels." Copying the draft during the next two months at Unalaska while performing his other parish duties, he handed the finished copy "to the Aleut interpreter" Daniel Kuziakin on 2 December.

> On every evening that he read it, many people would
> assemble at his home to listen. He (Kuziakin) read through
> the entire Gospel five times. He found a mistake in one
> place only, and that was not so much an error as a matter
> of weak and unsuitable phrasing. He corrected it well.

The last three chapters of the Gospel were read again that spring on 29 April 1830, now by the priest Veniaminov at the village of Recheshnoe (Nikolski) on Umnak Island: "All listened attentively and expressed their agreement."

The two Ivans, Veniaminov and Pan'kov, resumed the translation of the catechism at Tigalda that August, with Veniaminov finishing the project on his own, working at it constantly from the 15th. They then checked the translated catechism and checked yet again the translated Gospel by reading before another group from the 22nd to the 25th to receive constructive criticism. No errors were found in the Gospel translation "other than problems in orthography." The priest handed the draft of the translated catechism to Daniel Kuziakin to read in October, just as Veniaminov had done earlier with the Gospel. That same month, this priest himself introduced the Aleut catechism in school at the Unalaska harbor village where the pupils were Russian, Creole, and Aleut.

On Easter 1831 during the Divine Liturgy, he had the Gospel passage read from the perfected Aleut translation:

> April 19. Easter. I celebrated Matins at twelve o'clock
> (midnight). At six o'clock I celebrated the Liturgy during
> which the Gospel was read in Slavonic, Russian, and Fox-
> Aleut. There was a cannon salute. The texts were read by
> the priest, the cantor, and the Creole Zach. Chichinev.

Every subsequent Easter in the journals includes the Gospel reading in
Aleut.

This creativity continued throughout the time of the journals. As
orthography was perfected for the publication of the completed Aleut texts,
new projects were assumed, including: the adaptation of the translations
from Unalaskan Aleut to Atkan Aleut; the compilation of an Unalaskan
Aleut grammar and of an Unalaskan Aleut-Russian dictionary; and the
authoring of a work in Aleut by Veniaminov himself.[65] The details are
contained in the journal entries and can be brought to light thematically, as
the portion developed in this section may have indicated.

(5) A Source for Veniaminov's Ministry and Character

While many of Veniaminov's personal qualities become evident through
his activities in the existing parish as recorded in these journals, there is a
characteristic that might be less readily evident. It is indicated twice: (.i)
during an excursion into California in 1836; and very succinctly (.ii) during
a pastoral visit to Akun in 1828. It is his own Far Northern-ness.

(.i) On 15 July 1836 Veniaminov traveled from Sitka south to Fort Ross
where he wrote:

> I must admit the healthful air, the pure sky, the geographi-
> cal position, and the native vegetation all immediately
> strike and captivate one who was born north of 52 degrees
> and had never been south of that latitude....

He then crossed "the borders of Russia" (as he expressed it) into the newly
independent Republic of California, and toured the San Francisco Bay area
while awaiting his return transportation to Sitka. The journal's format
changes to a narrative here, its style to a travel diary: we see Veniaminov
enjoying a brief holiday until his vessel arrived on the 14th of September.
Indeed this is the only holiday reflected in the journals' thirteen-year span.
We see him experiencing and enjoying another culture, and making use of

yet another language, the Latin he had learned at school. From San Francisco he made a tour to Mission San Jose, situated on the southeastern side of the bay. He perceived it on the "left-hand shore."

(.ii) The perception was Far Northern, as was an insight that he demonstrated at Akun on 23 April 1828. "One of the local elders Ivan Smirennikov is considered a shaman in these parts," he noted on that day; but he continued, "I have found the facts quite to the contrary." He provided details in a report that he promised to send.[66] Veniaminov distinguished Smirennikov from shamans-of-old because the pastor was familiar with Orthodoxy and relied on patristic principles;[67] yet moreover and more so because he was familiar with Far Northern cultures and relied on regional insights.[68]

His discernment was reflected three generations later at the turn of the twentieth century by the Russian-Aleut priest (and trilingual curator of the Alaska Territorial Museum in Juneau) Fr. Andrew Kashevarov who, in retrospect, articulated the conclusion implicit in Veniaminov's response: that the baptized elder was a prophet; in Kashevarov's own words, "the Aleut prophet."[69]

Veniaminov's insight derived in vital part from familiarity with the Far North. Indeed he had spent his life in Arctic regions. Born in an eastern Siberian village, he may have been partly Native Siberian himself (while the details of his parentage are unknown, an indication exists: he was born in a village from local parentage). Schooled, married and ordained in the town of Irkutsk, he volunteered there for the Unalaska assignment and was dispatched through northeastern Asia. He then remained in the Unalaska and Sitka parishes, except for the brief excursion south, until he departed Sitka for Petersburg in 1838, after the span of these journals, a journey he made primarily to promote and oversee the publication of his work in the Aleut language and about the Aleutian Islands.

A conceptual inversion by scholars may therefore be valuable: for Veniaminov may be interpreted not so much as a type of European who assumed leadership in Russia's easternmost regions (northeastern Asia, the Aleutians, and Alaska), but instead as a native Far Northerner who assumed leadership in Europe as the Metropolitan of Moscow—inasmuch as such a dichotomy can be applied to traditional Eurasian Russia.

Epilogue. Subsequent to the period encompassed by these journals, Ivan Veniaminov made his first journey to Petersburg, his first journey to the

West. A series of coincidences then occurred that resulted in a hitherto unpredictable event that affected the course of the rest of his life. In November 1839 his wife died at Irkutsk, and he was advised to become a monastic. Tonsured with the name Innokentii, he was, in due time, chosen to be the bishop (Orthodox bishops must be monastics) of a new diocese for the easternmost parishes: the diocese of Kamchatka, the Kurile Islands and the Aleutians.

Returning to Sitka, Bishop Innokentii remained there from September 1841 until February 1842 when he commenced the first of his energetic tours through his diocese. He visited Aleut villages of his former parish, firstly; and while he then concentrated his own presence mainly at Kamchatka and Sitka until 1850, his numerous sailings to and fro would have included subsequent landings at Unalaska for comparatively frequent visits to his former parish home. He also visited Atka,[70] the Pribilofs, Mikhailovskii redoubt (St. Michael) on the northeast Bering Sea coast,[71] and Kodiak. He established a parish at Nushagak. He had religious missions opened at the Kenai and at Ikogmiut.

In 1850 the bishop's residence was moved to Aian in northeastern Asia. Eight years later in 1858 the diocese was enlarged to an archdiocese that extended westward into Yakutia. It eventually came to encompass the Amur as well. Thus his ministry came to encompass many people of northeastern Asia and easternmost Siberia in addition to the Kamchadals and the Kurile Island Ainus: particularly the Yakuts, as well as Evenks (or Tungus), Evens (or Lamuts), and the Yukaghirs. He had a religious mission opened among the Chukchi. In August 1868, Innokentii was chosen to be the Metropolitan of Moscow, a high if not the highest position among contemporary Russian ecclesiarchs, that he held until his repose in 1879. Nearly a century later in 1977, he was formally recognized as a saint by the Moscow Patriarchate.

The scope of his episcopal activities would subsume his initial parish ministries in a comprehensive biography. These journals are therefore all the more valuable, for they provide immediate insights into the activities and the character of this man while he was Unalaska's and Sitka's parish priest.

S. A. Mousalimas, Ph.D.
Pembroke, Oxford

NOTES

1. Veniaminov, Journals, 29 June to 10 July 1829, 8 July to 14 July 1832. See also "The Condition of the Orthodox Church in Russian America: Innokentii Veniaminov's History of the Russian Church in Alaska," trans. and eds. Robert Nichols and Robert Croskey, *Pacific Northwest Quarterly* 63, no. 2 (April, 1972), · 53-54.

2. Veniaminov, Journals, 26 Oct. 1823, 8 Nov. 1823, 12 March 1824, point 2 of entry beginning 23 August 1834, and point 2 of summary 1836. See also id., "Condition," 46-49.

3. Veniaminov, Journals, 16 July, 1 August, and 16 August 1836 .

4. Ibid., 12 July to 16 July 1836.

5. Ibid., 2 September to 7 September 1836.

6. See also Lydia T. Black, Appendix 5, Glossary: (b) Ecclesiastical Terms, in *The Journals of Iakov Netsvetov: The Atkha Years, 1828-1844*, trans. Lydia T. Black (Kingston, Ontario: Limestone Press, 1980), 307. For detail, see "The Symbolism of the Church," in Isabel Florence Habgood, *Service Book of the Holy Orthodox-Catholic Apostolic Church* (Englewood, New Jersey: Antiochian Archdiocese, 1975), xxviii-xl.

7. E.g., Veniaminov, Journals, 8-10 July 1827, 3 May 1829, 26 July 1829, 17 April 1830, 10 August and 14 August 1830, 20 April 1832; see also 27 May 1826.

8. See *Journals of Netsvetov: Atkha Years*. See also *The Journals of Iakov Netsvetov: The Yukon Years, 1845-1863*, trans. Lydia T. Black, ed. Richard A. Pierce (Kingston, Ontario: Limestone Press, 1984).

9. See e.g., Veniaminov, Journals, 1 August 1824; *Journals of Netsvetov: Atkha Years*, 6 January for the years 1829, 1834, 1835, 1841. See also, Richard Dauenhauer, "Fr. Michael Oleksa Blessing the North Pacific," *Frames of Reference* (Haines, Alaska: Black Current Press, 1987), 64-65.

10. See Pierre Pascal, *The Religion of the Russian People*, trans. Rowan Williams (London and Oxford: Mowbrays, 1976), 8-24 passim.

11. For Makarii, see sec. 3.4.ii below.

12. Gavriil A. Sarychev [Gawrila Sarytschew], *Account of Voyage of Discovery to the North-east of Siberia, the Frozen Ocean and the Northeast Sea* (London, 1807), 2:13.

13. Archimandrite Ioasaph, 19 May 1795, Synodal Archive 643:48, Yudin Collection, Manuscript Division, Library of Congress; Herman to Nazarii, May 1795, in Michael Oleksa, *Alaskan Missionary Spirituality*, ed. Michael Oleksa (New York: Paulist Press, 1987), 40.

14. *The Round the World Voyage of Hieromonk Gideon, 1803-1809*, trans. Lydia T. Black, ed. Richard A. Pierce (Kingston, Ontario, and Fairbanks, AK: Limestone Press, 1989), 131-143; Richard A. Pierce, *Russian America: A Biographical Dictionary* (Kingston, Ontario, and Fairbanks, Alaska: Limestone Press, 1990), 161.

15. N. A. Ivashintsov, *Russian Round-the-World Voyages, 1803-1849*, trans. Glynn R. Barratt, ed. Richard A. Pierce (Kingston, Ontario: Limestone Press, 1980), 141.

16. Ivan Veniaminov, *Notes on the Islands of the Unalashka District*, trans. Lydia T. Black and R. H. Geoghegan, ed. Richard A. Pierce (Kingston, Ontario: Limestone Press, 1984), 238. He overlooked only point (b) in the chronology: the missionaries in transit to Kodiak.

17. See sec. 2.5 above.

18. Appendix 3, "Inscription on the Gravestone of Egor Vasil'evich Netsvetov," *Journals of Netsvetov: Atkha Years*, 271. For first baptisms, see e.g. sec. 3.2.ii below.

19. *Voyage of Gideon*, 137-138, 141. Gideon administered chrismation instead of Holy Communion, because he was without an antimins: see sec. 2.1 above. For Maria's age, cf. (ibid.) where she is listed as twenty, with (ibid., 132) where she is listed as twenty-five. Notice (ibid., 132) that Maria is recorded among the "children born to Russian promyshlennye." Was she a Russian-Aleut herself? An intermarriage in her parents' generation would be very early indeed.

20. Veniaminov's brother Stefan had accompanied him and later became a missionary priest to the Chukchi; Veniaminov's son-in-law Petelin became the priest of Nushagak and subsequently of Kodiak, then a missionary priest in northern Asia (Pierce, *Biographical Dictionary*, 527). See Appendix, "Aleut and Creole Churchmen in Alaska: Nineteenth and Early Twentieth Centuries," in Oleksa, *Alaska Missionary Spirituality*, 377-386.

21. For an analysis of types of Aleut-Russian contacts, see Mari Sardy, "Early Contacts between Aleuts and Russians, 1741-1780," *Alaska History* 1, no. 2 (Fall/Winter 1985/86): 43-58. For a summary historical analysis, see Lydia T. Black, The European Fur Trade, in "The Nature of Evil: Of Whales and Sea Otters," in *Indians, Animals, and the Fur Trade*, ed. Shepard Krech III (Athens: University of Georgia Press, 1981), 117-121; and for a summary description of social

interactions, see id., "Russia's American Adventure," *Natural History* (December, 1989), 46-57.

22. See Pierce, *Biographical Dictionary*, 169.

23. *Voyage of Gideon*, 122.

24. Stepan Cherepanov, 3 August 1762, in *Russkie otkrytiia v Tikhom okeane i Severnoi Amerike v XVIII veka*, ed. A. I. Andreev (Moscow, 1948), 117-118.

25. For these voyages, see Lydia T. Black, *Atka: An Ethnohistory of the Western Aleutians* (Kingston, Ontario: Limestone Press, 1984), 67, 83; see also Raisa V. Makarova, *Russians on the Pacific, 1743-1799*, trans. R. A. Pierce and A. S. Donnelly (Kingston, Ontario: Limestone Press, 1975), 60-61, 63.

26. Veniaminov, *Notes*, 244; Iakov Netsvetov "Atkha Aleuts," in Veniaminov, *Notes*, 370. For the toions' patriarchal, or conciliar, manner of leadership, see Veniaminov, *Notes*, 241; Netsvetov, "Atkha Aleuts," 370.

Aleutian Island societies comprised several regional groups. See map, *Unangam Ungiikangin kayux Tunusangin...*, comp. Waldemar Jochelson, ed. Knut Bergsland and Moses L. Dirks (Fairbanks: Alaska Native Language Center, University of Alaska Fairbanks, 1990), xviii; cf., Lydia T. Black, Early History, in "The Aleutians," *Alaska Geographic Quarterly* 7, no. 3 (1980):83 (reprinted, id., *Atka*, x). For analyses see: Black, *Atka*, 41-71; id., Early History, 82-84; Knut Bergsland, Introduction to *Unangam Ungiikangin*, 2-5.

27. Black, *Atka*, 94, 187-188.

28. Ibid., 83-84; id., "Ivan Pan'kov—An Architect of Aleut Literacy," *Arctic Anthropology* 14, no. 1 (1977): 99.

29. Netsvetov, "Atkha Aleuts," 369; Veniaminov, *Notes*, 191.

30. See Veniaminov, *Notes*, 184, 191, 206, 229.

31. Stepan P. Krasheninnikov, *The History of Kamtschatka and the Kurilski Islands*, trans. James Grieve (1764; reprint, Surrey: Richmond Publishing Co., 1973), 180, 205, 263-267. See also James King, *A Voyage to the Pacific Ocean ... performed under Captains Cook ... [et al.] in the years 1776... [to] 1780* (London: W. & A. Strahan, 1784), 3: 303-304, 367, 368. See also *Voyage of Gideon*, 124-126. Cf. Krasheninnikov with Gideon: the former's contemporary observation in the early 1740s, deriving from successive years there, reports four churches/chapels at that time, while the latter's retrospective history, deriving from a brief tour, reports two churches/chapels from the 1740s and others from the 1760s to 1790s. Regarding the Kamchadals' religiosity, the three unrelated sources are unanimous, from the early 1740s, 1779, and 1808, respectively.

32. Josef Glazik, *Die Russische-orthodoxe Heidensmission seit Peter dem Grossen* (Munster: Aschendorffsche Verlagsbuchhandlung, 1954), 92; Eugene Smirnoff, *A Short Account of...Russian Orthodox Missions* (London: Rivington, 1903), 12.

33. King, *Voyage under Cook*, 368; see also J. C. Beaglehole, ed., *Journals of Captain James Cook*, Hakluyt Society (Cambridge: University Press, 1967), 1253.

34. Black, *Atka*, 77; id., Early History, 92. Other Russians during the initial contact period were mainly from Siberian towns and from the White Sea region (id., *Atka*, 77). The latter would include, as well as the northernmost Slavs, the Komi, the Karelians, and the eastern Sami (eastern Lapps). These Finnic-speaking peoples are related to the Ugric-speaking Mansi and Khants of Siberia. The eastern Sami were Eastern Orthodox from the 16th century; the Mansi and Khants, from approximately the same time; the Komi, from the 14th century at the latest; and the Karelians, beginning as early as the 10th century. Their Russian-ness may be found in their Eastern Orthodoxy (ritual life and worldview), in their shared Eurasian language, Russian, and in their social alliances.

References to cultural and physical affinities are noted below. For affinities between Russians and Itelmens (Kamchadals) at Kamchatka in 1779 and the early 1740s, see: King, *Voyage under Cook*, 189-219 passim; Krasheninnikov, *History of Kamtschatka*, 191, 195, 218. For affinities between the Russian Orthodox Kamchadals and the Aleuts at Unalaska in 1778, see John Ledyard, *A Journal of Captain Cook's Last Voyage* (1783; Corvallis: Oregon State University, 1963), 95; note that the "Indians" are Kamchadals and Aleuts, indistinguishable from each other in the text until Ledyard lists some of their vocabulary. For affinities between the Russians and the Alaskans in the Kodiak and Chugach regions in 1794, see George Vancouver, *Voyage of Discovery to the North Pacific Ocean and Round the World* (1798; Amsterdam: N. Israel, Bibliotheca Australiana, 1967), 3:122, 200.

Contrast these north Eurasian Russians who came for the sea hunts beginning in 1745 with the Westernized entrepreneurs and administrators who followed in the 1770s, particularly from 1784. Contrast, e.g., the descriptions by Vancouver (cited above) with the portraits of Grigorii Shelikhov (in Pierce, *Biographical Dictionary*, 556; also in Grigorii I. Shelikhov, *A Voyage to America, 1783-1786* [Kingston, Ontario: Limestone Press, 1981], 58-59). For an interpretation quite possibly applicable to this contrast and therefore to Aleutian and southern Alaskan history, see Pascal, *The Religion of the Russian People*, 3: "a single nation with two totally different peoples"; see also, Nicholos Zernov, *The Russians and Their Church*, 3rd ed. (London: S.P.C.K., 1978), 106, 123: "The unity of Russia during the Moscow period [before ca. 1725] was neither national nor political: it depended mainly on the knowledge of 'obriad' [ritual life].... The new Empire and Capital [Petersburg] were foreign plants in Russian soil."

35. G. Kozlov-Ugrenin, 15 June 1787, Okhotsk, in P. A. Tikhmenev, *A History of the Russian-American Company*, vol. 2: *Documents*, trans. Dmitri Krenov, eds. Richard A. Pierce and Alton S. Donnelly (Kingston, Ontario: Limestone Press, 1979), 16. See also, R. G. Liapunova, "Relations with the Natives of Russian America," in *Russia's American Colony*, ed. S. Frederick Starr (Durham: Duke University Press, 1987), 116.

36. Ugrenin in Tikhmenev, *Documents*, 16; Liapunova, "Relations," 116.

37. Natives of the Unalaska district to government inspectors, 1789-1790, Appendix 6 to Shelikhov, *Voyage to America*, 128. For this task given to the Billings/Sarychev expedition, see Liapunova, "Relations," 117-118.

38. Liapunova, "Relations," 124.

39. Makarii to Synod, 5 October 1797, trans. Lydia T. Black, in Oleksa, *Alaska Missionary Spirituality*, 290.

40. Black, *Atka*, 94.

41. Ugrenin in Tikhmenev, *Documents*, 15-16; Liapunova, "Relations," 116.

42. Black, *Atka*, 95

43. Veniaminov, "Conditions," 47. Veniaminov's primary knowledge was of the Unalaska district (eastern Aleutian Islands). For autonomy in the Atka district (central and western Aleutians), see *Journals of Netsvetov: Atkha Years*, 12; for specifically Atka Island and Amchitka Island (central Aleutians), see respectively, ibid., 18-19, 30; and for specifically the Near Islands (western Aleutians), with adaptation to a commercial economy, see Appendix 1, "Notes on the Western Aleutians and the Commander Islands by Navigator Vasil'ev (1811-1812)," in Black, *Atka*, 151-170 passim, esp. 160-161.

44. Veniaminov, "Conditions," 50-52; id., *Notes*, 166-188, 319-320, 323. But not for company dependents at Sitka: id., "Conditions," 47.

45. See *Unangam Ungiikangin*, photographs as well as various texts. See also the artifact collections from the Aleutians, e.g.: under Etholen and Wrangell 1820s-1830s; by Voznesenskii, 1840s; by Pinart, 1870-1872.

46. See sec. 3.3 above.

47. Black, "Ivan Pan'kov," 97; Pierce, *Biographical Dictionary*, 391.

48. Pierce, *Biographical Dictionary*, 325.

49. For possible kinship between these toions, see Lydia T. Black, Epilogue to "Ivan Pan'kov: an Architect of Aleut Literacy," *Orthodox Alaska* 7, no. 4 (October, 1978):32-33.

50. Veniaminov, Journals, comment, 24 April 1828.

51. Black, "Ivan Pan'kov," 97.

52. Veniaminov, Journals, 13 April and 24 April 1828, 16 September 1829. In 1824, Pan'kov was forty-six years old (Black, "Ivan Pan'kov," 96), Veniaminov was twenty-seven years old (b. 1797).

53. Black, "Epilogue," 29-32; id., "Ivan Pan'kov," 98; Pierce, *Biographical Dictionary*, 392. See sec. 4 below.

54. *Voyage of Gideon*, 142.

55. Ibid., 122.

56. Veniaminov, *Notes*, 233.

57. Veniaminov, *Notes*, 229; id., "Conditions," 51. See also note 46 above.

58. See notes 37-41 above: where a Shelikhov enterprise is not named, cf. the location with the enterprise(s) operative at that place at that time.

59. Appendix 8, "Inscriptions for the monument to Grigorii Shelikhov," in Shelikhov, *Voyage to America*, 136.

60. P. A. Tikhmenev, *A History of the Russian-American Company*, trans. and ed. Richard A. Pierce and Alton S. Donnelly (Seattle and London: University of Washington Press, 1978), 15-16, 35-36.

61. Appendix 9, "Extract from Iurii Radchenko," in Shelikhov, *Voyage to America*, 143-144.

62. Based on an ecclesiology from, e.g., England. See Gregory L. Freeze, "Introduction," *I. S. Belliustin: Description of the Clergy in Rural Russia* (Ithaca and London: Cornell University Press, 1985), 17.

63. Veniaminov, "Glance at the Aleuts' Present Enlightenment," in *Notes*, 317-323.

64. Veniaminov, Journals, comment, 24 April 1828. See Black, "Ivan Pan'kov," 97.

65. For the latter, see Veniaminov, Journals, summaries for the month of March 1833 and for the year 1836. This work was published in its Russian version in forty

editions and translated into a number of languages (Pierce, *Biographical Dictionary*, 522), including English from the Russian version: "The Way into the Kingdom of Heaven," trans. Paul Garret, in Oleksa, *Alaskan Missionary Spirituality*, 80-119

66. Veniaminov to Archbishop Mikhail of Irkutsk, 5 November 1829, Attestation by toion Ivan Pan'kov, Miscellaneous Papers, Russian Church, Alaska Historical Library, trans. Lydia T. Black, in Black, "Ivan Pan'kov," 100-102 (reprinted in Oleksa, *Alaska Missionary Spirituality*, 132-135): translated from a handwritten copy in Alaskan archives. A published version may be found in Innokentii (Ivan) Veniaminov, *Pis'ma*, ed. Ivan Barsukov (Petersburg, 1897-1901); but Barsukov's edition has not yet received a critical study.

67. S. A. Mousalimas, "Russian Orthodox Missionaries and Southern Alaskan Shamans," in *Russia in North America*, ed. Richard A. Pierce (Kingston, Ontario, and Fairbanks, Alaska: Limestone Press, 1990), 318-319. But Veniaminov was a parish priest, not a missionary. See also, id., "Contrasting Theological Outlooks on Ancient Kodiak Culture," *Greek Orthodox Theological Review* 34, no. 4 (1989): 365-378.

68. Veniaminov, *Notes*, 219-220. He had his own roots in the region where the term "shaman" derived, assimilated into the Russian language from the Evenk (Tungus): he had been born and raised in the Irkutsk gubernia, Siberia. For two perspectives on shamanism, see S. A. Mousalimas, "Shamans of Old in Southern Alaska," in *Shamanism: Past and Present,* ed. M. Hoppal and O. J. von Sadovsky (Budapest: Ethnographic Institute of the Hungarian Academy of Sciences, and Los Angeles: ISTOR Books, 1989), 307-316.

69. Andrew P. Kashevarov, "John Veniaminov, Innocent, Metropolitan of Moscow and Kolomna," in Oleksa, *Alaska Missionary Spirituality*, 346 (first published in *Alaska Magazine* 1 [1927]).

70. See *Journals of Netsvetov: Atkha Years*, 241-244.

71. See *Journals of Netsvetov: Yukon Years*, 103-105.

JOURNALS OF THE PRIEST
IOANN VENIAMINOV
IN ALASKA, 1823 TO 1836

JOURNAL NO. 1

*Kept by the priest Ioann Veniaminov during his stay
on the island of Sitka from October 20, 1823, to May 1, 1824,
in which he describes his activities relative to his duties.*

On August 30, 1823, between 1:00 and 2:00 in the afternoon, I set out from Okhotsk on the sloop *Konstantin*. I finally caught sight of Sitka [Baranof Island], and, after enduring a severe storm all night while sailing among many rocks, anchored safely at 8:00 P.M. on October 20th.

October 20. Saturday. 10:00. I appeared for the first time before the Chief Manager of the Russian colonies in America, Captain Lieutenant of the Navy and Bearer of the Cross of St. George, Matvei Ivanovich Murav'ev.

October 23. Tuesday. I spoke with Mr. Murav'ev, stating that, in order not to live idly here for so long, I intended and desired to teach the students of the local school as much as possible of God's law. I would teach the Catechism and the Sunday Gospel readings, since no one here has devoted himself to this teaching. I would teach the Catechism at the school on Wednesdays and Fridays from 9:00 to 11:00 and the readings at the church on Sunday[1] from 8:00 to 9:00, before the Liturgy. My proposal was accepted, approved, and complied with.

October 24. Wednesday. It was also proposed that I be introduced to a person knowing both the Russian and Unalaskan Aleut languages, and Russian grammar as well. From this person I could acquire in advance at least a few words of the language that I will need to know perfectly in order to address and edify the inhabitants of Unalaska. I have heard that they know Russian, but not all know it, and those who do, know it quite poorly. An instruction was issued in accordance with my proposal.

October 26. Friday. 10:00. I went to the school[2] and sang with the students the prayer "O Heavenly King" and the Lord's Prayer. I gave a brief explanation of the learning that is so important and necessary for all, a learning which I intend to give them. As much as possible according to my convictions, I began to teach the Short Catechism and went through the first chapter of its first part, giving all possible explanations and proofs for every word requiring elucidation, and adding the natural proofs for the existence of God that are found in the Full Catechism. Finally, we concluded with the prayer "It is Truly Meet."

October 27. Saturday. Today, a person such as I had requested, a Creole, appeared to show me the Unalaskan Aleut language.[3]

October 28. Sunday. 9:00. In church I explained the Gospel reading for the Nineteenth Sunday [after Pentecost]: selections 12 and 26. The moral: love your enemies and return good for evil, not only without bearing any grudges, but with love. This is the highest and most useful Christian virtue, a Christian's distinguishing trait, and so forth.

October 31. Wednesday. 10:00 and 11:00. In school I taught the second chapter of the first part of the Catechism. This chapter concerns the existence of God—who He is and the image or form which we can form of Him, and the perfection which must necessarily be found in Him, and its consequences.

Besides the aforementioned very slight pursuits in connection with my actual duties, I read a book by Thomas à Kempis, *The Imitation of Christ*. I am told that it was translated from the Latin by M. M. Speranskii.[4] I also occupied myself with noting down and memorizing Aleut words.

1823
November

November 2. Friday. 10:00; 11:00; and 11:45. At school I briefly went over the first lecture, and then read through the third chapter, on Divine Worship. This chapter describes the gratitude, reverence, and obedience that we owe to the Supreme Being without any expectation of reward, due only by the right of creation, and so on.

November 4. Sunday. 9:00 A.M. At church I explained the Gospel reading for the Twentieth and Twenty-first Sundays after Pentecost, Luke, selections 30 and 35.

The moral lesson of the first is that the omnipotence and mercy of Jesus Christ are boundless, and that He can work the very same wonders both today and forever into the future. The second passage treats the Word of God and the different people who obey it.

November 7. Wednesday. 10:00; 11:00; and 11:30. In school, I briefly went over the first part of the Catechism. I then began the second, which is on Evangelical faith. It teaches that faith does not demand any further tests or coercion, but rather requires only a good and obedient will; such is the very meaning of the word "faith." Therefore, faith, even if it is without works and is dead, can still change into truth, into justification, as in the case of Abraham in Genesis 15:6. [It explains] the difference between the faith of our forefathers and our faith, and so on. After that I began to explain the first statement of the Nicene Creed, and the mystery of the Holy Trinity. I discussed in particular the first person of the Trinity, using, when possible, proofs and explanations from the Holy Scriptures for each word in the Creed.

November 8. Thursday. I concelebrated the Liturgy. After the Liturgy I conducted the appropriate prayer service with proclamations for the Imperial Family and for Mikhail, Bishop of Irkutsk, Nerchinsk, and Yakutsk.

Before the dismissal at the end of the Liturgy, some Koloshi were admitted into the church by their request and our agreement.

November 9. Friday. 10:00; 11:00. In school I taught the first and second statements of the Creed, about the pre-eternal birth of the Son of God, about the origin of the Holy Spirit, and about the unified equality [of the three members of the Trinity], and so forth. Since he did not know, I informed the local priest, Aleksei Sokolov, of the birth of the Grand Princess Ol'ga Nikolaevna, and of the fact that the Bishop of Irkutsk is now called the Bishop of Irkutsk, Nerchinsk, and Yakutsk, according to [dispatch] No. 13.

November 11. Sunday. 9:00 and 9:30. In church I explained the Gospel reading, which tells the story of the rich man and Lazarus. The moral has to do with the reasons why the rich man, who only celebrated every day and could not bear to see Lazarus standing at his gate, was deprived of the enjoyment of the Heavenly Kingdom, while Lazarus, who may even have caused his own illness, was favored.

November 14. Wednesday. 10:00 and 11:00. At school I taught the third statement of the Nicene Creed: the Son of God descended to earth by His own will alone, and through His mercy toward mankind. We had nothing else besides the hope restored by Him through His mercy [?one word illegible].

November 15. Thursday. I led a service of thanksgiving to the Lord God on this, the birthday of my son Innokentii, in return for all the blessings that He has generously showered upon us up until now.

November 16. Friday. 10:00 and 11:00.[5] In school I taught the fourth statement of the Nicene Creed, as to how the death of Jesus Christ was carried out as a sacrifice for our sins, how He suffered by His own will, and so on.

November 18. Sunday. 9:00. In church I discussed the Gospel passage about the rich man and Lazarus. Not all of the students were present at 9:00, and there was only one visitor. By the end, though, they began to gather. Because of this experience, and with the agreement of the Chief Manager, I have established that, starting the Sunday after next (i.e., December 2), I will teach the Gospel lesson in school on Mondays. This change results from the fact that at nine o'clock it is still dark, and it is cold in the church.[6]

November 21. Wednesday. 8:30 and 9:30 [?]. In church I explained the Gospel reading for the Festival of the Most Holy Mother of God: Luke, selection 54. The moral: to listen to the Word of God is a duty that one must hold above all worldly troubles, since a man has only one need: salvation. After the Gospel lesson, I celebrated the Liturgy.

November 23. Friday. 10:00 and 11:00. In school I taught the fifth and sixth statements of the Nicene Creed, and there was a reading from Matthew, selections 114, 115, and 116.

November 25. Sunday. 10:00. In church I explained the Gospel for the Twenty-fourth Sunday after Pentecost, Luke, selection 39. The moral: just as in Biblical times, firm and true faith in Jesus Christ can still cure all illness today.

November 26. Monday. I celebrated the Vigil Service, the Liturgy, and a prayer service to St. Innokentii.

November 28. Wednesday. 10:00 and 11:00. In school I taught the seventh and eighth statements of the Nicene Creed, which concern the Last Judgement. They tell how it is not known when it will come, so that it is necessary always to be ready, and so on. I also spoke about the Third Person of the Holy Trinity.

November 30. Friday. 10:00 and 11:00. In school I taught the ninth and tenth statements of the Nicene Creed, in particular about the Sacrament of Holy Baptism and about Divine Grace.

In addition to the above activities, I read Plutarch's book for youth; and (2) the first part of Mr. Karamzin's *History of Russia*. I also copied down Aleut words.

1823
December

December 3. Monday. 10:00. In school I explained the Gospel reading for the Twenty-fifth Sunday, Luke, selection 53. The moral: each man must do good to every other man, no matter who he may be, as long as he needs the help of others. We must do this without expectation of reward or recompense, without thought of reward.

December 5. Wednesday. 10:00 and 11:00. I taught about the sacraments of Baptism, Chrismation, Confession, and Communion; I spoke of them as the only means to gain Divine Grace and the Heavenly Kingdom.

December 6. Thursday. I celebrated the appointed prayer service.

December 7. Friday. 10:00 and 11:00. I taught about the sacraments of Priesthood, Marriage, and Extreme Unction. I also taught about the eleventh and twelfth statements of the Nicene Creed concerning the future reckoning of the righteous and the sinful, and so on.

December 10. Monday. 10:00 and 11:00. In school I explained the Gospel reading for the Twenty-sixth Sunday after Pentecost, and the Gospel read in memory of Righteous Anna: Luke, selections 66 and 36. The moral of the first is to avoid envying the wealthy or passionately giving oneself over and rather to feel satisfied with one's state. The moral of the second is how beloved to God are all who obey His Word, and so on.

December 12. Wednesday. I celebrated the Liturgy and a prayer service of thanksgiving.

December 14. Friday. 10:00 and 11:00. I taught about the Law of God in general. I discussed the fact that this Law is known a priori, for it has been written in the heart of every man, and so on. I then taught the First Commandment of the Law.

December 17. Monday. 10:00 and 11:00. I explained the Gospel readings for the Sunday of the Forefathers and the Twenty-seventh Sunday after Pentecost: Luke, selections 76 and 77. The moral lesson of the first is that we act baselessly when we heedlessly ignore the voice calling us to salvation. I discussed the excuses we give for this failure to hear. The second reading teaches us that we must try harder to show love to those nearby than to observe the external forms of piety, and so on.

December 18. Tuesday. 11:00. In school I taught the Second Commandment of the Law of God.

December 19. Wednesday. 10:00 and 11:00. I taught the Third Commandment after reviewing the Second.

December 21. Friday. 10:00 and 11:00. I taught the Fourth Commandment after reviewing the first three. I concluded by saying that all of these Commandments are encompassed in the words "love the Lord thy God with all your heart," and so on. Thus, I ended the year 1823.

December 25. Tuesday. I concelebrated the Liturgy and a prayer service.

This month I read the following books: [?*Dukh Ekkarstgauzeneo*], the second part of the *History of Russia*, and a glossary of technical words. I also took notes on Aleut words.[7]

1824
January

January 1. Tuesday. I celebrated the Liturgy and then a prayer service.

January 2. Wednesday. 10:00. In school I reviewed the first four Commandments, since not all present had been students earlier.

January 4. Friday. 10:00 and 11:00. I taught the Fifth Commandment.

January 6. Sunday. I concelebrated the Liturgy and performed a Blessing of the Water.

January 7. Monday. 11:00. I explained the Gospel reading for the Twenty-ninth Sunday after Pentecost, and for the week before Epiphany: Luke, selection 85, and Mark, selection 1. The moral of the first concerns how we ought to give thanks to God—for what and when. The second teaches that the baptism spread by John the Baptist and that now carried out by the Christian Church are one in the same, and that this baptism is the sole means to our reconciliation with God.

January 9. Wednesday. 10:00 and 11:00. I taught the Fifth Commandment and spoke of respect for [?one word illegible] one's superiors.

January 10. Friday. 10:00 and 11:00. I taught the Sixth Commandment.

January 13. After the Hours I performed a prayer service on this day instead of on the 12th.

January 14. Monday. 11:00. I explained the Gospel readings for the Sunday before Epiphany and the Thirty-first Sunday after Pentecost—Matthew, selection 8, and Luke, selection 93. The moral of the first is that there is no need to postpone the time of repentance, and as much as you have fallen, that much will you be exalted. The second states that the Lord is always ready to fulfill any of our requests that are truly beneficial for us, if only we ask Him with zeal and faith.

January 16. Wednesday. 10:00 and 11:00. I taught the Seventh and Eighth Commandments.

January 18. Friday. 10:00 and 11:00. I taught the Ninth and Tenth Commandments, and spoke generally about love toward those near us, giving examples of this love.

January 21. Monday. 11:00. I explained the Gospel reading for Zacchaeus Sunday: Luke, selection 94. The moral lesson is that God accepts and forgives every sinner who will just repent sincerely.

January 23. Wednesday. 10:00 and 11:00. As a supplement to, or an elucidation of, the Ten Commandments, I interpreted excerpts from Matthew, chapters 5, 6, and 7.

January 25. Friday. 10:00 and 11:00. I taught the nature of true prayer and explained how we have a right to call God the Creator "Our Father." I also covered other aspects of the preface to the Lord's Prayer.

January 28. Monday. 11:00. I explained the Gospel reading for this Sunday, the story of the tax collector and the Pharisee. The moral concerns the reasons why a tax collector—an obvious sinner who recognizes himself to be just that—is absolved, while the Pharisee—who gives thanks to God—is condemned.

January 30. Wednesday. 10:00 and 11:00. I taught the first petition of the Lord's Prayer, and spoke of what benefit it holds for us.

This month I read the third, fourth, fifth, and sixth parts of the *History of Russia*. I also read a book on the memorable features of St. Petersburg.

1824
February

February 1. Friday. 10:00 and 11:00. I taught the second and third petitions of the Lord's Prayer.

February 3. Sunday. After the Hours I performed a prayer service to Simeon and Anna.

February 4. Monday. 11:00. I explained the Gospel story of the Prodigal Son and the Gospel reading for the day marking the Presentation of Christ in the Temple ["Candlemas"]. The moral: if we follow the prodigal son's example by living dissolutely, then we should also follow his example by turning to our Heavenly Father. He is already ready to be merciful to us, even before we turn to Him, if we only form a firm intention of doing so. He also, so to speak, has already gone far toward meeting us with His help.

February 6. Wednesday. 10:00 and 11:00. I taught the fourth and fifth petitions of the Lord's Prayer.

February 8. Friday. 10:00 and 11:00. The sixth and seventh petitions and conclusion of the Lord's Prayer. With that I finished the Catechism.

February 10. Sunday. After the Liturgy I performed a prayer service to St. Innocent.

February 11. Monday. 11:00. I explained the Gospel reading for Shrovetide. This reading concerns the Last Judgement. The moral: how highly the Judge values our acts of mercy, and how sternly He makes us answer for our unmerciful acts, and so on.

February 13. Wednesday. 10:00 and 11:00. I began to review the Catechism and taught the obvious, natural, and innate proofs of the existence of God.

February 17. Sunday. I celebrated the Liturgy.

February 18. Monday. 11:00. I explained the Gospel reading for the First Sunday in Lent, Matthew, verse 17. The moral concerns how we should keep the fast and forgive our brothers their trespasses.

February 19. Tuesday. 10:00 and 11:00. I taught about the substance, properties, and perfections that are necessarily found in God, of whom we have a natural conception, and who must exist, and so on.

February 20. 10:00 and 11:00. I taught about the reverence that our reason and heart inspire us to show to the Source of All Existence. He is also the source of both our present prosperity, and, more especially, our future well-being, and so on.

February 23. Saturday. I attended the Liturgy and gave a sermon before Communion. [Missing footnote in original.]

February 24. Sunday. I celebrated the Liturgy, and thus began the first week of Lent.

February 25. Monday. 10:00. I discussed the Gospel reading for the First Sunday of Lent, John, selection 5. The moral: a firm and unquestioning faith in Jesus Christ is beneficial for us and is our redemption, and so on.

February 27. Wednesday. 10:00. I taught about faith and about why the Holy Scripture is holy and worthy of our acceptance.

February 29. Friday. 10:00. I taught about the mystery of the Holy Trinity, particularly in regard to the first Person, and about Sacred History in brief up to the birth of Christ.

This month I read the following books: (1) the seventh, eighth, and ninth parts of the *History of Russia*; (2) [a book on] the Crusades by Voltaire; (3) a book on the death of Jean Calais, who was martyred by fervor, written by Voltaire; (4) [a book on] Napoleonic policies by Neverov; and (5) a story about the pernicious thoughts of Bonaparte, translated by Shishkov.

1824
March

March 3. Monday. 11:00. I discussed the Gospel reading for the Saturday and Sunday of the second week of Lent: Mark, selections 6 and 7. The moral of the first is that no matter how zealous prayer might be, without faith it is ineffectual. The moral of the second is that he who does not want to believe in Jesus Christ cannot be persuaded by anyone through any means, and so on.

March 5. Wednesday. 10:00 and 11:00. I taught about the second and third Persons of the Holy Trinity. I also spoke briefly about the Sacred History of the New Testament.

March 7. Friday. 10:00 and 11:00. I spoke about Jesus Christ's mercy, descent to earth, incarnation, birth, life, and teachings. I also spoke about why it was necessary that He be made flesh on earth.

March 10. Monday. 11:00. I discussed the Gospel readings for the Third Sunday in Lent and for the remembrance of martyrs—Mark 37 and Luke 106. The moral lesson concerns the nature of the cross, and what it means to walk in the footsteps of Jesus Christ. Each offense and insult that we bear from others is a cross on the way to the Heavenly Kingdom.

To bear these patiently is to carry His cross. In the end the patience animated by faith, hope, and love, overcomes everything and makes us sharers in Christ's paradise, and so on.

Wednesday. March 12. I concelebrated the Liturgy and then a prayer service during which the newly arrived Kolosh toions [leaders] were allowed into the church. Two of these pray in Russian and say that they have been baptized.

Friday. March 14. 9:00 and 10:00. I taught about the death of Jesus Christ, speaking about its necessity and the time chosen for its occurrence, and then I interpreted the Gospel reading for the evening of Holy Friday.

Saturday. March 15. I attended the Liturgy and delivered a sermon before Communion.

Sunday. March 16. I celebrated the Liturgy. On this day I began another week.

Monday. March 17. 10:00. I explained the Gospel reading for the Fourth Sunday in Lent, Mark, selection 40. The moral: fasting is the confirmation of prayer. Prayer strengthened by fasting and faith can drive out demons and work great wonders, for God's omnipotence is inexhaustible.

Wednesday. March 19. 8:30; 10:00. I taught about Jesus Christ's resurrection and His appearance before His disciples after His resurrection.

Friday. March 21. 8:30 and 10:00. I spoke of the Ascension of Christ. I also spoke about the Last Judgement, describing when it will occur and what it will entail.

Monday. March 24. 8:30 and 10:00. I interpreted the Gospel readings for the Fifth Sunday in Lent and for the commemoration of Saint Mary of Egypt: Mark, selection 41 and Luke, selection 33. The moral: why it is that our prayer sometimes goes unfulfilled, even though it is sent to God with faith. There is only one way to be greater than others: serve others with sincerity and zeal, following the example of the Savior. The second Gospel reading, instead of giving a moral, gives an example of a fornicating woman in the Gospels. The passage shows her zealous and complete repentance and the mercy of God, who absolves man's numerous sins.

Tuesday. March 25. I celebrated the Liturgy.

Wednesday. March 26. 10:00. I spoke about the Holy Spirit and about the Church that Christ heads, a Church spread by the Apostles, and confirmed by the councils of the Holy Fathers. I spoke of the Church's unity, composition, and marks [*chrekhakh*]. I spoke briefly of the History of the Apostles and of the Seven Ecumenical Councils.

Thursday. March 27. 10:00 and 11:00. I taught about the sacraments of the Holy Church. Like faith, the sacraments, by virtue of the very meaning of the word sacrament, require neither further proofs nor coercion. I also taught about God's grace, which every man needs.

Friday. March 28. 10:00 and 11:00. I taught about the resurrection of the dead, and about the fact that such resurrection is possible. I also spoke of the changes to occur in those who will live, as taught by the Apostle Paul. [I taught about] the eternal life to come. Finally, I reviewed all the essentials of the Christian religion, and reiterated that this religion should be, and surely will be, untouched by the passage of time through the ages.

Saturday. March 29. I attended the Liturgy and delivered a sermon before Communion.

Monday. March 31. On this day, I began to conduct the church services and continued to conduct them until the eighth day of April.

During this month I read the following books: (1) *On Unification of Reason and the Heart,* by Zimmerman; (2) *On the Advantages of Free Trade*, by Candillac; (3) *On the Recognition of One's True Self,* by John Mason; and

(4) *The Dogmatics of the Orthodox Christian Church*, translated from the work by Bishop Theofilakt. [Most likely title; Veniaminov does not give the exact title of Bishop Theofilakt's work.]

1824
April

Wednesday. April 2. I heard Confession from some officers of the Navy frigate *Kreiser*; this Confession took place by their own desire. I also heard Confession from the head of the local office and from the supply sargeant.[8]

Sunday. April 6. On this bright day I delivered a catechetical homily at Matins and concelebrated the Liturgy.[9]

Monday. April 7. I celebrated the Liturgy.

Monday. April 14 [date of April 11th is apparently an error in the original]. 10:00 and 11:00. At the school I taught the Gospel readings for Palm Sunday and Thomas Sunday: John, selections 41 and 65. The moral lesson concerns the degree to which envy is harmful and baneful to the envious one himself, and how it is unbearable, harmful, and worthy of the contempt of others, since an envious man not only does not want to see others who are spared of misfortune and who prosper, but acts the same way in regard to himself. The second moral lesson is about how blissful are those who believe in Jesus Christ without [demanding] any unnecessary proofs, without seeing any kind of signs or miracles, but rather only holding to the simple conviction of a minister of the Gospel; I taught other things from that Gospel selection.

Tuesday. April 15. I celebrated the Liturgy.

Wednesday. April 16. 10:00 and 11:00. I taught about Natural Law in general. I taught that it is known to every man, inasmuch as it is innate, and written on his heart with ineffaceable letters. [I also taught] that it is imperfect in comparison to the Law of the Gospel, and so on.

Friday. April 18. 10:00; 11:00; and 11:30. I taught a general lesson about the Ten Commandments, and about the fact that all of these Commandments are contained in the following two: "Love the Lord Thy God," and "Love Thy Neighbor as Thyself." The moral "Do not do unto others what you do not want done to you" falls far short of expressing the spirit and force of the Law of the Gospel.

I taught the advantages that the Law of the Gospel has as against Natural Law, and about its perfection, simplicity, obvious truth and clarity (which is very great), eternal constancy, and of its great and true value. Finally, I instructed them to remember the following: always put yourself in the place of the other person, and whatever it is that, being in that position, you truly and sincerely desire and require of others in dealing with you, so exactly should you treat that other person, and so on.

Monday. April 21. 11:00. I taught the Gospel reading for the Sunday of Myrrh-bearing Women. The moral is that we should defend the innocent who are oppressed by evil and injustice, and should adhere zealously to the truth, and so on.

Wednesday. April 23. 10:00 and 11:00. I taught about the Lord's Prayer, speaking of its perfection, spirit, and force. I taught the preface, explaining why we call God the Creator "Our Father."

Friday. April 25. 10:00 and 11:00. I taught three petitions of the Lord's Prayer, speaking of their indispensability and vital beneficialness.

April 27. Sunday of the Paralytic. I celebrated the appointed prayer service of thanksgiving.

Monday. April 28. 11:00. I taught the Gospel reading for the Sunday of the Paralytic: John, selection 14. The moral lesson is that many of the repentants will not obtain forgiveness of sins, although they may want it very much. I explained why, and so on.

Wednesday. April 30. 10:00 and 11:00. I taught the last four petitions of the Lord's Prayer. I taught about their indispensability and vitality for us, and about the fact that these petitions, no matter how zealously spoken, will not be granted if we do not do our part to assist in their fulfillment. Lastly I spoke about the importance and force of the conclusion of the Lord's Prayer.

This month I read *A Precise Guide to the Rearing of Children*, which was compiled from the teachings of Georg Joachim Zollikofer, and *The Mystery of the Cross* by Douzetems.

NOTES

1. My proposal was that, at the times of the week mentioned above, all could be freed from work, so that not only the students, but others with the desire, could attend and hear the Word of God. I do not intend merely to explain the Word of the Gospels—I myself still need to study it night and day—but I also intend to draw from it a moral lesson through discussion.

2. I found the school here to be better in all respects than I had expected it to be. Besides explaining Russian grammar, the Short Catechism, and Sacred History in brief, the teacher—a simple, but good man—teaches the students to know by heart arithmetic up to the second level. The students are Creoles—born of Aleuts, Kolosh, and Creoles—as well as several legitimate children of promyshlenniki. The former category of students is maintained at Company expense. The school itself is a house where the teacher and students live; it is old, but quite decent and clean.

3. The inhabitants of almost every island in the Fox chain speak different languages. Some, however, are similar.

4. I do not see it as necessary to indicate what I read on each day, since this would be superfluous information—all the more so because, I admit, I did not spend all of my free time reading.

5. My daughter Ekaterina was born on this date, and baptized on the 24th. The godparents were the Chief Manager, Matvei Ivanovich Murav'ev, and Paraskeva Petrova Prokof'eva, the wife of the Russian-American Company Navigator Mikhail Vasiliev Prokof'ev.

6. The zeal of the visiting listeners had begun to cool as well; at first more than fifteen people assembled, but fewer and fewer came as time went on.

7. I stopped trying to learn them by heart after I had collected over 200, since my teacher would pronounce the same word a certain way one day and quite differently at some later time.

8. Their names are as follows: the captain of the ship was Mikhail Petrovich Lazarev, a captain of the second rank and cavalier. The lieutenant was Mikhail Dmitrievich Annenkov. The midshipmen were Dmitrii Irinarkovich Zavalishin, Pavel Matveevich Murav'ev and Ivan Petrovich Butenin. The managers are Kirill Timofeevich Khlebnikov and Grigorii Ivanovich Sungurov.

9. The concelebration included Father Ilarii, a monk from the Aleksandr Nevskii Monastery [*Lavra*] who had arrived on the frigate *Kreiser*, where he lives; the priest Ioann Veniaminov; and the priest Aleksei Sokolov.

JOURNAL NO. 2

*Kept by IoannVeniaminov in accordance with his duty
as priest of the church in Unalaska from
July 29, 1824, until July 1, 1825, in which he describes
his service in connection with his duties.*

1824

On **July 29th** at nine o'clock I stood anchored in the harbor at Unalaska. I had set off from Sitka on July 1st of this year, at seven o'clock in the morning, aboard the brig *Riurik*, and had a successful, though prolonged, voyage—successful, except for its ending. [Note missing in text?]

Tuesday. July 29. At two o'clock I took Confession from, and administered the Eucharist to, the wife of the Russian Merkul'ev. She had been suffering from consumption, and finally had not risen from her bed for more than seven months. She died two hours after I had seen her; it was as though she had expected this to happen.

Thursday. July 31. At nine o'clock, I chrismated the two children of the local administrator, adding the prayers for public ablution and baptism. At four o'clock I performed a funeral service for the deceased woman, and celebrated Vespers.

August

Friday. August 1. Having celebrated Matins at the appointed time, I celebrated the Liturgy in the chapel sanctuary on the portable communion cloth for the first time since the birth of Christ and even since the creation of the world. I administered Communion to the young people [one word illeglible]. Then I attended a blessing of the water at a small river, which is a more proper setting for a ceremony that is both a church and folk ceremony. Then I returned to the church. Upon celebrating the Liturgy, I instructed that an official document be read along with some items from a decree sent to me from the Irkutsk Holy Consistory. After reading this decree, I delivered a speech of greeting instead of one of instruction.

I led a Prayer of Thanksgiving to the Lord God, who by His grace had allowed me to reach this region successfully and in good health, to the God

17

who has gladdened the inhabitants here, inhabitants of many years, by my arrival. I proclaimed the "Many Years" for His Majesty the Emperor, and for the Right Reverend Mikhail, Bishop of Irkutsk, Nerchinsk, and Yakutsk. This proclamation was accompanied by a cannon salute, after which the head of the office presented me with a document on which he and the clerk greeted me on behalf of the Russian-American Company and expressed their joy and zeal.[1] They expressed themselves both in word and in deed: they attached to the document a list of volunteers who had donated more than 900 units of local currency for my use.[2]

August 3. Sunday. Having celebrated Vespers and Matins at their appointed times, I celebrated the Hours at nine o'clock and then chrismated and married Aleuts who were setting out for the small islands.[3]

August 4. Monday. I sacramentally blessed three marriages.

August 6. Wednesday. At their appointed time I celebrated Vespers and the Vigil Service. At ten o'clock I celebrated the Liturgy and a prayer service. Before the prayer service, I taught the Aleuts, through an interpreter, about the Divine Existence and Essence, using all possible proofs.
   Comment: At six o'clock the vessel *Riurik* went to the small islands.

August 7. Thursday. I gave an exhortation to the departing Aleuts, especially to their leader, who knows the Aleut language perfectly, but also knows Russian very well.

August 9. Saturday. At Vespers I gave instructions to the Aleuts departing for their own villages.

August 10. Sunday. I taught the Aleuts about reverence for God. I celebrated the Hours, and then the prayer service for the 9th.

August 10; August 11, Monday; August 12, Tuesday. At four o'clock I celebrated Vespers, and from this day forward celebrated services for those Aleuts who are keeping the fast [of the Dormition].

August 13. Wednesday. After Vespers I chrismated twenty-four persons.

August 14. Thursday. After Matins I explained to the fasting Aleuts through an interpreter, about the Sacrament of Confession. We are forgiven of sin through it, and we need it in order to receive that forgiveness. After the Hours, having reviewed the previous material, I explained the Sacrament of the Eucharist, and then spoke about everything that is required for this sacrament—what is needed and what is proper. After hearing Confession from eighteen people, and after conducting Vespers, I celebrated the Vigil Service.

August 15. Friday. Upon reading the Common Rule of Prayer and reviewing my previous lessons, I celebrated the Liturgy and gave Communion to those who had confessed and to the children who had been chrismated.

August 17. Sunday. I celebrated the Hours, and then I chrismated eight people.

August 18. Monday. I gave Final Communion to an ill person.

August 24. Sunday. In the evening I celebrated Matins. I also celebrated the Hours and a prayer service in place of the one on the 12th.

Comment: At ten o'clock the vessel *Riurik,* returned from the islands, stood at anchor.

August 26. Tuesday. I baptized an infant.

August 27. Wednesday. I heard Confession from an ill person, to whom I then gave Communion.

August 28. Thursday. I celebrated the Vigil Service [one word illegible].

August 29. Friday. I celebrated a memorial service and the Hours.

August 30. Saturday. After Vespers, the Vigil, and the Liturgy at their appointed times, I celebrated the prayer service prescribed by the typicon with a cannon salute.

August 31. Sunday. I celebrated the Hours and a Royal memorial service for the month of August. [A Royal memorial service is given for a member of the imperial family who died on a given day.]

This month I read the first volume of Robertson's history of America and prepared papers and letters.

September

September 1. Monday. The papers prepared last month to send to Irkutsk and Sitka were sealed.

September 2. Tuesday. I celebrated a prayer service, as it was my name day.

   Comment: At six o'clock in the morning [?], the vessel *Riurik* departed for a voyage.

September 3. Wednesday. I baptized an infant.

September 5. Friday. Having celebrated Vespers and the Vigil Service at the appointed time, I celebrated the Liturgy and a prayer service at nine o'clock.

September 7. Sunday. Having celebrated Matins in the evening, I did not celebrate the Hours because of very high winds.

September 8. Monday. Having observed Vespers and the Vigil Service in the evening, in the morning I chrismated three persons, celebrated the Liturgy, and gave Communion to those who had been chrismated.

September 10. Wednesday. I performed a funeral service.

[September 11]. *Comment*: At noon the vessel *Riurik* departed.

September 14. Sunday. I read the Lesser Vespers in the evening. In the morning, I celebrated Matins with the Veneration of the Cross, and the Liturgy. In the evening, after Vespers, I celebrated the Vigil Service.

September 15. Monday. I celebrated the Liturgy and a prayer service, and sacramentally blessed eight marriages.

[September 16.] *Comment*: At 7:30 in the morning there was a moderate earthquake.

September 17-19. Wednesday, Thursday, and Friday. I was ill with a cold.

September 20. Saturday. I performed a funeral service.

September 21. Sunday. Having celebrated the Hours, I celebrated a Royal memorial service for all of September.

September 28. Sunday. Having celebrated Vespers, Matins, and the Hours at the appointed times, I celebrated a prayer service and chrismated and baptized an infant, and sacramentally blessed four marriages.

This month I read the Book of Martyrs and *The Victory of Faith* (in 3 parts) by Chateaubriand.

October

October 1. Wednesday. Before a congregation of those free from work, I celebrated in the chapel a prayer service to the Virgin Mary, accompanied by a ringing of the bells.

October 5. Sunday. I celebrated Matins and the Hours, and performed a funeral service.

October 9. Thursday. I performed a funeral service for an infant who had passed away.

October 12. Sunday. I celebrated Vespers at its appointed time. I celebrated Matins, the Hours, and the prayer service for the 11th.

October 14. Tuesday. I celebrated the Hours and a prayer service.

October 19. Sunday. I celebrated the Hours.

October 26. Sunday. I celebrated Matins, the Liturgy, and a Royal memorial service.

October 29. Wednesday. I baptized an infant.

As before, this month I sometimes read the Book of Martyrs. I was also occupied with the building of an organ.

November

November 2. Sunday. Having observed Vespers at its appointed time, I celebrated Matins and the Hours.

November 8. Saturday. Having celebrated Vespers at its appointed time, I celebrated Matins, the Hours, and a prayer service with a proclamation of the "Many Years" for His Imperial Majesty and for the Right Reverend Mikhail, Bishop of Irkutsk.

November 9. I celebrated Vespers, Matins, and the Hours.

November 15. Saturday. As it was the birthday of my son and daughter, I celebrated a prayer service of thanksgiving to the Lord God, who has blessed me.

November 16. Sunday. I celebrated Vespers, Matins, and the Hours.

November 23. Sunday. I celebrated Vespers, Matins, the Hours, and a Royal memorial service.

Comment: On the 23rd at nine o'clock, there was a large earthquake.

November 27. Thursday. Having celebrated Vespers and a Vigil in the evening, I celebrated the Liturgy. I celebrated a prayer service to St. Innocent at the appointed time.

November 30. Sunday. I celebrated Vespers, Matins, the Hours, and a prayer service.

This month I read *A Historical View of the Course of the Century* [?author not given], and was occupied with the construction of the organ mentioned previously.

December

December 6. Saturday. In the morning, after celebrating Vespers and the Vigil, I celebrated the Liturgy and a prayer service to St. Nicholas.

December 7. Sunday. I celebrated Vespers, Matins, and the Hours.

December 12. Friday. I celebrated Vespers, a Vigil, the Liturgy, and a prayer service.

December 14. Sunday. I celebrated Vespers, Matins, and the Hours.

December 21. Sunday. I celebrated Vespers and the Hours.

December 24. Wednesday. I celebrated the Hours and Vespers without the Liturgy.

December 25. I celebrated Matins with a Blessing of the Breads, the Liturgy, and a prayer service with a cannon salute. Moreover, since by this day many Aleuts had gathered,[4] at the proper place in the Liturgy I gave a speech that I had composed on the essence, incarnation, and birth of Jesus Christ, and on the purpose of his having come to Earth.

December 26. Friday. I celebrated Vespers, Matins, and the Hours.

December 28. Sunday. I celebrated Vespers, Matins, the Hours, and a Royal memorial service for all of December.

This month I finished the organ. Sometimes I read *A Historical View of the Course of the Century*.

1825
January

January 1. Thursday. Having celebrated Vespers and Matins at the appointed time, I celebrated the Liturgy and a prayer service. During the Liturgy I delivered a sermon that I had written about the life of Jesus Christ from His birth until Epiphany. The main moral lesson is that we, in imitation of Jesus Christ, should obey without a grumble any superior that has been placed over us—no matter what he is like—and should fulfill his legitimate commands.

January 2. Friday. I chrismated one person and I sacramentally blessed one marriage between Aleuts who are leaving for their own villages.

January 4. Sunday. I celebrated Vespers, Matins, and the Hours.

January 5. Monday. I baptized an infant, and celebrated the Hours and Vespers without the Liturgy, but with a Blessing of the Water.

January 6. Tuesday. After conducting Matins, I celebrated the Liturgy and attended a Blessing of the Water at a stream. This rite was accompanied by a cannon salute.

January 7. I celebrated Vespers, Matins, the Hours and a prayer service.

January 11. Sunday. I celebrated Vespers, Matins, and the Hours.

January 13. Tuesday. I celebrated Vespers, Matins, the Hours, and a prayer service.

January 18. Sunday. I celebrated Vespers, Matins, and the Hours.

January 25. Sunday. I celebrated Vespers, the Hours, and a memorial service for all of January.

This month I read the following books: *A Historical View of the Course of the Century*, volume 4, and *Notes of the Naval Officer Bronevskii* in 4 volumes [?possibly Vladimir Bogdanovich Bronevskii, who published a two-volume account of a journey from Trieste to St. Petersburg in 1810]. I was also occupied with the writing of church books and other matters.

February

February 1. Sunday. I celebrated the Hours.

February 2. Monday. At their appointed times, I celebrated Vespers and the Vigil Service, and then I celebrated the Liturgy.

February 3. Tuesday. I celebrated the Hours and a prayer service.

February 8. Sunday. Having observed Vespers and the Vigil Service in the evening, I celebrated the Liturgy and a prayer service to St. Innocent. I spoke at Vespers, clarifying the present holy Christian rite of asking forgiveness, which we perform on this day.

From this day up until the 16th, I celebrated daily services for those fasting.

February 11. Wednesday. I celebrated the Liturgy of the Presanctified.

February 13. Friday. After Matins I spoke to the observant Aleuts through a translator, instructing them on the Sacrament of Confession, and on the requirements for Confession. I also taught them about faith. After the Hours and the Liturgy of the Presanctified, I celebrated the traditional blessing of the cereal [*koliva*] for the first Saturday of Lent and then heard Confession from ninty-two people.

February 14. Saturday. Having celebrated Matins and the Rule of Prayer, I celebrated the Liturgy and gave Communion to all those who had confessed. Before Communion, I instructed them through a translator about the Sacrament of the Holy Eucharist, with a historical explanation. I instructed them on what is considered to be required, necessary, and appropriate for celebrating the Eucharist.

After Vespers I chrismated seven persons, both men and women, and baptized two infants.

February 15. I celebrated Matins and the Liturgy and gave Communion to those just chrismated. Six youngsters took Confession. Vespers took place at its appointed time.

February 21. Saturday. I celebrated Matins, with a memorial service.

February 22. I celebrated Vespers and Matins at their appointed time, and then I celebrated the Liturgy. Later I celebrated Vespers.

February 28. Saturday. I celebrated Vespers and Matins, with a memorial service for the *afashchiki* [?] buried here.

March

March 1. Sunday. At their appointed times, I celebrated Vespers and Matins with the Veneration of the Cross. I celebrated the Liturgy, and later on, Vespers.

From this date until the 16th of March, I celebrated daily services.

March 4. Wednesday. I celebrated the Liturgy of the Presanctified.

March 6. Friday. After Matins, I instructed the fasting Aleuts through a translator, speaking on the Sacrament of Confession and on all that is necessary for our salvation.

After the Hours and the Liturgy of the Presanctified, I heard Confession.

March 7. Saturday. I observed Matins with a memorial service, and then I celebrated the Liturgy and gave Communion to all those who had confessed.

March 8. Sunday. I celebrated Vespers, Matins, and the Liturgy.

March 9. Monday. I celebrated the Liturgy of the Presanctified.

March 10. Tuesday. In the evening I celebrated Matins with the Great Canon. I also celebrated the Liturgy of the Presanctified.

March 11. Wednesday. After Matins I instructed the fasting Aleuts on Faith, Confession, and the Eucharist. Then I celebrated the Hours and the Liturgy of the Presanctified. After that I heard Confession.

March 12. Thursday. Matins was celebrated with the requisite blessing of the wine and breads. At nine o'clock I celebrated the Liturgy and gave Communion to those who had confessed. I also celebrated a prayer service.

On this day the school here was opened.[5] At present it serves twenty-two students.[6] It was opened with the following ceremony. Having celebrated a suitable prayer service for the health of His Majesty the Emperor, with a cannon salute, I celebrated a prayer service for before the beginning of studies, including a proclamation of the "Many Years" for: (1) His Majesty the Emperor; (2) the Holy Synod and Mikhail, Bishop of Irkutsk, Nerchinsk, and Yakutsk; and (3) all those who desire to teach and to learn, as well as all who assist this good intention. A cannon salute was fired for each. Afterwards the students, who had taken Confession and had received Holy Communion on this day, kissed the cross two-by-two, and entered the school to the ringing of bells. Before them went the local cantor vested in a sticharion and carrying the Gospels. Behind them went I, with the cross, singing the "Our Father" and "Most Blessed Art Thou, O Christ Our God..." [the chief hymn of Pentecost]. Behind me came all of the people attending the ceremony.

The students took their seats. After I had read a prayer, and sprinkled both the building and children with Holy Water, I said another prayer. Then, taking off my outer vestments, I distributed books to the students and read aloud three times the first three letters, pointing on the board with a stick and pronouncing the letters "a," "be," and "ve."

After this, congratulating the assembly, I gave a speech that I had prepared for this occasion, addressing it to the Russians and the Creoles. Moreover, the interpreter spoke to the Aleuts on my behalf, delivering a speech that I had composed on the benefits of learning. After this, as the organ played the Imperial National Anthem, the students congratulated one another on the opening of school. The enthusiasm of each led him to volunteer support for the school and for the poor students. Then, the students rose from their places and read the Lord's Prayer. We left the school in the same order. After this day, teaching was to be daily, with the exception of the last Sunday in Lent, Easter, and most Sundays and holidays.

March 13. Friday. I celebrated the Liturgy of the Presanctified.

March 14. Saturday. I celebrated Matins with the Akathistos, and then I celebrated the Liturgy.

Before the service I preached to those Aleuts who are observing the fast—I spoke about repentance, and so on. I heard Confession both before and after Vespers.

March 15. Sunday. I celebrated Vespers and Matins at the proper time, and [word illegible], and then I celebrated the Liturgy and gave Communion to all those who had confessed. Afterwards I celebrated Vespers.

March 20. Friday. I celebrated Vespers without the Liturgy, and henceforth celebrated every day until April 6.

March 21. I celebrated Matins and the Liturgy.

March 22. Sunday. At the appropriate time I celebrated Vespers and the Vigil Service, with a Liturgy for the deceased buried here. I then celebrated the Liturgy.

March 23. Monday. I celebrated the Hours, with a reading from the Gospels of Matthew and Mark, before the Liturgy [?]. After Vespers I chrismated nineteen persons.

March 24. Tuesday. After Matins I instructed the Aleuts on Faith and the Law, using a translator. Then I celebrated the Hours, with a reading from the Gospel of Luke, and before that [?] the Divine Liturgy. Before Vespers I heard Confession from fourteen people, and I chrismated these afterwards.

March 25. Wednesday. After celebrating Matins and the Hours, with a reading from the Gospel of John, I instructed the Aleuts about the Mysteries and about Holy Communion. Afterwards I celebrated the Liturgy and gave Communion to all those who had confessed. I heard Confession before and after Vespers.

March 26. Thursday. At its appointed time, I celebrated Matins and the Liturgy, and gave Communion to those who had confessed. On this day I gathered a store of gifts for the ill.

March 27. Friday. Having celebrated Matins in the evening, after the Hours I preached on Faith, and so on, to the Aleuts who had recently arrived from Umnak Island. I celebrated the Hours with the Burial Service and a procession around the chapel. I heard Confession in the evening. [?illegible]

March 28. Saturday. After conducting Matins and the Hours at the appointed time, I celebrated Vespers with the Liturgy and gave Communion to those who had confessed.

March 29. Easter. Beginning at midnight, I celebrated Matins in the presence of a multitude of people, with the usual church ceremony. At this ceremony I delivered a catechetical homily.

At 6:30 I celebrated the Liturgy and gave Communion to the youngsters, and then held a procession, accompanied, around the houses and iurts.

March 30. Monday. I celebrated Vespers, Matins, and the Liturgy, and gave Communion to the youngsters.

March 31. The same. [Indicated in original by parentheses with entry for March 30.]

April

April 1. Wednesday. I celebrated Vespers, Matins, and the Hours.
   Comment: On this day I began to prepare for a trip, and the office informed me of an allowance given to support me.

April 2. Thursday. I celebrated Vespers, Matins, and the Hours.

April 3. Friday. I celebrated Vespers, Matins, and the Hours, and celebrated a prayer service for the [hunting] party Aleuts.[7]

April 4. Saturday. I celebrated the Liturgy and divided up the [*artos?*— illegible].

April 5. Sunday. Beginning in the evening, I celebrated Vespers, the Vigil Service, and the Liturgy.

April 7. Tuesday. I celebrated the Liturgy for the deceased buried here and then a general memorial service.

April 12. Sunday. After the Hours had been celebrated, a prayer service was celebrated [text illegible]. A translator was dispatched to accompany me, the Creole Stefan Kriukov,…[text illegible] so that he could translate exactly my instructions.
   By this date I was prepared for my trip, having given to cantor Stefan Veniaminov suitable written instructions on how to act in my absence in regard to the newborn, to ailing people, and to the students in the school.

April 13. Monday. At three o'clock in the afternoon we set out on the proper course, accompanied by a favorable wind. We sailed in a new ten-oar baidara, under sail. However, after we had sailed out of [Unalaska] Bay the wind grew stronger and we turned back into a harbor along the northern side of the island of Amaknak, rowing in at 6:30.

April 16. Thursday. Six o'clock in the morning. We rowed out from the harbor under a calm wind, and then traveled on from here approximately thirty-five versts into a headwind, to arrive at the village of Veselovskoe, where there were no inhabitants to be seen, since they live at different settlements in the winter.

April 17. Friday. Nine o'clock in the evening. We rowed out from Veselovskoe, and had gone no more than twenty versts into a headwind, when we stopped at a spot known as Ermoshak [Cape Kovrizhka].[8]

April 18. Saturday. A strong southerly wind made it impossible to depart, and so we spent the day at Ermoshak.

April 19. Sunday. Since the strong southerly wind had given way to just as strong a westerly wind, we still could not set out to sea, and so, in order not to waste time and to be of some use to the Company [?], I formed the intention of traveling by foot through the mountains to the village of Makushin and I instructed that preparations for this be made.

At 8:30, taking with them everything necessary for the performance of religious rites and the sacraments, approximately twenty persons set out on foot. The wind remained the same. They continued on their way until nine o'clock at night, encountering along the way all possible obstacles: there was no road and not even a path; an excessive amount of snow on the mountain ridges, snow that was quite deep and covered with ice on top; a wind that sometimes stopped the travelers with its strong gusts;[9] and, at times, large flakes of snow falling. I began to regret that we had gone, but finally, although we were exhausted, we reached the village of Makushin. We had traveled nearly twenty-five versts.[10]

At eleven o'clock, I blessed the water, and blessed the sites for the tents and the [two words illegible].

April 20. Monday. 2:00; 3:00. I chrismated twenty persons of both genders and various ages. Afterwards I sat down and explained to them about Chrismation and Baptism.

April 21. Tuesday. The wind was very strong, so that it was impossible to pitch the tents.

April 22. Wednesday. 10:00. I celebrated the Hours and performed a funeral service in the cemetery for the deceased who are resting here [?*afishchiki*]. I then gave Communion to an ill person after due instruction.

April 23. Thursday. 2:00; 3:00. I set up the tent and assembled all of the local inhabitants. Then, through an interpreter, I preached on Faith and the Law, and on the Mysteries of Confession and Communion.

Comment: The baidara arrived from Ermoshak at three o'clock.

4:00; 5:00. I celebrated the Vigil Service and read the Rule of Prayer for the Eucharist.

April 24. Friday. 7:00; 8:00; and 9:00. I read the Rule of Prayer and the Hours. Then, in a tent, I celebrated the full Liturgy and gave Communion to those who had confessed and to the young people.

2:00. I sacramentally blessed seven marriages among Aleuts of the local [one word illegible] villages.

At this time all of the inhabitants of this village had been chrismated, married, heard in Confession, and given Communion.

4:00. I gave all-purpose and legal instructions to the local toion.

April 25. Saturday. A southwesterly wind made it impossible to depart.

April 26. Sunday. [See entry for April 25.] I celebrated a prayer service in the iurt of the toion.

April 27. Monday. [See April 25.]

April 28. Tuesday. At 5:30 in the morning we set out from the village of Makush[in], and, under variable winds, successfully reached the next village, Koshiga [Kashega], at two o'clock in the afternoon.

6:00; 7:00. I chrismated twenty-three people.

April 29. Wednesday. 2:00; 3:00; 4:00; and 5:00. Having duly instructed the local inhabitants on all that which is necessary for our salvation, I heard Confession from them.[11]

7:00 and 8:00. I celebrated the Vigil Service and read the Rule of Prayer.

April 30. Thursday. 6:00; 7:00; 8:00; and 9:00. After a reading of the Rule of Prayer and the Hours, I celebrated the Liturgy in a tent and gave Communion to all those who had confessed and to the youngsters. At the cemetery, I performed a funeral service and memorial service for the deceased. Then, I sacramentally blessed six marriages.

At this time, all the local inhabitants had been chrismated, married, heard in Confession, and given Communion. At 9:45 we set off from Koshiga and sailed with a variable wind to reach the village of Chernovskoe [Chernofski] at 2:45 in the afternoon.

4:00; 5:00; 6:00; 7:00; 8:00; and 9:00. After instructing the local inhabitants sufficiently in regard to the Faith and the Sacraments, I heard

Confession from them, celebrated the Vigil Service, and then sacramentally blessed the marriages of six couples.

May

May 1. Friday. 5:00; 6:00; 7:00; and 8:00. After reading the Rule of Prayer and the Hours in the tent, I chrismated thirteen people, celebrated the Liturgy, and gave Communion to all who had confessed and to the young people.

At this time, all of the local inhabitants had been chrismated, married, heard in Confession and given the Sacrament of Holy Communion.

At nine o'clock we set off under sail with a favorable wind, and at eleven o'clock we reached the village of Tanamykta, having covered a distance of more than fourteen miles or twenty-five versts.

5:00; 6:00; 7:00; 8:00; and 8:30. Upon arriving in the village I gave sufficient instruction concerning Faith and the Law and the sacraments. Then, I chrismated two persons, heard Confession, celebrated the Vigil Service, and sacramentally blessed two marriages.

May 2. Saturday. 4:30; 6:00; 7:00; and 8:00. After a reading of the Rule of Prayer and the Hours, I celebrated the Liturgy and gave Communion to those who had confessed and to the youngsters. Then, after giving the usual general instructions, I set off at eight o'clock.

At this time, all of the local inhabitants had been chrismated, married (except one), heard in Confession, and given Communion.

At 9 P.M. we reached the village of Tulik, which is seven miles distant across Umnak Strait.

At twelve o'clock I chrismated twenty inhabitants of Tulik.

4:00; 5:00; 6:00; 7:00; 8:00. After giving sufficient instruction on the Faith and the Law, I heard Confession, celebrated the Vigil Service, and sacramentally blessed six marriages.

May 3. Sunday. 4:30; 6:00; 7:00; 8:00. After a reading of the Rule of Prayer and the Hours, I celebrated the Liturgy and gave Communion to those who had confessed and to all the youngsters.

At this time, all the local inhabitants had been chrismated, married, heard in Confession, and given Communion.

At eight o'clock, having given the usual general instructions to the toion,[12] we set off from Tulik, following the southern side of Umnak Island. We traveled using oar and sail, under a tailwind. At 9:30 in the evening we reached the large neck of land (from which one can cross over to the village of Recheshnoe [Nikolski] on the northern side). We had traveled around 100 versts.

May 4. Monday. Leaving the baidara on the neck of land, we crossed over on foot to the village of Recheshnoe. We crossed through grass- and white-moss-covered valleys between lakes, a distance of around eight versts. A beautiful place! And how completely unlike mountainous and rocky Unalaska! At the village we were met in an unusual way—with a rifle salute, and with the presence of each and every inhabitant.[13]

May 5. Tuesday. 2:00; 3:00. I chrismated twenty-seven people of both genders and various ages.

6:00; 7:00. I celebrated Matins in the evening.

Comment: Today, as a test, I planted barley in five different places.

May 6. Wednesday. 8:00; 9:00; 10:00. After celebrating the Hours, I chrismated twenty persons, both men and women, of various ages.

5:00. I read through the Lesser Vespers, and then, instead of Confession, I gave instructions to the children in the presence of their fathers and godfathers.

5:30; 7:00; 8:00. I celebrated a Vigil Service, with a blessing of the bread and wine.

May 7. Thursday. 9:00 and 10:00. I celebrated the full Liturgy of St. John of Chrysostom in the local chapel and gave Communion to the young people.

3:00 and 4:00. I sacramentally blessed fourteen marriages.

5:30; 7:30. Instead of conducting the Vigil, I assembled all of the local inhabitants in the chapel, and then preached as usual on Faith and the Law, using interpreters.

May 8. Friday. After celebrating the Hours at its appointed time, I heard Confession from fifty-six persons from among the local inhabitants.

5:00. I read the Lesser Vespers and the Rule of Prayer.

7:00; 8:00. I celebrated the Vigil Service with a blessing of the breads.

May 9. Saturday. 6:00; 7:00. After a reading of the Rule of Prayer and the Hours, I celebrated the full Liturgy in the chapel and gave Communion to those who had confessed. After the Liturgy I celebrated a prayer service to St. Nicholas, with a proclamation of the "Many Years" for His Majesty the

Emperor and for the Right Reverend Mikhail. After this service I held a procession around all the local iurts, carrying the cross.

At 11:30 we set out on foot from the village of Recheshnoe,[14] and went back to the neck of land. We were sent off with another similar ceremony—there was a gun salute, and almost everyone in the village saw us back as far as the neck of land.

At twenty minutes after 1:00 we set out in our baidara, under sail, to make our return journey. We were sent off by another volley of fire. At 4:45 we stopped on the deserted Sevidovskii Island [Vsevidof Island], having gone twenty miles, or thirty-five versts.

May 10. Sunday. Although we set out and covered about ten miles on our return course, we turned around after encountering headwinds and arrived back at the very same island.

May 11. Monday. We set out at eight o'clock, using sail and oar. We reached the village of Tulik. In the sound we encountered a riptide [*suloi*].[15] [Two words illegible.] How horrible it was!

May 12. It was impossible to set out because of a strong headwind and rain.

May 13. Wednesday. We set out by sail at six o'clock. At ten o'clock we arrived at the village of Chernovskoe. After leaving here, we arrived at the village of Koshiga at eight o'clock, having faced a fresh headwind.

May 14. Thursday. Having set out by oar from Koshiga at 8:30, we reached the small town of Ermoshak at eight o'clock in the evening.

May 15. Friday. Having left Ermoshak by oar at nine o'clock, we arrived at the village of Vesovskoe [Veselovskoe?] at three o'clock. Although the inhabitants had already assembled, I did not stay there, because very many of the locals had already been chrismated, married, heard in Confession, and given Communion at [Unalaska] Harbor, and because I was hurrying to reach home by the Feast of the Trinity. I did not stop, but hope to go there again this summer. Setting out hence by oar, we reached the village of Pestriakovskoe, which is no more than twenty versts from our Harbor.

We did not remain here for similar reasons, and we set out by oar at 6:30 and arrived safely at [Unalaska] Harbor at nine o'clock.

May 17. Sunday. Having celebrated the Vigil Service at the appointed time, I celebrated the Liturgy, Vespers, and a prayer service to the Lord God who had blessed us with a successful completion of the journey.

May 18. Monday. I celebrated Matins and the Hours. After these, there was a procession of the cross around the village and a Blessing of the Water.

May 19. Tuesday. I visited the school[16] and was satisfied with the progress of the students.

May 24. Sunday. Having celebrated a Vigil Service in the evening, I celebrated the Hours and a prayer service in place of that for the 21st.

May 31. Sunday. Having celebrated a Vigil Service in the evening, I celebrated the Hours and a memorial service for all of May.

June

June 6. *Comment*: On the sixth we received papers from Irkutsk and Sitka, brought aboard the vessel *Konstantin*, which had arrived.

June 7. Sunday. Having celebrated Vespers and the Vigil Service in the evening, I celebrated the Liturgy.

June 9. Tuesday. I chrismated two people.

June 14. Sunday. I celebrated the Vigil Service and the Hours.

June 21. Sunday. I celebrated the Vigil Service and the Hours.

June 22. *Comment*: On June 22 the vessel *Buldakov* arrived with wood for the church.

June 28. Sunday. I celebrated the Vigil Service, the Hours, and a prayer service instead of that done on the 27th.

June 29. Monday. I celebrated Vespers, the Vigil Service, the Liturgy, and a memorial service. I baptized infants before the Liturgy.

June 30. Tuesday. I baptized an infant. On this date there was an examination of the students of the local school in the presence of the head of the Novo-Arkhangel'sk [Sitka] office, Mr. K. T. Khlebnikov, and others.

This month I prepared papers and responded to the correspondence received.

NOTES

1. A copy of this document was forwarded in September, 1824.

2. Later on this sum grew to 1200 rubles.

3. Every year the [Russian-American] Company sends local Aleuts to the islands of St. Paul and St. George [the Pribilofs]. These Aleuts only now are being replaced after three years by others...[eight words illegible], since not a single Aleut arrives or departs without having received the blessing of the priest—or so they say.

4. [Three mostly illegible lines explaining the gathering of Aleuts and details of the work schedule set by the Company.]

5. At that time there were seventeen people.

6. The school building and my house are nothing more than iurts edged around with sod. In this iurt there are only two windows. Moreover, this building was barely...[four words illegible], so much so that the manager is unhappy with it.

7. From this time until the middle of July, many Aleuts go off in baidarkas to hunt sea otter. During these absences, they live on small islands and go far out to sea, but only on the calmest days.

8. It is clear from ...[illegible] that there has been a settlement here, but these days there is only one person remaining. Not only this, but other settlement sites as well, show clearly that there was formerly a much more numerous population—here the iurts extended for more than sixteen sazhens. And where is this population now?

9. Here only I learned the use and benefit of the local dress, made from the gut of *siuch*, or sea lions—neither wind nor rain can penetrate this very thin garment.

10. Here I must remark on the physical fortitude of the Aleuts. They had eaten very little on the day before, and on this day they ate absolutely nothing except for water. [Two nearly illegible lines, probably stating: they walked carrying fairly heavy loads —some weighed around 2 poods [1 pood=36 lbs.]—and went with such loads along a very bad road. They interpreted into Russian for me.] Furthermore, they did all this without any rest, and in a mood as merry as though they were not facing any kind of hardship.

11. I taught all of the Aleuts using a set sequence, and even identical wording. I have written instructions for this practice [one word illegible]. I omit nothing that is essential for the preservation of faith and the redemption of each man.

12. There were two toions here, the one from Tulik and the one from Egorkovskoi.

13. It is impossible to remain silent about the zeal, devotion, and affectionate manner of all of the local Aleuts. They have only to catch sight of the baidara, and all—from the small to the great, and even those on crutches—come to receive us, to greet us, and to receive the blessing with great joy. They see us off in the same manner.

14. [Veniaminov provides a note describing the location and condition of the village of Recheshnoe. He also names the fish that supply food from the surrounding lakes. He mentions that the dwellings in the village are adequately clean, but the chapel is decrepit and near collapse. The note is too illegible for exact translation.]

15. An irregular choppiness.

16. I think it unnecessary to note down when I visited the school when I go there only to supervise both the instructor and the students; when I go there to teach [three words illegible] I will describe the visit in detail.

JOURNAL NO. 3
July 1, 1825, to July 1, 1826

1825
July

July 2. Thursday. After celebrating the Hours, I directed that the local icons and the altar cross be taken out. I myself took the cross. We went to the site designated for the new church. Here I celebrated a prayer service with a Blessing of the Water. After the ground, the workers, and the lumber had been sprinkled with Holy Water, I myself began the cutting of the wood, and then all the officials in attendance followed suit. When the cross had been raised up into the air, a salute was fired from the shore and from three vessels that happened to be here at this time.[1]

July 5. Sunday. I celebrated the Hours.

July 8. Wednesday. I celebrated the Hours.
   Comment: On July 8 the *Baikal* departed.

July 12. Sunday. I celebrated the Hours.

July 19. Sunday. I celebrated the Hours.

[July 22. Wednesday.] On July 22 the brig *Buldakov* departed.

July 26. Sunday. I celebrated the Hours.

Up until the 20th of this month I prepared papers, and on the 21st I sent them off. After that, I read the supplement to *Syn otechestva* for 1823, and oversaw the construction of the church, for which the entire lower story was cut by August 1.

August

August 1. Saturday. I celebrated Matins with the Veneration of the Cross and the Liturgy, and attended a Blessing of the Water at the river. Upon returning from this ceremony, I celebrated a special prayer service of

37

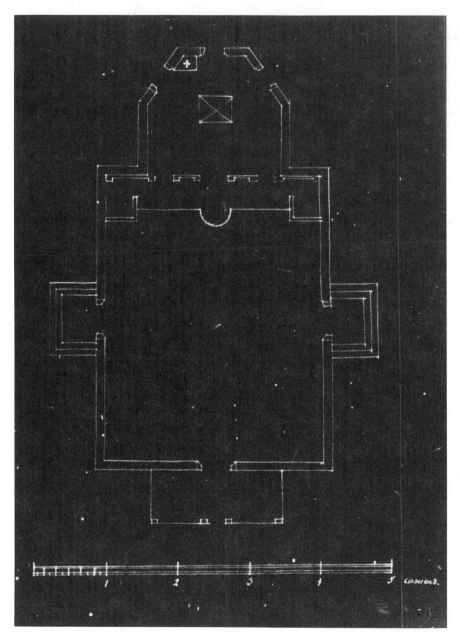

Veniaminov's diagram showing the floor plan for the
construction of the church at Unalaska.

thanksgiving to the Lord God, who had so kindly allowed me to success-fully finish one year.

August 2. Sunday. I celebrated the Hours.

August 6. I celebrated the Liturgy and a prayer service.

August 9. Sunday. I celebrated the Hours and a prayer service, with a proclamation of "Many Years" for His Majesty the Emperor and the entire imperial family, and for the Right Reverend Mikhail, Bishop of Irkutsk, Nerchinsk, and Yakutsk.

August 15. Saturday. I celebrated the Liturgy.

August 16. Sunday. I celebrated the Hours.

August 23. Sunday. I celebrated the Hours.

August 29. Saturday. I celebrated a memorial service and the Liturgy.

August 30. Sunday. I celebrated the Liturgy and a prayer service, accom-panied by a cannon salute.

This month, besides supervising the construction of the church, I read the Literary Supplements to *Syn otechestva* for 1821.

September

September 2. Wednesday. I celebrated a prayer service to St. John.

September 5. Saturday. I celebrated the Liturgy and a prayer service.

September 6. Sunday. I celebrated the Hours.

[September 7. Monday.] *Comment*: On the 7th there was a moderate earthquake.

September 13. Sunday. I celebrated the Hours.

September 14. Holy Cross Day. I celebrated the Vigil Service in the morning, together with the Veneration of the Cross and the Liturgy.

September 15. Monday. I celebrated the Vigil Service in the evening, and then I celebrated the Liturgy with a prayer service, accompanied by a cannon salute.

September 20. Sunday. I celebrated Matins in the morning and the Hours. Beginning with this day, the Vigil Service began in the morning.

September 27. Sunday. I celebrated the Hours, at which I read a lesson from Ambrose.

This month I read *Syn otechestva* for 1823. The master builder from Sitka, who had finished the frame, could work no further [on the construction] and declined to do so. Therefore, at the request of the office manager, and in order not to stop entirely the construction of the church, I took upon myself the direction of further construction.

October

October 4. Sunday. I celebrated the Hours, at which was read a lesson from [one word illegible].

October 11. Sunday. I celebrated the Hours.

October 13. Wednesday. I celebrated the Hours and a prayer service.

October 18. Sunday. I celebrated the Hours.

October 22. Thursday. I celebrated a prayer service to the Virgin Mary.

October 25. Sunday. I celebrated the Hours, and read the appointed service.

This month, besides being busy with the construction of the church, I read a book on the politics of Europe after the battle of Leipzig.

November

November 1. Sunday. I celebrated the Hours.

November 8. Sunday. I celebrated the Liturgy and a prayer service with a proclamation of "Many Years" for his Majesty the Emperor and for the Right Reverend Mikhail, Bishop of Irkutsk.

November 15. Sunday. I celebrated the Hours and delivered a sermon.

November 22. Sunday. I celebrated the Hours and delivered a sermon.

November 28. The Day of St. Innocent. I celebrated the Liturgy and a prayer service to St. Innocent with a ringing of the bells.

November 29. I celebrated the Hours and a prayer service for the 30th.

This month, besides working on the construction, I read *A Description of Kamchatka* [*Opisanie Kamchatki* by S. P. Krasheninnikov], and *Syn otechestva* for 1821.

December

December 6. I celebrated the Liturgy and a prayer service.

December 12. Saturday. I celebrated the Liturgy and a prayer service.

December 13. Sunday. I celebrated the Hours and delivered a sermon.

December 20. Sunday. I celebrated the Hours.

December 24. Thursday. I celebrated the Hours and Vespers, without the Liturgy.

December 25. Christmas. I celebrated the Liturgy and a prayer service, accompanied by a day-long ringing of the bells. At the Liturgy I delivered a sermon that I had written for that day, based on the text: "He has saved His people from their sins."

December 26. I celebrated the Liturgy.

December 27. I celebrated the Hours.

This month, besides working on construction of the church, I read *A Description of Kamchatka*.

In the church, all the doors have been built, as have been the entire lower story, all the windows, and the ceiling in the sanctuary. The entire church is roofed.

1826
January

January 1. Friday. I performed the Vigil Service, the Liturgy, and a prayer service. At the Liturgy I delivered a sermon that I had written and given in Irkutsk on ____[blank in original].

January 3. Sunday. I celebrated the Hours.

January 5. Tuesday. I celebrated the Hours, and Vespers with a Blessing of the Water.

January 6. Epiphany. I celebrated the Liturgy and visited the river for the Blessing of the Water. Before the Liturgy I baptized two infants. At the Liturgy, I delivered a sermon that I had written and delivered in Irkutsk.

January 7. Thursday. I celebrated the Hours and a prayer service.

January 9. Saturday. I held a procession with the icons to the house of the manager.
    Comment: On this day the office clerk, S. S. Petelin, passed away.

January 10. Sunday. I celebrated the Liturgy and delivered a sermon before the interment of the body of the late office clerk, S. S. Petelin. I chose the theme that it is necessary to be always prepared for death.

January 13. Wednesday. I celebrated the Hours and a prayer service.

January 16. Saturday. I celebrated Vespers and a funeral service for the deceased.

January 17. Sunday. I celebrated the Hours.

January 24. Sunday. I celebrated the Hours.

January 30. Saturday. I celebrated the Hours.

January 31. Sunday. I celebrated the Hours.

This month I prepared church records and wrote church books. I also began to translate the Catechism into the Fox-Aleut language.

February

February 2. Tuesday. I celebrated the Vigil Service and the Liturgy.

February 3. Wednesday. I celebrated the Hours and a prayer service.

February 4. Thursday. I celebrated the Hours and a prayer service.

February 7. Sunday. I celebrated the Hours.

February 8. Monday. I celebrated the Vigil Service in the evening.

February 9. Tuesday. I celebrated the Liturgy and celebrated a prayer service to St. Innocent, with a ringing of the bells.

February 14. Sunday. I celebrated the Hours.

February 16. I heard Confession from an ill person and gave Communion to him.

February 17. I celebrated a Liturgy for the repose of the dead and heard Confession from an ill person.

February 20. [Saturday.] *Comment*: On the 20th there was a moderate earthquake.

February 21. Sunday. I celebrated the Hours.

February 28. Sunday. I celebrated the Liturgy, and Vespers. During the service I delivered a sermon appropriate for this day.

This month, besides working on the construction of the church, I was busy with translating the Catechism.

March

March 1. Monday. Lent. I celebrated Matins, the Hours, and then Vespers.

March 2. Tuesday. I celebrated Matins, the Hours, and then Vespers.

March 3. Wednesday. I celebrated Matins, the Hours, and the Liturgy of the Presanctified, and then Vespers.

March 4. Thursday. I celebrated Matins and the Hours.

March 5. Friday. After Matins I instructed those preparing for the sacraments. After the Hours and the Liturgy of the Presanctified, I heard Confession from sixty-four people.

March 6. Saturday. I celebrated the Liturgy and gave Communion to those who had confessed.

March 7. Sunday. I celebrated the Liturgy.

March 8. Monday. There was no service because of a strong wind and drizzle.
Comment: On March 8th there was a slight earthquake. On the 11th there was a strong rumbling under the earth that continued for a long time. Afterwards we learned that the northeastern ridge on Unimak Island had collapsed.

March 9. Tuesday. I celebrated Matins, the Hours, and Vespers.

March 10. Wednesday. I celebrated Matins, the Hours, the Liturgy of the Presanctified, and Vespers.

March 11. Thursday. After Matins, I instructed those preparing for the sacraments, and then I celebrated the Liturgy of the Presanctified. I heard Confession from forty people.
    Comment: [See March 8.]

March 12. Friday. I celebrated Chrysostom's Liturgy and a prayer service, as appointed. I gave Communion to those who had confessed. Before the Liturgy I chrismated five people.

March 14. Sunday. I celebrated the Liturgy.

[**March 15.** *Comment*:] On March 15 there was a small earthquake, after which the coastline in the harbor slid.

March 21. I celebrated the Liturgy. Before the Liturgy, I baptized an infant.

March 22. Monday. I celebrated Matins, the Hours, and Vespers.

March 23. Tuesday. I celebrated Matins, the Hours, and Vespers.

March 24. Wednesday. After Matins I instructed those preparing for the sacraments. After I had celebrated the Liturgy of the Presanctified, I heard Confession from thirty-four persons.

March 25. The Annunciation. I celebrated Matins with the Akathistos, and then I celebrated the Liturgy and gave Communion to all those who had confessed.

March 26. Friday. I celebrated Matins, the Hours, and Vespers.

March 27. Saturday. After Matins, I instructed those preparing for the sacraments. Then I celebrated the Liturgy and heard Confession from twenty-five people.

March 28. Sunday. I celebrated the Liturgy and gave Communion to all those who had confessed. Before the Liturgy, I chrismated two people.

March 30. Tuesday. I heard Confession from an ill person and gave Communion to him.

At the beginning of this month the toion of Tigalda, Ivan Pan'kov, arrived, at my invitation and request. The two of us corrected the portion of the

Catechism that I had translated, i.e., up to the Nicene Creed. We continued the translation.

Besides doing this work, I oversaw the construction of the church.

April

April 1. I heard Confession from an ill person and gave Communion to him.

April 4. Sunday. I celebrated the Liturgy.

April 5. I performed a funeral service for one who had drowned.

April 10. Lazarus Saturday. I celebrated the Liturgy.

April 11. Palm Sunday. I celebrated the Vigil Service and chrismated five people. I celebrated the Liturgy and Vespers.

April 12. Monday. I celebrated Matins, the Hours, the Liturgy of the Presanctified, and Vespers.

April 13. Tuesday. I celebrated Matins, the Hours, the Liturgy of the Presanctified, and Vespers.

April 14. Wednesday. I celebrated Matins, the Hours, the Liturgy of the Presanctified, and Vespers. Before the Hours, I instructed those preparing for the sacraments. Afterwards I heard Confession from fifty-two people.

April 15. Thursday. I celebrated the Liturgy and gave Communion to those who had confessed.

April 16. Friday. After Matins, I instructed those preparing for the sacraments. After the Hours and Vespers, I heard Confession from 86 people. I celebrated Vespers together with the Burial Service of Jesus Christ.

April 17. Saturday. At one o'clock, I celebrated the Liturgy and gave Communion to those who had confessed.

April 18. Easter. I celebrated the Liturgy. At the service the Gospel was read in two dialects [sic]: Slavonic and Russian. I myself read in Slavonic and the cantor in Russian.

April 19. Monday. I celebrated the Liturgy.

April 20. Tuesday. I celebrated the Hours.

April 21. I celebrated the Liturgy and a prayer service. The cross was raised in the new church with a Blessing of the Water and a sprinkling of the water, accompanied by a cannon salute.

April 22. Thursday. I celebrated the Hours.

April 23. Friday. I celebrated the Hours.

April 24. Saturday. I celebrated the Hours.

 April 25. Sunday. In the chapel I celebrated the Hours and a prayer service of thanksgiving to the Lord God, for blessing us in the construction work. On the 26th we began to break the old chapel apart.

By Easter we had finished the Catechism, and we checked it on Easter.

May

May 2. Sunday. I celebrated the Hours in a tent.

May 6. I performed a funeral service for one who had died.

May 9. Sunday. I celebrated the Hours in a tent.

May 16. Sunday. I celebrated the Hours in a tent.

May 23. Sunday. I celebrated the Hours in a tent, and then I heard Confession from, and gave Communion to, an ill person.

May 25. Tuesday. I celebrated Matins in a tent.

May 26. I celebrated the Hours in a tent.

 May 27. Thursday. Ascension Day. In a tent, I celebrated the Liturgy, and a prayer service, having placed the tent on the spot where the chapel had stood, and, moreover, on the spot where the altar had stood in the chapel.

Before the Liturgy there was a ringing of the church bells for the call to worship and a Blessing of the Water.

This month I prepared papers and rewrote the translated Catechism in a clean copy. By June the inside of the church had been completed entirely, and they began to raise the iconostasis that had stood in the chapel.

June

June 5. I celebrated the Vigil Service in the evening.

June 6. Trinity Sunday. I celebrated the Liturgy in a tent located on the former chapel site.

The arrival of the sloop *Konstantin* had brought dispatches and letters from Russia. It also brought the news that Grand Princess Elena Pavlovna had successfully given birth to Grand Princess Maria Mikhailovna.

June 12. Saturday. After going over [one word illegible] with the office, I celebrated the Vigil Service.

June 13. Sunday. Using the tent, I celebrated the Hours and a prayer service with kneeling prayers. There was an all-day ringing of the bells.

June 14. Monday. I baptized an infant.

June 15. Tuesday. I gave Holy Unction to an ill person.

June 19. I performed a funeral service.

June 20. Sunday. I celebrated the Hours in the tent.

June 27. Sunday. I celebrated the Hours in the tent, and celebrated a prayer service thanking God for the victory at Poltava.

Comment: On the morning of the 27th the brig *Baikal* arrived, and on board was the new chief manager, his Honor Lieutenant Peter Egorovich Chistiakov.

This month I prepared papers. By the 15th, the new church was entirely ready and was decorated with an iconostasis and Holy Icons as much as circumstances permit.

June 29. See the next journal, No. 4.

NOTES

1. The *Baikal*, the *Buldakav*, and the *Konstantin*.

JOURNAL NO. 4

April 17, 1827, through July 15 of the same year.
Travel journal of Ivan (Ioann) Veniaminov, priest of the Ascension
Church of Unalaska Island, Northwest America, Irkutsk diocese. Kept
by him during his visit to the Aleut inhabitants of the eastern regions
belonging to the Unalaska church. The journal records his service in
fulfillment of his duties.

April

April 17. Sunday. After a celebration of the Liturgy, an oath was administered to the Aleut translator sent me by the office, one Daniil Kuziakin. After the oath was completed, I celebrated a prayer service to the Lord God, requesting a successful voyage and return.

On this day I was ready to depart, and remained [in Unalaska] awaiting a favorable wind.

April 24. Sunday. At five o'clock in the afternoon, we weighed anchor and moved out from the bay into the sea to the north, into a slight headwind.

The next day we sailed out into the sea to the south of Unalaska, through Unalga Strait. We sailed from this date until the 5th of May. This voyage was prolonged by the presence of either strong headwinds or calms; with a tailwind, this same ship could cover the same distance in sixty hours or less.

During the first four days I suffered from the usual seasickness, i.e., vomiting.

May

May 1. Sunday. I celebrated the Hours at sea, adding a prayer service for those traveling by sea.

May 5. Thursday. At 9:00 in the morning, into a steady wind that was partly against us, we entered the harbor on Unga Island [Delarof Harbor] at the village of Grekodeliarovskii [Unga]. This village is located at 55 and 23/60 degrees north latitude and 160 and 20/60 degrees west longitude.[1] This village is considered the most important and last settlement belonging to the Unalaskan church between Unalaska and Kodiak. I was met with obvious joy by each and every person there.

All of the able-bodied men had left to hunt sea otter. I did not wish to prolong my stay there, nor did I wish to interfere with this hunting.

Therefore, at that time I recommended to the local manager that the men be sent for, since they would not yet have gone far away. This was done.

May 6. Friday. Strong winds made it impossible to pitch the tent. Therefore, today I only took a census of all the local inhabitants. Then, after careful questioning of the elder inhabitants, I resolved the following dispute:

One of the Creoles, one Iuda Balamutov, had lived with an Aleut woman for more than five years. He had made an agreement with her to marry her. Finally, after living with her and [their?] children, he left her without providing the slightest support for the subsistence of her and the children. He gained influence over another woman, his relative—although not a close one. This second woman was already married to another Aleut. He took her as a wife and lived with her for nearly four years.

I questioned in detail all persons, except for Balamutov himself; he had temporarily gone far away. I then decided the matter in the following manner. Since the woman whom he had taken as a second wife had long been living with him against her will and now wanted to be married to her first husband, and since the latter was still unmarried and had long waited to take her as wife, I decided to marry them. After taking some time to think it over, they were married.

As for Iuda Balamutov, I warned that if he did not agree to take his first wife, then he would not be allowed to marry another. As for the support of his wife and children, I suggested to the chief manager that he might order that full support for the family be taken from Balamutov's salary.[2]

May 7. Saturday. I set up the tent, gathered all the adults, and taught them sufficiently, using an interpreter. I chrismated them in the afternoon, and celebrated a Vigil Service in the evening.

Comment: On May 7 at eight o'clock in the evening, some local Aleuts arrived, twenty in number.

May 8. Sunday. I celebrated the Hours. After teaching a second time, I chrismated people. After the Vigil Service I heard Confession from forty-six adults, giving them sufficient Confessional instruction in their own language. I left the young ones for the return trip.

May 9. After a reading of the Rule of Prayer, I celebrated the Liturgy and gave Communion to all those who had confessed. The service took place in the tent. In the afternoon, I sacramentally blessed eighteen marriages and chrismated three persons.

Since I intended to depart the following day, in the evening I gathered all of the adult Aleuts and gave them instructions on morals. Above all, I told them that in the future they should enter into matrimony, and declared the age limits for those entering into such a union, advising these, my children, not to marry too late or too early.

May 10. Tuesday. A strong headwind prevented our departure. Many of the Aleuts departed on [Russian-American] Company business. I visited the Aleuts in their dwellings, giving them general instructions.

In the evening I celebrated the Vigil Service.

May 11. Wednesday. I celebrated the Hours and added a prayer service. Then, at eight o'clock in the morning, I set out in a baidara to visit other inhabitants. I faced a headwind.

An increase in the strength of the wind prevented us from going more than twenty versts before putting in at an uninhabited island named Popovskii [Popof]. This island lies alongside Unga and the Alaska Peninsula.

There I celebrated the Vigil Service for Ascension Day Eve.

May 12. Ascension Day. After the Hours and a prayer service, we set out into a slight headwind.

Having gone at least sixty versts, we stopped on the uninhabited island of Nerpechii, near the village of Pavlovskoe [Pavlof].

May 13. Friday. We set out by oar, with calm winds, and reached the village of Pavlovskoe at two o'clock in the afternoon. This village is located on the Alaska Peninsula at 55 and 1/2 degrees latitude, 162 and 10/60 degrees longitude.

May 14. Saturday. I gathered all the local inhabitants into a tent and instructed them. I chrismated thirty-one people, heard Confession from thirty-two people, and celebrated the Vigil Service. In the evening [we gathered] in the iurt of the toion, and those who knew Russian heard me read from the Catechism that I had translated into their language. They heard the translation with pleasure and showed a desire to have copies for themselves.

May 15. After a reading of the Rule of Prayer at four o'clock in the morning, I celebrated the Liturgy and gave Communion to those who had confessed and to the youngsters.

Then, after visiting all of the inhabitants in their dwellings, and giving general instructions to them, we set out at eight o'clock. Because of a headwind we did not reach a village, and we put in at an uninhabited island named Dolgoi Island.

May 16. Monday. Having set out at five o'clock, we arrived at the village of Bel'kovskoe [Belkofski], which is located on the Alaska Peninsula at 55 degrees latitude and 162 and 45/60 degrees longitude. Since not all of the local inhabitants were home, and since some Unga Aleuts are now living on a little island in the sea near Bel'kovskoe for the purposes of hunting sea lion, I sent for these Aleuts. I did not wish to be delayed here long.

I chrismated twenty-five infants and celebrated Vespers and the Vigil Service.

Comment: In the evening everyone gathered and the Unga Aleuts arrived from the small island.

May 17. Tuesday. At seven o'clock I celebrated the Liturgy and gave Communion to the young ones who had been chrismated. At nine o'clock I gathered all the adults in the tent, and taught them sufficiently. I chrismated forty-two people. In the afternoon I sacramentally blessed eighteen marriages, celebrated the Vigil Service, and heard Confession from sixty-six people, both men and women.

May 18. After a reading of the Rule of Prayer, I celebrated the Liturgy and gave Communion to those who had confessed and to several youngsters. Then I visited the inhabitants in their dwellings, and we set out. We sailed with a tailwind, and at ten o'clock in the evening reached the very tip of Morzhevskii [Morzhovoi] Bay, on the southern side, having gone about twenty-five versts or more. From here one may easily cross over to a village on the northern side of the Alaska Peninsula.

May 19. Thursday. I did not wish to prolong my voyage, nor to keep for long those traveling with me in the baidara, who needed to be engaged in sea otter hunting at this time. Therefore, for their sakes and the Company's benefit, decided to cross the neck of land on foot, rather than spend a whole day (or more if the weather were not good) sailing through Isannakhskii [Isanotski] Strait and another day sailing back. On a calm and clear day we crossed over to the village of Morzhevskoe [Morzhovoi], on almost the very tip of the Alaska Peninsula at 55 degrees latitude and 163 and 45/60 degrees longitude. We immediately sent for those inhabitants, men and women, who were hunting sea lion on a small island approximately thirty versts distant.

May 20. Friday. All of the local inhabitants who had been on the small island arrived in the evening.

May 21. Saturday. In the morning I gathered all of the inhabitants in the tent and taught and chrismated them. In the afternoon I sacramentally blessed seven marriages. After conducting the Vigil Service, I heard Confession from forty-five people, both men and women.

May 22. Trinity Sunday. In the morning, after a reading of the Rule of Prayer, I celebrated a prayer service in the iurt of the manager. Then, at 9:30 and 12:00, I celebrated the Liturgy with Vespers and gave Communion to those who had confessed and to the youngsters.

At 5:30, after visiting all of the inhabitants in their dwellings, we set out on the return trip to Unga across the neck of land, and crossed over to the southern side of the Alaska Peninsula. We were accompanied by almost all of the inhabitants, who had been greatly gladdened by my presence.

Not only these inhabitants, but, in a word, every resident of every place I visited, thanked me emotionally upon parting for having visited and explained the Faith and the Christian Law.

Still, I always told them to thank God, Who had shown the kindness to allow me to reach this remote region and stop here, and Who had illumined them with the light of the Gospel. As for me, I told them to pray to Him so that I might again spend some time among them.

May 23. Monday. I celebrated the Liturgy in the tent, adding a prayer service for those traveling by sea. We could not leave because of a strong headwind.

May 24. Tuesday. We set out into a slight wind that was partly against us. After going about twenty versts, we put in on the Alaska Peninsula because the wind had grown dangerously strong.[3]

May 25. Wednesday. A headwind prevented us from sailing out.

May 26. Thursday. We set out with a moderate tailwind. After covering around 40 versts, we put in at Olenii Island [Deer Island].

May 27. Friday. We set out into a slight wind that was partly against us and rowed into the village of Bel'kovskoe. In the evening I sacramentally blessed three marriages.

May 28. Saturday. I chrismated one man and heard Confession from one woman.

We could not depart because of a strong headwind.

May 29. Sunday. I celebrated the Hours in the tent, and celebrated an additional prayer service.

A strong headwind prevented our departure.

May 30. Monday. After replacing the baidara, we set off with a tailwind at seven o'clock in the morning. At nine o'clock in the evening we arrived at [Delarof] Harbor on Unga Island, having gone more than 100 versts. Thus, my journey in the baidara ended safely.

The reasons we arrived so quickly at Unga on this day were as follows: (1) we sailed straight through, not stopping at the village of Pavlovskoe; and (2) we had a tailwind, with which one can cover more than ten versts per hour in a good baidara.

This day's voyage was not without danger, however. Firstly, the sea was rather highly agitated after the strong easterly winds that had blown on the 28th and 29th. Secondly, the skin of the baidara tore as the boat was being lowered into the water; the boat contained Company cargo weighing more than fifty poods. It was necessary to bail water at least four times an hour. However, things calmed down once we had found the hole and stopped it up. Thirdly, we traveled at a great distance from the shore: before we had traveled about thirty-five versts toward Unga, the Alaska Peninsula was already more than fifty versts distant on our left, and there was no land on our right. It was impossible to turn back because of the wind.

Still, our familiarity with being at sea, and even more our hope in God Who directs the course of men, overcame our fear of danger. Besides seasickness, I experienced no fear or unpleasantness, either on this day's journey or on earlier ones, except for on the 24th. Still, I was in constant danger of losing my life, since, as the saying goes, out here a man is separated from death by not even the thickness of a board, only that of a little skin.

June

June 1. Wednesday. After pitching the tent, I baptized two infants and chrismated one who had been born here during my absence. Then I celebrated a prayer service of thanksgiving to the Lord God who had kindly allowed us to complete in safety the voyage back to Unga—and in such an infirm boat at that. I celebrated this service before a general congregation of the inhabitants, and then I celebrated a prayer service for the Aleuts who had been with me on the journey and were now departing.

I celebrated Vespers and the Vigil Service and heard Confession from twenty-one persons, after first instructing them. To the young ones—age eight and lower—I gave instruction in place of Confession.

Comment: The Aleuts who had been with me set off this day at eleven o'clock.

June 2. Thursday. After a reading of the Rule of Prayer, I celebrated the Liturgy and gave Communion to those who had confessed and to the youngsters.

By this time, the inhabitants of all of the local villages (except one) had been chrismated, heard in Confession, married, and, with a few exceptions, given the sacrament of Holy Communion.

June 3. Friday. I sacramentally blessed two marriages. As of this day, I was prepared for the return trip to Unalaska.

June 4. Saturday. We stood at anchor because of a problem with the ship.

June 5. Sunday. After celebrating the Hours and a prayer service, we weighed anchor at nine o'clock and left [Delarof] Harbor on Unga Island. We sailed from this date until the 11th of June. Our arrival was so delayed because of a headwind and a calm.

June 11. Saturday. We approached Unalaska with a slight tailwind, in the fog. We hoped to make it into the harbor and home on this date, especially since the wind had become colder. However, beginning at noon, the wind, now a headwind, increased until it was extremely strong; we entered Bobrovskii Bay [Beaver Inlet] on the eastern side of Unalaska. Fearing that the current might carry us beyond the strait, we spent the entire night at this spot under sail.

June 12. Sunday. At six o'clock in the morning, we dropped anchor in the above-mentioned bay. Since it is easy to reach the Harbor settlement [Unalaska] from this point, and since I did not want to waste time because I had many things to do (in the way of written work), I set out in a baidarka for the isthmus. From there I hiked over the mountains with a guide. After covering about ten versts, I arrived home in [Unalaska] at one o'clock in the afternoon. The ship remained at anchor in the above-mentioned bay.

Comment: The ship arrived safely on the 14th, after fifty days of absence.

Thus ended my journey to the eastern region, my visit to the inhabitants there who belong to the church. It had lasted forty-nine days, and —Thanks Be to the Most High God!—it had been safe, healthy, and joyous. Furthermore, if I may be so bold as to say it, it had been truly and sincerely useful and successful as well (for mine was but to plant and water—it was God's to make grow).

And so, with a feeling of simple pleasure in my soul and heart, I can say that this trip was not without its success and value. There had not been one village in which I had failed to perform or teach a single sacrament, to teach each and every person sufficiently about Faith and the Law, and to explain the sacraments that I administered. The Aleuts thanked me, and still thank me, for this service.

[Signed:] Priest Ivan Veniaminov.

NOTES

1. This longitude is measured west from Greenwich.

2. While I was traveling through the village of Bel'kovskoe [Belkofski] Balamutov asked for forgiveness [one word illegible] and promised to take his first wife, with the children, and get married at the first opportunity. Thus, the entire matter was concluded.

3. In the interest of the Company, I had permitted at least 50 poods [1 pood=36 lbs.] of walrus tusk to be loaded into the baidara; this caused the baidara to become unwieldy. When we had set out from shore and the wind had begun to pick up, we began to take on water, and the wind would not allow us to reach the shore. However—and Praise Be to God!—the wind died down and we put in to shore safely.

JOURNAL NO. 5
July 1, 1827, through July 1, 1828

July

July 1. Friday. Morning. I celebrated the Hours, adding a prayer service for those traveling by sea (for my own sake), and the appointed prayer service for the imperial family.

Afternoon. I moved onto the ship.

July 2. Saturday. Morning. We weighed anchor at nine o'clock. The winds were calm. We sailed out of the bay and set our course for the islands of St. George and St. Paul [the Pribilofs].

July 3. Sunday. Morning. At sea, but within sight of the shore, I celebrated a prayer service for those traveling by sea, with kneeling prayers.

July 6. Wednesday. Nine o'clock. We caught sight of the island of St. George in the fog. This island lies in the northern, or Kamchatkan, sea, at 56 degrees north latitude and 170 degrees longitude, as measured from Greenwich.

At one o'clock in the afternoon we dropped anchor in the open sea opposite a village on the shore, and in the evening we moved over to the shore.[1]

July 7. Thursday. Because of work that needed to be done for the Company, I did nothing on this date.

July 8. Friday. 8:00; 9:00; 10:00; 11:00; and 11:30. After everyone had assembled in the tent, I celebrated the Hours and gave adequate instruction through an interpreter. Then I chrismated thirty-two people. In the afternoon I sacramentally blessed four marriages. Then, I celebrated a Vigil Service and heard Confession from fifty-one people, both men and women.

July 9. Saturday. After a reading of the Rule of Prayer, I celebrated the Liturgy in the tent, and gave Communion to those who had confessed and to the youngsters. I sacramentally blessed one marriage.

At this point, all of the local inhabitants had been chrismated, heard in Confession, blessed in marriage, and (with the exception of two) given Holy Communion.

July 10. Sunday. 8:00; 9:00. I celebrated the Hours in the tent, adding a prayer service for those traveling by sea. To all the Russians, Creoles, and Aleuts I administered an oath of allegiance to His Majesty the Emperor Nicholas Pavlovich and to His Heir, Alexander Nikolaevich.

After lunch I visited the inhabitants in their dwellings.[2]

We stood at anchor because of a calm.

July 11. Monday. Morning. We weighed anchor at six o'clock, and sailed, with little wind, to the island of St. Paul, ninty versts away.

July 12. Tuesday. With little wind, we dropped anchor at six o'clock at the island of St. Paul. I went ashore at this time, and after being met by each and every person, I went straight to the chapel and then to a room in the house of the manager.[3]

July 13. Wednesday. Morning. At the request of the local inhabitants, I celebrated a prayer service to the Apostles Peter and Paul, with a Blessing of the Water. After giving sufficient instruction through an interpreter, I chrismated twenty persons. In addition, I chrismated twenty-one people in the afternoon.

Comment: Our ship sailed off from shore and went to the southwest to explore. There is a rumor of an unknown island in that direction.

July 14. Thursday. Morning. I chrismated thirty-two people. At the appointed times, I celebrated Vespers and the Vigil Service. After that, I spoke to the youngsters—ages five to ten—giving them instruction instead of Confession.

July 15. Friday. 9:00; 10:00; and 11:00. After a reading of the Rule of Prayer, I celebrated the Liturgy in the chapel and gave Communion to all the young people. Also, I sacramentally blessed eleven marriages. In the afternoon, I heard Confession from fifty-nine people and celebrated Vespers and the Vigil Service.

July 16. Saturday. 9:00; 10:00; and 11:00. After a reading of the Rule of Prayer, I celebrated the Liturgy and gave Communion to those who had confessed. In addition, I sacramentally blessed two marriages.

In the afternoon I sacramentally blessed eleven marriages and heard Confession from fifty-one people. I also celebrated Vespers and the Vigil Service.

July 17. Sunday. 9:00; 10:00; and 11:00. After a reading of the Rule of Prayer, I celebrated the Liturgy and gave Communion to those who had confessed. Then, I administered to all the Russians, Creoles, and Aleuts the oath of allegiance to His Majesty the Emperor and His Heir, after exhorting them and explaining the force of an oath. In the afternoon I visited all the dwellings of the Aleuts[4] here and found them to be as clean as possible. In the evening I prayed over an infant.

At this time everyone living here had been chrismated, heard in Confession (except for two Russians), given the sacrament of Holy Communion, and married.

July 18 through July 23. I spent these days waiting for the ship.

July 20. Wednesday. I celebrated the Hours and prayed over an infant.

July 22. [Friday.] *Comment*: Our ship was sighted in the morning.

July 23. Saturday. I celebrated the Hours and then the Vigil Service.
Comment: The ship arrived at twelve o'clock, having had no success.

July 24. I celebrated the Hours, adding a prayer service for those traveling by sea. Before the Hours I baptized two infants.

July 25. Monday. 9:00. Having been seen off by all of the inhabitants, I left St. Paul and sailed for St. George against a headwind.

July 26. Tuesday. Morning. At eight o'clock, in the fog, we approached St. George Island and dropped anchor. After receiving a load of cargo, we set out for Unalaska at four o'clock.

I need not describe here the joy and gratitude evoked in the local inhabitants by this visit, for they are the same Aleut people as live on Unalaska, Umnak, and Unga.

We sailed from this date until August 1, delayed by headwinds and lack of wind.

July 31. Sunday. Morning. I celebrated the Hours at sea.

At noon we caught sight of the shores of Unalaska and Umnak. I was extremely desirous of being in Unalaska by August 1; in the evening, however, the wind died down, and I fell into complete despair, since we were still very far from shore and even farther from the harbor. However, faith in God will not be put to shame!

August

August 1. Morning. At sunrise a fresh breeze suddenly began to blow; it was a partial tailwind. Since we picked up a tailwind outside the harbor, we arrived at Unalaska Harbor at eleven o'clock. At this time, in accordance with an order I had made in advance, bells were rung to summon the people. Once the anchor was set, I went ashore. Then began the bells for the Hours. I, together with a greeting party of all of the inhabitants, went directly to the church. Once there, I began to celebrate the Hours.

After the "Our Father" had been sung, a glorification was sung. Then, during the last Prosagion, the cross was carried out in accordance with custom. After the Veneration of the Cross and a celebration of the Hours, I went with the icons to the river. After a Blessing of the Water there was a procession of the cross around the village, accompanied by a ringing of the bells.

Upon returning to the church, I celebrated a prayer service of thanksgiving to the Lord God, who had kindly allowed me to stay three years here in good health, with good success, and without misfortune, and allowed me to complete my voyage to the Pribilof Islands. This visit had allowed me to comfort, console, and instruct the local inhabitants.

Praise be to God! Praise to Him, Who gives me His Word in measure with my abilities, and Who through this Word comforts and instructs His Rational Flock.

Thus ended my second trip of the summer.

August 5. Friday. 6:00; 7:00. I celebrated the Vigil Service.

August 6. The Feast of the Transfiguration. 10:00; 11:00. I celebrated the Liturgy and a prayer service.

August 7. Sunday. 10:00. I celebrated the Hours and a prayer service for the 9th.

August 9. Our ship again went to Unga.

August 11. Thursday. Evening. A Russian government ship, the sloop *Seniavin*, arrived under the command of Captain Lieutenant Fedor Pavlovich Lütke. I received dispatches from the Main Office.

August 13. Saturday. 7:00; 8:00. I celebrated the Vigil Service.

August 14. I celebrated the Liturgy and then the Vigil Service.

August 15. Feast of the Dormition. 10:00; 11:00. I celebrated the Liturgy and then the Vigil Service.

August 16. I celebrated the Hours. On board ship I celebrated a prayer service for the voyage.

August 20. Saturday. Morning. At ten o'clock the ship *Seniavin* weighed anchor and left for the Pribilofs. From there it would go on to Bering Strait and then to Kamchatka.

7:00 and 8:00. I celebrated the Vigil Service.

August 21. Sunday. 10:00; 11:00. I celebrated the Liturgy and a prayer service of thanksgiving.

August 28. Sunday. 10:00; 11:00. I celebrated the Hours. Later, I celebrated Vespers and the Vigil Service.

August 29. The beheading of St. John the Baptist. I celebrated the Liturgy. Before that I celebrated a memorial service.

7:00; 8:00. I celebrated Vespers and the Vigil Service. During the Vigil Service, a Russian government ship arrived from Kamchatka, the sloop *Moller*, under the command of Captain Lieutenant Mikhail Nikolaevich Stanikovich [Staniukovich].

August 30. Tuesday. 10:00; 11:00; and 12:00. After a reading of the Hours, I performed a memorial service for His Majesty the Emperor Alexander Pavlovich. Then I celebrated the Liturgy and a prayer service.

This month I read the following books: (1) *The First Russian Marine Expedition*; and (2) *A Chronological History of all Expeditions to the Northern Polar Regions*, by Mr. Berkh.

September

September 1. Thursday. 5:00. I celibrated Vespers.

September 2. My name day. Morning. I celebrated Matins, the Liturgy, and a prayer service of thanksgiving at the request of those who had been on board the ship.

September 4. Sunday. I celebrated the Liturgy and then the Vigil Service.

September 5. Monday. Morning. I celebrated the Hours and a prayer service.

At eight o'clock the sloop *Moller* weighed anchor and sailed for the southern coast of the Alaska Peninsula in order to reconnoiter the area. Such description is the goal of their expedition, which will go on from there to Sitka.

September 8. Thursday. I celebrated the Liturgy.

September 11. Sunday. I celebrated the Liturgy.

September 14. I celebrated the Vigil Service with the Veneration of the Cross, and celebrated the Liturgy.

[September 16. Friday.] *Comment*: Our ship arrived from Unga.

September 18. Sunday. I celebrated the Liturgy.

September 23. Friday. I celebrated the Hours.

September 25. Sunday. I celebrated the Liturgy and sacramentally blessed one marriage.

September 28. Wednesday. I celebrated a prayer service for the students. They began studying today. Before this day they had been idle, since I had been living with my household in the school building while my house was being repaired.

This month I read the following books:[5] (1) the most recent edition of the *Tales* of Krylov; and (2) the works of Dmitriev. [Probably the poet and author Ivan Ivanovich Dmitriev, who was a colleague of Karamzin and whose collected works were published in Moscow in 1810 and 1818.]

October

October 2. Sunday. I celebrated Matins and the Liturgy.

October 9. Sunday. I celebrated Matins and the Liturgy and sacramentally blessed one marriage.

October 10. Monday. I sacramentally blessed one marriage.

October 16. Sunday. I celebrated the Liturgy, at which was read the appointed sermon.

Comment: On October 16 our ship arrived from Unga.

October 22. Saturday. I celebrated a prayer service to the Virgin Mary, and then Vespers.

October 23. Sunday. I celebrated Matins and the Liturgy, and the appointed sermon was read.

October 30. Sunday. I celebrated Matins and the Liturgy, and the appointed sermon was read.

This month I read the [book title unintelligible], and was busy with finishing the organ.

November

November 2. Wednesday. 10:00 and 11:00. I went to the school, and this day began to teach the older students the Full Catechism, using the text composed and translated by me into the local language. With the help of God I explained the nature of the Catechism, and the Nature of Him Whom we call God. I read and explained in Aleut, since some students do not know Russian terribly well.[6]

November 4. Friday. 10:00 and 11:00. In school I went over my previous lesson and taught the proofs of the existence of God.

November 6. Sunday. I celebrated the Liturgy, at which a standard sermon was given.

November 8. Tuesday. I celebrated the Liturgy, and then celebrated a prayer service followed by a proclamation of "Many Years" for the imperial family and for the Right Reverend Mikhail, Bishop of Irkutsk, Nerchinsk, and Yakutsk.

November 9. Wednesday. 10:00 and 9:30. After going over the previous lecture, I taught in school about the properties of God—who God is. I finished the second chapter [of the Catechism].

November 11. Friday. 10:00 and 11:00. In school I taught about the veneration of God—why and in what manner we ought to venerate Him. Then, having reviewed the entire first part of the Catechism, I asked questions of each of the students and was satisfied with their answers. Praise be to God and to His Word!

November 13. Sunday. 10:00 and 11:00. I celebrated the Liturgy, at which was read the appointed sermon.

November 14. I gave Final Communion to an ill person.

November 16. Wednesday. 10:00 and 11:00. In school I taught about the Holy Scriptures and why they deserve our faith.

   Comment: On the 16th, at night, there was an earthquake—one moderate shock.

November 17. Thursday. 10:00 and 11:00. I performed a funeral service for a deceased woman, the Aleut to whom I had given final Communion on the 14th.

November 18. Friday. 9:30 and 11:00. In school I went over the previous lecture and read through the section on faith in the Unity, both in Russian and in Aleut. I started teaching about the Holy Trinity.

   7:00 and 8:00. I celebrated the Vigil Service in honor of St. Joseph.

   Since I had no kind of tables or written instructions concerning when to celebrate the accession to the throne of His Majesty the Emperor, Tsar Nicholas the First, I decided to celebrate on the 19th, going by the Imperial Manifesto, in which it is written: "the date of my accession to the throne is to be assumed to be November 19."

   Comment: The manager of the office was informed of my intention to teach the Gospel to the students of our school on some Sundays and holidays, either in the church or in the school building. Special ringings of the church bells will inform the inhabitants that services will begin at other than the usual times.

November 19. Saturday. 7:00 and 8:00. After a reading of the Hours, I performed a memorial service for His Majesty the Emperor Alexander, accompanied by a ringing of the bells. Then I celebrated the Liturgy and, at the proper point in the service, delivered a sermon that I had composed for this day, based on no particular passage of scripture. I spoke of the reasons for and manner of our obedience to the sovereign and all the powers established by him. Then I celebrated a prayer service for the day of accession [to the throne of Nicholas I] with kneeling prayers and an all-day ringing of the bells.

   Comment: …accompanied by a seven-shot cannon salute from the shore batteries and the ship.

November 20. Sunday. 9:00. In school I explained the Gospel reading for the 26th Sunday, the story of the rich man.[7] The moral lesson is that one should not be attached to the blessings of this world. However, one should also not live in idle laziness, and one should give to the poor everything that is superfluous or inessential, and thereby grow rich in God.

Comment: The students were summoned to this lesson by a special ringing of the bells.

10:00. I celebrated the Hours.

Comment: There was no Matins or Liturgy Service because of a leak in the church.

November 21. Feast of the Presentation of the Blessed Virgin. I celebrated the Vigil Service and the Liturgy.

November 23. Wednesday. 10:00 and 11:00. In school I taught about the Holy Trinity. I discussed the distinction which is professed between each Person of the Trinity, and what actions are ascribed to each Person.

4:00. I went to the school, and I was satisfied to see that the arithmetic class has achieved some success at this point. The students who began in the middle of October can count and write up to six figures. I began to teach addition and instructed that [this teaching] be continued.[8]

November 25. Friday. 9:30 and 11:00. In school I taught about Divine Creation—about how God created the World and Man, his reasons for doing so, and the nature of the first people.

7:00 and 8:00. I celebrated a Vigil Service dedicated to St. Innocent.

November 26. Saturday. 7:00 and 8:00. I celebrated the Liturgy and a prayer service to St. Innocent.

November 27. Sunday. 9:00. In school I explained the Gospel reading for the 27th Sunday, and for the Feast of the Blessed Virgin. The moral lesson of the first is that Christ can heal any illness, both now and at all times. The second teaches that one must hear and preserve the Word of God, for "Blessed art those who hear the Word of God and keep it."

10:00 and 11:00. I celebrated the Liturgy, at which the appointed sermon was read.

November 30. Wednesday. 10:00 and 11:00. In school, after going over the previous two lectures, I taught about the image of God, which was imprinted on the first human beings. Although they were driven out of Paradise and subjected to a just punishment after losing this image, they were still not left without hope.

65

This month, besides being busy with the matters described above, I occasionally read a book, Volume 7 of the *Global Traveler* [*Vsemirnaia puteshestvovatel'*], and spent more time finishing the organ.

December

December 1. Thursday. I celebrated a funeral service for a deceased infant.

December 2. Friday. 11:00. In school I taught about Divine Providence, teaching that the salvation of mankind is the sole goal of God's caring about us, direction of us, actions in regard to us, and love for us. All else exists for the sake of mankind.

December 4. Sunday. I celebrated the Liturgy, at which the appointed sermon was read.

December 5. Monday. I gave Final Communion to an ailing Aleut.

December 6. Tuesday. I celebrated the Liturgy, during which, at its appointed time, I gave a sermon that I had prepared for this day based on the following text: "The shepherd enters through the doors…and the sheep listen to his voice and follow him." I spoke about how every Christian should listen to his shepherd, who teaches, instructs, admonishes, and advises him. He should follow these teachings, instructions, exhortations, and words of advice. After the Liturgy I celebrated a prayer service for the health of His Majesty the Emperor Nicholas and the entire imperial family; this service was accompanied by a cannon salute.

Comment: At eight o'clock in the morning death came to the Aleut to whom I had given Final Communion on the 5th. He died fully conscious and filled with Christian hope.

December 7. Wednesday. 9:30 and 11:00. In school I taught about the incarnation of the Son of God—about how, when, and why he took on human flesh.

December 8. Thursday. I performed a funeral service for the deceased Aleut and gave Final Communion to an ailing Aleut woman.

December 9. Friday. 9:30 and 11:00. In school, after reviewing the previous lecture, I taught briefly about the earthly life of Jesus Christ: His teachings, Passion, death, and resurrection. I also explained his death as a sacrifice made for the sins of all people. With this lesson I finished the review that I had intended of the entire Catechism from the beginning.

December 11. I celebrated the Liturgy, at which the appointed sermon was read.

December 12. I gave Final Communion to an ailing Aleut woman.

December 14. Wednesday. 10:00 and 11:00. In school I went over the first part of the Catechism and was satisfied with the answers given by the students. There is a God—the Most High—the Creator, and one must love Him—there is the Short Catechism as written on the hearts of each! However, if not discovered, it can be altered, although it cannot be destroyed or effaced.

December 15. Thursday. I heard Confession from an ill person.

December 16. Friday. 10:00 and 11:00. In school I taught about the Evangelical Faith, as given in the Holy Scriptures. It merits our full acceptance. I also taught about the Holy Trinity. God is Three-in-One: this one must know, be convinced of, and believe. One cannot, however, fully understand this concept or subject it to tests.

December 18. Sunday. I celebrated the Liturgy.

December 19. Monday. I celebrated the Liturgy and gave Communion to an ailing infant and another [one word illegible].

December 21. Wednesday. 10:00; 11:00; and 11:45. In school I taught about the creation and Divine Providence, and about the incarnation and Passion of Jesus Christ. Bliss for mankind is the cause and goal of these acts of infinite love. At the end of class the students were dismissed until January 9, 1828.

December 22. Thursday. I celebrated a funeral service for a deceased woman, the woman to whom I had given Final Communion on the 12th.

December 23. Friday. I celebrated the Hours for the Feast of the Nativity of Christ [Christmas].

December 24. Saturday. I celebrated the Vespers Service for Christmas.

December 25. Christmas. I celebrated Matins, the Liturgy of St. Basil and at its appointed time I led an informal discussion that I had prepared for this day using the following text:

> Now when Jesus was born in Bethlehem of Judea in the
> days of Herod the King, behold, wise men from the east

came to Jerusalem, saying "where is he who has been born King of the Jews? For we have seen his star in the East, and have come to worship him." [Matthew 2:1-2 RSV]

I spoke of how we should bow before God. After the Liturgy, I performed the appropriate prayer service accompanied by a cannon salute.

December 26. I celebrated the Liturgy.

December 27. I celebrated the Hours and prayed over an infant.

Beyond this, I was busy with the organ, and with writing church and school books and accounts.

December 29. We received word that the construction of the chapel on Umnak had been completed,[9] except for the porch and outside paneling.

1828
January

January 1. Sunday. After baptizing an infant, I celebrated the Liturgy of St. Basil the Great, and at its appointed time gave a sermon that I had composed for this day based on no particular scriptural text. I spoke on the subject of how the path that Jesus Christ took is the most promising path, and, in fact, the only one to the Heavenly Kingdom. After the Liturgy I celebrated a prayer service.

January 2. Monday. I sacramentally blessed one marriage between Aleuts who were departing for their own village.

January 5. Thursday. I celebrated Matins, the Hours, Vespers with the Liturgy of St. Basil the Great, and a Blessing of the Water.

January 6. Epiphany. I celebrated Matins, the Liturgy, and a Blessing of the Water at the river, the last being accompanied by a three-shot cannon salute.

January 7. Saturday. I celebrated the Liturgy and a prayer service.

January 8. Sunday. I celebrated the Hours.

January 11. Wednesday. 10:00 and 11:00. In school, after going over all that I had previously taught, I began to teach of God's Grace, stating that it is an invisible gift of the Holy Trinity granted to every person who desires it, and not granted by merit. It is invisible and, one might say, ineffable, for one can better feel the Grace than define its essence. It is better, therefore, to receive it than to try to come to know it theoretically. I also spoke briefly of the means for obtaining Grace.

January 13. Friday. 10:00 and 11:00. In school I reviewed the preceding lesson, and then taught briefly about the Lord's Prayer, after reading it both in Russian and in Aleut. I got through the preface and the first three petitions. [I covered all this] briefly, because my spiritual poverty and the young age of the students prevented me from expanding my remarks; I only explained, therefore, why, and by what right, we use the name of "Father" to refer to God the Creator and Judge: we are His offspring, made by Him...vices...[vices, *pokhoti*, unintelligible in this context].

The First Petition concerns neither our spiritual nor our bodily life, but relates to the Glory of the Name of God, which is the first cause and goal of the existence of mankind and of all sentient beings. The other two petitions concern our own spiritual wants and those of all man's entire being. Our primary desire and sole want is to receive the Kingdom of God. The second of the two states that the sole means or method for doing this is through the fulfillment of the Will of God, which entails a casting aside of the will and desires of an ardent heart.

January 15. Sunday. After baptizing an infant, I celebrated the Liturgy, at which the first appointed service was read.

January 16. *Comment*: On the 16th, Innocent, my oldest son, began to study reading and writing. He is five years and two months old.

January 18. Wednesday. 9:30 and 11:00. In school I taught the last four petitions and the conclusion to the Lord's Prayer. Daily bread, or moderate and simple food, is a necessity and a means to the continuation of life, while excess and luxury are an abridgement of life, and therefore... and so on.

Debts. Jesus Christ foresaw that it would be impossible for any man to live without becoming indebted—not only to God, but to other men as well. Therefore, we ought to forgive in advance, and continue to forgive, our debtors, and in the same way pray that we will be forgiven.

Temptation. There are many and various temptations, internal and external, big and small, and a man cannot live without facing them. But here our petition concerns those temptations that can cause us to grumble against Providence, or even to reject the faith. There is cunning in everything that can turn us from the pathway to the kingdom of God's glory, and so...etc.

The Kingdom. The Kingdom of God is present for all ages, His strength is insuperable, and His glory is magnificent. Therefore, every petition of every man should be brought up before the one God of the Ages, and no one can satisfy these petitions or true needs of ours other than the Almighty, for Whom all things are possible. His glory should be, and is, the consequence of all of these petitions...and so on.

January 20. Friday. 10:00 and 11:00. In school I taught about the Word of God. I taught about its nature and about its value, and began to teach in general about the sacraments of our Church. I stated that faith is necessary for a man to receive Grace through the sacraments.

January 22. Sunday. 9:00. In school I explained the Gospel reading for Sunday, the story of the Prodigal Son. The moral lesson is that we need never despair of God's mercy. We imitate the Prodigal Son in our corruption, and we should also imitate him in turning to God. We must not just stop along the road or cling to our sins, but rather return and come to His eternal mercy.

10:00 and 11:00. Then I celebrated the Liturgy, at which was read the appointed sermon.

January 25. Wednesday. 10:00 and 10:30. In school I went over the last lesson from the Catechism and then taught about the Mysteries of Baptism and Holy Communion: these sacraments are necessary in order to receive the right to enter God's Kingdom.

January 27. 10:00 and 11:00. In school, after reviewing the lesson on Baptism and Communion, I taught about the other five sacraments, speaking most of all about repentance. I said that it is necessary for the absolution of our sins.

4:00. I went to the school. Since the students were able to perform addition correctly, I began to teach them subtraction and instructed that such teaching be continued.

January 28. Saturday. I celebrated the Hours and a prayer service.

January 29. Sunday. In school I explained the appointed Gospel reading for this day, the moral lesson of which is that everyone, be he rich or poor, should try to do good as often as possible. I celebrated the Liturgy, at which was read the sermon read on the Sunday of the Exaltation of the Cross.

January 30. Monday. I celebrated the Hours (without Matins).

This month I read the following books: (1) a general geography book; and (2) *A Detailed Guide to the Raising of Children*, by Zollikofer.

February

February 1. Wednesday. 10:00. In school I taught about the sacred Church.

February 2. Thursday. I celebrated the Vigil Service and the Liturgy.

February 3. Friday. I celebrated the Vigil Service, the Liturgy, and a prayer service.

February 4. Saturday. I celebrated the Vigil Service, the Liturgy, and a prayer service. I performed a funeral service for a deceased infant. In the evening I celebrated a Vigil Service in honor of St. Innocent.

February 5. Sunday. After baptizing an infant, I celebrated the Liturgy. At the appointed time in the Liturgy I read a sermon that I had written for this day. It had no scriptural text, but concerned the reasons why Lent had been established and the ways in which we ought to fulfill the obligations that it places on us.

February 6. Monday. Services began on this day for those observing Lent.

February 8. Wednesday. I celebrated the Liturgy of the Presanctified.

February 10. Friday. Morning. I taught those preparing for the sacraments. After giving a brief explanation of God and the incarnation, Passion, and death of His Son, I spoke of repentance and the Holy Eucharist. Beyond that, I taught about the way in which we wear the cross, and depict it on ourselves as a sign that we have been baptized, that we believe, and that we find hope in the crucifixion. We also do this because we have vowed to, ought to, and desire to imitate Christ in forbearance... and so on.

12:00. I celebrated the Liturgy of the Presanctified. In the afternoon, I heard Confession from fourteen Aleuts, both men and women.

February 11. Saturday. I celebrated the Liturgy and gave Communion to all those who had confessed. In place of the sacrament text, the appointed sermon was read.

February 12. I celebrated the Liturgy and Vespers, and with this the services were completed.[10]

February 15. Wednesday. 9:30 and 11:00. In school I taught about the Church of Christ. Every true believer is a part of the body of the United Church, which is universal and eternal, founded and established with Jesus Christ as its cornerstone.

February 17. Friday. 11:00. In school I taught about the Second Coming of Christ and the resurrection of the dead. The death of our body is something both knowable and unknowable, as are the Second Coming of Christ and the resurrection of the dead. Death is a call to the Day of Judgement, and the Coming of Christ will be the time of retribution, so that one must always be ready for it...and so on.

February 18. *Comment*: At eleven o'clock in the morning there was a rather strong earthquake with one shock.

February 19. Sunday. I celebrated Matins and the Liturgy. Later, I celebrated Vespers.

February 24. Friday. 10:00 and 11:00. In school I taught about the futures awaiting the righteous man and sinner, and began to speak about the Law of God.

February 26. Sunday. I celebrated Matins with the Veneration of the Cross. I celebrated the Liturgy, and Vespers at its appointed time. Daily service began on this day and continued until March 12.

February 29. Wednesday. I celebrated the Liturgy of the Presanctified.

This month I read the following books: (1) *On the Mystery of the Cross*, by Douzetems; and (2) something from *The Practical Mariner* by Gamalei [?]. I was also busy with finishing the organ.

March

March 2. Friday. After Matins I exhorted those observing Lent. Then, I celebrated the Liturgy of the Presanctified and heard Confession from forty Aleuts and Creoles, both men and women.

At twelve o'clock midnight a daughter was born to me prematurely. She was in her sixth month and barely alive. She was marked with the sign of the cross and baptized with plain water, which was poured three times over her head. She died immediately.

March 3. Saturday. I performed Matins with a memorial service. Also, I celebrated the Liturgy and gave Communion to all those who had confessed. A sermon was read prior to Communion.

March 4. Sunday. I celebrated the Liturgy.

March 7. Wednesday. I celebrated the Liturgy of the Presanctified. In the evening I celebrated Matins with the Great Canon.

March 8. Thursday. I celebrated the Liturgy of the Presanctified.

March 9. Friday. I celebrated the Liturgy of the Presanctified. Following a brief exhortation, I heard Confession from fourteen Aleut women and one Aleut man.

March 10. Saturday. I celebrated the Liturgy and gave Communion to all those who had confessed.

March 11. Sunday. I celebrated the Liturgy and concluded the fifteen days of services with Vespers.

March 16. Friday. I celebrated the Liturgy and Vespers. Services began on this day and continued daily up until April 2.

March 17. Lazarus Saturday. I celebrated the Liturgy.

March 18. Palm Sunday. I celebrated the customary Vigil and the Liturgy.

March 19. Holy Monday. I celebrated Matins and the Hours, during which there were Gospel readings from Matthew and Mark. In addition, I celebrated the Liturgy of the Presanctified.

March 20. Holy Tuesday. I celebrated Matins and the Hours, during which there were Gospel readings from Luke. In addition, I celebrated the Liturgy of the Presanctified.

March 21. Holy Wednesday. I celebrated Matins and the Hours. Along with the Hours there was a reading from the Gospel of John. After Matins, I instructed those observing Lent, and before Vespers I heard Confession from thirty-three people, both Aleut and Russian. One of the Russians is in danger of his mortal soul, and in order to correct this he remained without absolution until Easter (it remained a secret between us). He submitted to this obediently.

March 22. Holy Thursday. Beginning at two o'clock, I celebrated Vespers with the Liturgy and gave Communion to all those who had confessed except for the one man mentioned above.

March 23. Holy Friday. I celebrated the Matins of Holy Suffering, the Hours, and Vespers with the Burial Service at three o'clock.

March 24. Holy Saturday. I celebrated Matins and the Hours. After baptizing an infant starting at 2:30, I celebrated Vespers with the Liturgy. Starting at seven o'clock in the evening, I heard Confession from thirty Aleuts who had arrived today, including the one who had remained without absolution; upon his repentance and the giving of sufficient admonitions, I absolved him.

March 25. Easter. Matins began at twelve o'clock. At Matins I read the Catechetical Oration of St. John of Chrysostom. The Liturgy took place at 6:30, and all who had confessed and all the youngsters took Communion. Vespers took place at five o'clock.

March 26. Easter Monday. I celebrated the Liturgy, during which I gave Communion to as many as thirty youngsters.

March 27. Easter Tuesday. I celebrated the Liturgy.

March 28. Easter Wednesday. I celebrated the Liturgy. Afterwards, I sacramentally blessed seven marriages among Aleuts who needed to set out for their own villages.

March 29. Easter Thursday. I celebrated the Liturgy.

March 30. Easter Friday. I celebrated the Liturgy.

March 31. Easter Saturday. I celebrated the Liturgy. At 4:30 I celebrated the Lesser Vespers. At six o'clock I celebrated the Vigil Service. Beginning on this day, I determined that on holidays I would celebrate Matins in the evening.

This month I read Church and Bible history and was busy finishing the organ.

April

April 1. Sunday. I celebrated the Liturgy, and Vespers afterwards. By order of the local office, at five o'clock some Aleuts from Akun arrived to take me to Akun. This was done because last March I had informed the office that I intended to spend some time on Akun and Umnak during the present year. I requested them to provide me with the means of doing so.

However, since the Aleuts from Unimak who had arrived here on March 26 wished to take Confession and receive Communion, I decided to delay my departure until the following Sunday.

April 2. *Comment*: Beginning April 2 the students began to study again. They had not been studying since the beginning of March because of freezing weather caused by winds from the north.

April 3. Tuesday. I celebrated Matins and the Liturgy.

April 4. Wednesday. Starting with the Hours, services began for those who wanted to take Communion.

April 7. Saturday. After Matins I taught those intending to take Communion, and after Vespers I heard Confession from fifteen persons.

April 8. Sunday. I celebrated the Liturgy and gave Communion to all those who had confessed. After the Liturgy, I celebrated a prayer service for those traveling by sea. Then I swore in those provided me by the office, giving them an oath of loyalty to His Majesty Nicholas Pavlovich and to His Heir. I explained ahead of time the force of an oath.

April 9, 10, and 11. Monday, Tuesday, and Wednesday. Although I was ready for the trip, strong winds prevented our departure.

April 11. Wednesday. 11:00. I went to the school. Since the students were able to add and subtract correctly, I began to teach them multiplication and instructed that such teaching be continued.[11]

April 12. Thursday. Morning. I set out at nine o'clock in a three-man baidarka, in the company of four two-seaters. After sailing through the three straits between islands, we arrived safely at eight o'clock at the village of Artel'novskoe on the island of Akun. Akun lies off the northeastern coast of Unalaska at a distance of at least 120 versts past the islands of Unalga and Akutan.[12] We passed the former on the left and the latter on the right. We encountered no riptides, rough winds, or opposing currents, and met only with a slight headwind and occasional sleet that fell for short periods.

Comment: The cantor remained here [in Unalaska].

April 13. Friday. 10:00; 11:00; and 12:00. Since all of the inhabitants of the three settlements on Akun Island had gathered here in anticipation of my visit, I assembled them all in the tent and taught them adequately, through the interpreter Ivan Pan'kov, toion of the island of Tigalda.[13]

In the afternoon I visited the inhabitants in their dwellings and found these places to be adequately clean.

April 14. Saturday. I chrismated forty-six persons, both men and women, and various ages. Before Vespers and after the Vigil Service I heard Confession from fifty-three people from the two other villages. I held off on the locals, planning to serve them on my return trip. For the youngsters aged nine or lower, I gave instruction in place of Confession.

April 15. Sunday. 6:00 and 7:00. After a reading of the Rule of Prayer, I celebrated the Liturgy in the tent and gave Communion to all those who had confessed and to fifteen young people.

We set out at 8:30 in an eight-man baidara. The weather was calm and clear. At 4:30 we arrived safely at the island of Tigalda, at a village located on the northeastern side of the island at a distance of at least sixty-five versts from the main village on Akun. We had sailed through three straits that can be very bad with riptides. The third strait is particularly bad. They are bad when there is wind and rough water, but we met no unpleasantness because the wind was perfectly calm and the sea was quiet.

April 16. Monday. 8:00, 9:00, and 10:00. We assembled all of the inhabitants in the tent, together with all the inhabitants of the island of Ugamak. Ugamak is located approximately fifteen versts from here.[14] I then taught them sufficiently through the interpreter, the local toion Pan'kov.

11:00 and 12:00. I chrismated thirty-seven persons, both men and women, and various ages.

From 5:00 to 10:00 I celebrated Vespers together with Matins in the barracks[15] and heard Confession from forty-three persons of both genders. For the youngsters I provided instructions instead of Confession.

Comment: In the morning the temperature went as low as one and one-half degrees below zero.

April 17. Tuesday. 9:00 and 10:00. After a reading of the Rule of Prayer, I celebrated the Liturgy in the tent and gave Communion to those who had confessed and to the youngsters, a total of sixty-three persons.

5:00. I sacramentally blessed nine marriages and visited the inhabitants in their dwellings, which were adequately clean.

At this time, all the local inhabitants had been chrismated, heard in Confession, given Communion, and married (the last except for two for whom it was impossible).[16]

Comment: The temperature went as low as two degrees below zero.

April 18. Wednesday. Morning. We set out for Tigalda at five o'clock with a calm southerly wind. We turned course back for Akun, and arrived at ten o'clock at the island of Avatanok [Avatanak], which is located next to Akun and Tigalda. We came to the village located on the island's northern side, having sailed at least forty-five versts. We encountered no misfortune in the middle of Derbenskoi [Derbin] Strait, which is one of those with bad riptides.

Comment: In the morning the temperature went as low as two degrees below zero.

11:00 and 12:00. I assembled all of the inhabitants in the tent and taught them sufficiently through the same interpreter, Pan'kov. In the afternoon, I chrismated sixteen people and sacramentally blessed five marriages. After the Vigil Service, I heard Confession from fourteen persons. For the youngsters, I provided instruction in place of Confession.

April 19. Thursday. 6:00 and 7:00. After a reading of the Rule of Prayer, I celebrated the Liturgy in the tent and gave Communion to all those who had confessed and to the youngsters—thirty persons in all.

Comment: The temperature went as low as one and one-half degrees below zero.

At this time all of the local inhabitants had been chrismated, married, heard in Confession, and given the sacrament.

We set out for Akun at eight o'clock. The wind was either somewhat against us or calm. The current was against us as we crossed Avatanok [Avatanak] Strait, in the midst of which we encountered a moderate riptide. Here I discovered the meaning of the word riptide.[17] Although we were in no small danger, since water began to pour into the baidara, we passed through safely, and arrived at eleven o'clock back at Artel'novskoe, the main village back on Akun.

Comment: Here we found a Harbor baidara [i.e. from the Harbor settlement on Unalaska] that had come for me the day before.

April 20. Friday. High winds made it impossible to use the tents.

April 21. Saturday. 6:00; 7:00; 8:00; and 9:00. I celebrated Vespers and heard Confession from twenty-nine people, the inhabitants of the local village.

April 22. Sunday. 7:00; 8:00; and 9:00. After a reading of the Rule of Prayer, I celebrated the Liturgy in the tent and gave Communion to all those who had confessed and to the youngsters. After the Liturgy, I performed a prayer service to St. Alexander, instead of having done this on the previous day, since a high wind had prevented us from using the tent.

11:00; 12:00. I sacramentally blessed twelve marriages.

At this time all of the local inhabitants had been chrismated, married, [and] (except for one elderly woman who was not here) heard in Confession and given Communion.

April 23. Monday. I had intended to go to a village some ten versts from here in order to give Final Communion to the aforesaid woman, but we were prevented from doing so because a chance infirmity afflicted the leg of Pan'kov, the interpreter. The Aleuts volunteered to bring the woman here.

5:00. And they did so. After brief instructions,[18] I heard Confession from her and gave her Communion from the reserved sacrament.

In the evening I conversed with one of the local elders, Ivan Smirennikov, who is considered a shaman in these parts. I found the facts quite to the contrary (I am presenting herein a report of conversation as proof of this).

April 24. Tuesday. Morning. We set out at five o'clock in a sixteen-man baidara that had been sent from [Unalaska] Harbor. En route we put in at Akutan Island, at the village of Golovskoe on the island's northern side. Through Pan'kov, the same interpreter, I instructed adequately [the] five very aged inhabitants of this place. Then, I heard Confession from them, and gave them Communion from the reserved sacrament.

We set out thence at 10:30 with a slight tailwind and arrived safely at the harbor on Unalaska at seven o'clock in the evening.

Comment: Pan'kov left to go back to Akun Island.

I need not write here of the manner in which the Aleuts received me and my teachings. To do so would be to repeat the same words many times over. Still, I cannot remain silent, and with heartfelt satisfaction will repeat that the inhabitants of the islands mentioned above are very zealous and fervent in their desire for God's word, and grateful for their instruction. It is further testimony to the special zeal of the interpreter Ivan Pan'kov, that on holidays he has many times instructed the intelligent men in the Christian Law, as they themselves have told me.

April 25. Wednesday. Morning. After explaining the power of an oath, I swore in an Aleut from Umnak whom the office had presented. I swore him to an oath of loyalty to His Majesty Nicholas Pavlovich and to His Heir.

April 27. Friday. 10:00 and 11:00. In school I briefly reviewed the teachings about Evangelical Faith, and then taught the first two commandments.[19]

April 29. Sunday. I celebrated the Liturgy. Before the Liturgy, I baptized one person and chrismated two others. I celebrated a prayer service after the Liturgy, instead of having done it on the 27th.

May

May 1. Tuesday. I celebrated Vespers.

May 2. Wednesday. I celebrated Matins, the Liturgy, Vespers, and the Vigil Service at its appointed time.

May 3. Ascension Day. Having performed a Blessing of the Water during a ringing of the bells summoning to worship, I celebrated the Liturgy and a prayer service for the parish's feast day. I led a Procession of the Cross and then celebrated Vespers.

May 4. Friday. 11:00. In school I taught the Third Commandment after reviewing the first two.

May 5. Saturday. I celebrated the Vigil Service.

May 6. Sunday. I celebrated the Hours.[20]

May 8. Tuesday. I celebrated Vespers and the Vigil Service.

May 9. Wednesday. I celebrated the Liturgy. Beforehand, I chrismated an infant.

May 11. Friday. 10:00 and 11:00. In school I reviewed the first three commandments and then taught the Fourth: to love God with all your soul and heart, and so on. I taught about what it means to fulfill these commandments and what it means to fail to fulfill them.

May 12. Saturday. I celebrated Vespers and the Vigil Service.

May 13. Trinity Sunday [Pentecost]. 11:30. I celebrated the Liturgy and Vespers.

May 14. Monday. I celebrated Matins and the Hours.

May 16. Wednesday. 9:30 and 11:00. I taught the Fifth Commandment, and a little bit about rules of courtesy. I anointed a sick person.[21]

May 18. Friday. I taught the Sixth and Seventh Commandments in school, and celebrated Vespers and the Vigil Service. During the Vigil a Russian government ship, the sloop *Moller*, arrived under the command of Captain Lieutenant M. N. Stanikovich [Staniukovich]. This was the second time it had come to Unalaska. It had sailed from Kamchatka.

May 19. I celebrated the Liturgy and a prayer service for the deceased. Afterwards I celebrated Vespers and the Vigil Service.

May 20. Sunday. I celebrated the Liturgy and Vespers at the appointed time.

May 21. Sunday. I celebrated the Hours and a prayer service.

May 23. Wednesday. 11:00. I taught the Eighth Commandment in school.

May 25. Friday. 10:00 and 11:00. I taught the last two commandments in school. Having briefly gone over the entire Law, I thus concluded the study of the entire Catechism, and still intend to review the second part.

May 26. I celebrated the Vigil Service.

May 27. I celebrated the Liturgy.

This month I read *Syn otechestva* for 1827 and *Severnaia pchela*.

June

June 1. Friday. 7:00. The sloop *Moller* sailed for the coasts of the Alaska Peninsula to explore there. They plan to come to Unalaska again in August.

June 2. Saturday. I celebrated Vespers and the Vigil Service.

June 3. Sunday. I celebrated the Liturgy. Beforehand, I baptized an infant.

[June 8. Friday]. *Comment*: A Russian-American Company ship, the brig *Golovnin*, arrived at eight o'clock.

June 9. I received decrees from the Irkutsk Church Consistory concerning the coronation and so on. In fulfillment of these decrees, I reported to the local office about a celebration to take place the following day.

5:00; 7:00; and 8:00. I celebrated Vespers and the Vigil Service.

June 10. Sunday. 11:00 and 12:00. After the Hours, I celebrated a prayer service to the Lord God, who had granted victory in the crushing of the sedition on the 14th of December, 1825 [the Decembrist Revolt]. Then, I celebrated the Liturgy, followed by a prayer service in honor of the coronation. In connection with this the church bells were rung for three days.

June 11. Monday. I celebrated the Hours. After that, I celebrated a prayer service of thanksgiving with a proclamation of "Many Years" for the Right Reverend Mikhail, Archbishop of Irkutsk, Nerchinsk, and Yakutsk.

June 12. Tuesday. I celebrated the Hours.

June 16. Saturday. I celebrated Vespers and the Vigil Service.

June 17. Sunday. I celebrated the Liturgy.

June 23. Saturday. I celebrated Vespers and the Vigil Service.

June 24. Sunday. I celebrated the Liturgy. Then, at the proper time, I celebrated Vespers and the Vigil Service.

June 25. The Tsar's birthday. I celebrated the Liturgy and a prayer service appropriate for the day.

June 28. Thursday. I celebrated Vespers and the Vigil Service.

June 29. Friday. I celebrated the Liturgy and a prayer service giving thanks to the Lord God for the victory at Poltava and for preserving our church, which was consecrated on this day in 1826.

This month I was primarily occupied with the preparation of papers to be sent to Russia and Novo-Arkhangel'sk.

[Signed:] Priest of the Unalaska Church of the Ascension,
Priest Ioann Veniaminov.
The 30th day of June, 1828.

NOTES

1. There is no harbor of any kind here. Throughout our visit here the winds were calm. The winds were very favorable for moorage, so favorable that the inhabitants here could not remember an instance when a ship had stood at anchor so successfully for such a long time.

2. There are few structures here, since it is a place entirely lacking in trees. There are only a barracks and four iurts.

3. The chapel here was built in honor of the Apostles Peter and Paul, and is a rather nice one. Even nicer is an icon of the apostles in a silver riza and a golden frame.

4. The Aleuts here live very well, especially under the present manager, Gomziakov, with whom they are very satisfied. If there is anything disadvantageous here, it is only that there are no fish other than the halibut that are sometimes caught; these, however, are good compensation, since they are abundant in meat. The Russians find the seal meat rather tasty as well.

5. I wanted, without fail, to spend some time on Akun this year. However, I did not do so because of the presence of the ships here, and by September it was already too late to go, since the Aleuts begin to disperse for fox hunting.

6. I tried to do everything possible so that all would understand, and with that purpose in mind I required each student to explain his own understanding of the concepts.

7. To explain the Gospel means to read it through in Slavonic and in Russian, and then to retell the whole story in my own words. Then I draw from the story some kind of moral lesson. I discuss this moral, questioning the students, and, of course, clarifying the difficult or obscure points.

8. Arithmetic is taught by my assistant, Stefan Veniaminov.

9. Nomadic Aleuts were seen on Unga [two words illegible]. As many as ten baidarkas were counted, including two two-seaters.

All of the Aleuts are unanimous in affirming that on the Alaska Peninsula there live Aleuts who have fled from this island chain or from Kodiak Island, and that they travel along the entire chain in secret. However, they do not do anything greatly offensive, except for removing foxes from traps and, when they can (which is very rarely), taking young men off with their group. For this last reason they are feared by all the inhabitants. My records show three males and one female to be missing, and the inhabitants believe that these people are among the nomadic Aleuts. (The company office, it seems, does not believe these rumors, for it has taken no measures in response.)

10. I did not teach a Gospel lesson on this or any other Sunday in Lent because of the freezing weather that began at the start of Lent and continued without interruption up until March 22. It got as cold as seven degrees Reaumur, often together with winds from the north. For the same reason, the students had no studies from the 6th to the 13th, and from the 25th of February until April; there is no stove in the school.

11. I did not teach the Catechism: before Easter I did not because of the freezing weather; after Easter, because of my intended trip and the performance of church services.

12. This distance is judged by the progress of the baidarka, assuming that a baidarka can cover up to ten versts an hour, or even more with a favorable current.

13. He is the manager there for the [Russian-American] Company.

14. These people had been living here for all of this spring because it was disadvantageous to live on Ugamak.

15. A strong northerly wind prevented us from using a tent.

16. One because he refused to take as wife a blind woman and her children, and the other because of the illness of his mate.

17. A riptide [*suloi*] is nothing other than an abnormally steep and frequent disturbance, rotary in some places, which curls up like a tube at the top. This phenomenon occurs when the wind and roughness of the sea go against the direction of the current. The faster the current—and the stronger the wind and the roughness—the more terrible the riptide. They occur more often in straits than elsewhere, though they do not exist to the same degree throughout an entire strait at any one time—in some places they will be less severe. There is no way to save oneself when in the middle of a strong riptide in a baidara, and even more so in a baidarka! However, in times of calm and smooth seas there are no riptides, even in the straits with the swiftest currents.

18. Because of her advanced age, I was barely able to provide her with the most necessary knowledge.

19. And I intended to continue this teaching from this day forward.

20. Because we did not have any flour [to prepare bread for Communion].

21. A Creole office clerk who died on the 17th.

JOURNAL NO. 6

In which Priest Ioann Veniaminov indicates with what he was occupied in connection with his duties. June 1, 1828, to June 21, 1829, Unalaska.

July

July 1. Sunday. I celebrated the Liturgy and the appropriate prayer service.

July 7. Saturday. I celebrated Vespers and the Vigil Service.

July 8. Sunday. I celebrated the Liturgy.

[July 10. Tuesday.] *Comment:* A Russian-American Company ship, the *Golovnin*, which had set out on the 12th of June for the north and for the Pribilof Islands, returned on the 10th of July.

July 14. Saturday. I celebrated Vespers and the Vigil Service.

July 15. Sunday. I celebrated the Liturgy.

July 19. Thursday. I celebrated Vespers and the Vigil Service.

July 20. Friday. I celebrated the Liturgy.

July 21. Saturday. I celebrated Vespers and the Vigil Service.

July 22. Sunday. I celebrated the Liturgy.

July 26. Thursday. The sloop *Moller* arrived at Unalaska for the third time, having come from the shore of the Alaska Peninsula.

[July 27. Friday.] *Comment*: A Russian-American Company ship, the brig *Finliandiia*, arrived with wood for the belfry. Also on board were dispatches from the chief manager.

July 29. Sunday. I celebrated the Liturgy. Before that service, I celebrated the July memorial service for the Tsar.

During this month I was occupied with the writing of papers to send to Russia and Sitka. I also read newspapers.

August

August 1. Wednesday. I celebrated the Liturgy. Afterwards I celebrated a Blessing of the Water at the river and held a procession with icons around the village. Returning to the church, I celebrated a prayer service of thanksgiving.

August 3. Friday. The sloop *Moller* weighed anchor and departed for Kamchatka. From there it will depart for Russia. Along with the *Moller*, the Company vessel *Golovnin* also weighed anchor. It sailed for Sitka. Dispatches for Russia and Sitka were sent on board the second ship.

August 4. Saturday. I celebrated Vespers and the Vigil Service.

August 5. Sunday. I celebrated the Liturgy. Afterwards, I celebrated a prayer service for those traveling by sea.

At twelve o'clock I set out in a boat from Unalaska, bound for Umnak Island to visit the inhabitants there. We had a tailwind.

It is remarkable that there were no more than twelve hours of tailwind throughout this entire journey, which lasted ten days and four hours. A strong headwind blew the rest of the time, and there was a dense fog, so that our voyage was very prolonged: instead of ten days, twenty hours at most would be needed to cover this distance [under normal conditions].

August 12. Sunday. At sea I celebrated a prayer service for those traveling by sea.

August 14. Tuesday. In the evening I read Vespers and Matins.

August 15. Feast of the Dormition. I celebrated the Hours at sea.

At four o'clock we dropped anchor in the harbor at the village of Recheshnoe [Nikolski], which is located on the northwest side of Umnak Island. In the evening I celebrated Vespers and the Vigil Service in the chapel.[1]

August 16. Thursday. After blessing the water, I consecrated the chapel with the following ceremony:

I sprinkled with Holy Water on both the inside and outside, during the customary procession of the cross. I then returned to the church. After the litany, I read the prayers for the blessing of a new home and followed that with requisite kneeling prayers. Then, I proclaimed the "Many Years" for His Majesty the Emperor; for the Holy Synod and Bishop Mikhail, Bishop of Irkutsk, Nerchinsk, and Yakutsk; for the church elders and creators of this sacred house. Then, after reading through the Hours, I celebrated the Liturgy in the chapel sanctuary and gave Communion to all of the youngsters from the local village. In the morning I chrismated eleven persons, both males and females. In the afternoon I assembled all of the inhabitants into the chapel, instructed them duly through an interpreter, and then heard Confession from fifty-four persons, both men and women. In addition, I celebrated Vespers and the Vigil Service.

August 17. After a reading of the Rule of Prayer, I celebrated the Liturgy in the chapel sanctuary and gave Communion to all those who had confessed. After the Liturgy, I visited three ill people, and brought them elements for Communion. In the afternoon I sacramentally blessed four marriages, including that of Ignatii Suvorov and Irina Kozhevnikova.[2]

August 18. Saturday. I celebrated the Vigil Service.

August 19. Sunday. I celebrated the Hours and a prayer service for those traveling by sea. After finishing all of this, I gave instructions to the local inhabitants, and most importantly told them that if anyone among them sees any of the nomadic Aleuts, then he should greet them for me and tell them that I feel sorry for them and desire that they should settle someplace permanently, and that they are pardoned....and so on.

In the afternoon the ship set out for Unalaska, sailing along the northern side of Umnak, while I remained behind with the intention of setting out along the southern side, so that I might visit all of the Aleuts living on Umnak and on the western coast of Unalaska.

August 20 and 21. Monday and Tuesday. A strong headwind and rain prevented us from setting out.

I celebrated the Vigil Service on the 21st.

August 22. Wednesday. I celebrated the Hours and the customary prayer service.

August 24. Friday. At six o'clock I set out on foot across the isthmus, heading for the southern side of Umnak. From there I set out in a baidarka, accompanied by three other such craft, in order to return to Unalaska. At four o'clock in the afternoon we arrived at the village of Egorkovskoi, which is located in the middle of Umnak.

August 25. Saturday. After duly teaching the inhabitants, I chrismated two infants, heard Confession from sixteen people, and celebrated the Vigil Service.

August 26. Sunday. After a reading of the Rule of Prayer, I celebrated the Liturgy in the tent and gave Communion to all those who had confessed and to the youngsters. I also sacramentally blessed two marriages.

We set out in four baidarkas at eleven o'clock, and arrived in the village of Tulik at five o'clock in the evening. The interpreter who had served both the cantor and me remained, out of necessity.

August 27. Monday. I chrismated three infants. Then, after teaching, I heard Confession from all of the inhabitants. To three of the very aged I gave Communion from the reserved sacrament.

We set out in five baidarkas at seven o'clock, crossing the strait to Unalaska. At eleven o'clock we arrived safely at the village of Chernovskoe. There are fairly many inhabitants there, since the Aleuts from Tanamykta are living there as well. At this time, however, no one was there except for two women of advanced age, one with an infant.[3] Since I had no hope of assembling all the inhabitants, I quickly heard Confession from the women, gave Communion from the reserved sacrament to the elderly ones, and chrismated the infant.

We left here at two o'clock, but a crosswind began to pick up strength. We barely made it across the bay, and that was not without facing considerable danger.[4] We stopped for the night at the first opportune landing.

August 28. Tuesday. We set out at six o'clock and arrived safely at the village of Koshiga.

In the afternoon I assembled everyone in the tent and then instructed them. I chrismated four infants, sacramentally blessed five marriages, heard Confession from thirty-four people, and read Vespers and Matins together.

August 29. After a reading of the Rule of Prayer and the Hours, I gave Communion from the reserved sacrament to those who had [just] been chrismated and to nine of those who had confessed—the very old and the ill.

At nine o'clock we set out with good weather, and at three o'clock we arrived safely at the village of Makushin.

In the evening I chrismated one infant, read Vespers and the Matins together, and read the Rule of Prayer.

August 30. Thursday. I heard Confession from twenty-two persons. Then, during the Hours, I gave Communion from the reserved sacrament to one very elderly person and to four ill people. After a prayer service, I sacramentally blessed two marriages.

At ten o'clock we set out in baidarkas for the inside of Makushin Bay. From there we proceeded on foot. We stopped for the night after covering about eight versts.

August 31. Friday. After covering around ten versts, we reached Captain's Harbor [Unalaska Bay], in the eastern portion of which is found Harbor village [Iliuliuk, present-day Unalaska]. We finally arrived at this village at eleven o'clock aboard a launch that had been sent us. Thus concluded my second trip through the western regions of my parish.

In my free time I read Buffon's *Book for Youth*, volumes 1 and 2. [Probably *Le Petit Buffon, ou Histoire naturelle dediee a la jeunesse*, by the French natural historian George Louis Leclerc, Comte de Buffon.]

September

September 1. Saturday. I celebrated Vespers and the Vigil Service. [See comment for September 2.]

September 2. Sunday. I celebrated the Liturgy after baptizing an infant.
    Comment: At night on both the 1st and the 2nd there were earthquakes; both were a single light shock.

September 5. Wednesday. I celebrated the Hours and a prayer service.

September 7. Friday. I celebrated Vespers and the Vigil Service.

September 8. Saturday. I celebrated the Liturgy. Later on, I celebrated Vespers and the Vigil Service.

September 9. Sunday. After hearing Confession from an ailing person, I celebrated the Liturgy and a prayer service for a journey. During the Liturgy, I gave Communion to the person who was ill. At eleven o'clock we set out in baidarkas to visit nearby villages at the request of the inhabitants. At two o'clock we reached the village of Kalekhta, which is located on the northeastern side of Unalaska. After assembling all of the inhabitants in the tent, I duly taught them. Then, after a reading of the Rule of Prayer for Vespers, I heard Confession from eight persons who had not been able to attend Confession and Holy Communion during the fast which had just concluded.

September 10. Monday. After a reading of the Rule of Prayer, I gave Communion from the reserved sacrament to seven very elderly persons. We departed at six o'clock and safely sailed across Unalga Pass, one of those which has riptides when opposite currents are present. At nine o'clock we arrived at the village of Unalga, which is found on the small island of Unalga, next to Unalaska. After assembling all of the inhabitants in the tent, I duly taught them. I chrismated six youngsters, and sacramentally blessed three marriages. Also, I heard Confession from three people who had not been at Confession and Holy Communion. I gave two of them Communion from the reserved sacrament. Shortly after one o'clock we set out across the strait again, and at three o'clock we arrived safely at Borkinskoe [Biorka] village on the island of Spirkin [Sedanka Island], off the southeastern shore of Unalaska.

I gathered all the inhabitants into the tent, instructed them, and chrismated them. Then, after a reading of the Rule of Prayer, I heard Confession from eight people who had not been able to attend Confession and Communion during previous fasts.

September 11. Sunday. After a reading of the Rule of Prayer, I gave Communion from the reserved sacrament to five very elderly and ill people.[5]

At seven o'clock we set out across Bobrovskii Bay [Beaver Inlet], and at nine o'clock arrived at Bobrovskii village [Beaver], on the eastern shore of Unalaska.

After gathering all of the inhabitants into the tent, I taught them, chrismated three people, sacramentally blessed three marriages, and heard Confession from six people. I gave four of these—the ill and the aged—Holy Communion from the reserved sacrament.

We departed at two o'clock, and at four o'clock we arrived at the nearby Sechkinskoe settlement, in Bobrovskii Bay on the southeastern coast of Unalaska.

After the usual teaching, I chrismated one infant. After a reading of the Rule of Prayer, I heard Confession from three very aged and ill persons.

September 12. Wednesday. After a reading of the Rule of Prayer, I gave Communion from the reserved sacrament to those who had confessed. Since a strong tailwind prevented us from setting off on our return by baidarka, and since we had reached the isthmus located farther along the bay, I started out on foot and arrived at [Unalaska] Harbor at twelve o'clock.[6]

September 13. I celebrated the Lesser Vespers.

September 14. Friday. I celebrated the Vigil Service and the Liturgy. Afterwards I celebrated a memorial service for the sixteen people who drowned on August 25.

September 15. Saturday. I celebrated Vespers.

September 16. Sunday. I celebrated Matins and the Liturgy. Afterwards, I performed a funeral service for a deceased infant.

September 18. Tuesday. I gave Final Communion to an ill person.

September 21. Friday. I celebrated a funeral service for the person to whom I gave Final Communion on the 18th.

September 22. Saturday. At eleven o'clock, after a Blessing of the Water and a ringing of the church bells, the foundation for the belfry was put in place next to the church itself. The construction of the tower began this day. In the evening I celebrated Vespers.

September 23. Sunday. I celebrated the Hours and sacramentally blessed one marriage. Matins was not held because of a strong southwesterly wind.

September 24. Monday. I gave Final Communion to an ill person.

September 29. Saturday. I celebrated Vespers.

September 30. Sunday. I celebrated Matins and the Liturgy.

This month I read the following books: (1) the physics writings of Eiler, volume 1 [probably Leonhard Euler, *Lettres a une princesse d'Allemagne sur divers sujets de physique et de philosophie*, which had been published in four volumes by the Russian Imperial Academy of Sciences, 1768-74]; (2) volume 1 of *Christian Philosophy*; and (3) the first two volumes of Karamzin's *A History of Russia*.

I attended to the construction of the belfry, supervising the carpenters at the request of the chief manager.

October

October 6. Saturday. I celebrated Vespers.

October 7. Sunday. I celebrated Matins and the Liturgy.

October 13. Saturday. I celebrated the Lesser Vespers.

October 14. Sunday. I celebrated the Vigil Service, the Liturgy, and a prayer service.

October 20. Saturday. I celebrated Vespers.

October 21. Sunday. I celebrated Matins and the Liturgy, and sacramentally blessed one marriage.

October 22. Monday. I celebrated a prayer service to the Virgin Mary.

October 27. Saturday. I celebrated a Vigil Service.

October 28. Sunday. I celebrated Matins and the Liturgy. Before the Liturgy I celebrated a memorial service for the Tsar.

During this month I was primarily occupied with the construction of the bell-tower. I read volumes 3, 4, and 5 of [Karamzin's] *A History of Russia.*

November

November 2. Friday. In school I began to teach the Catechism; I finished the first chapter.

November 3. Saturday. I celebrated Vespers.

November 4. Sunday. I celebrated Matins and the Liturgy.

November 7. Wednesday. I went to the school and reviewed the proofs of the existence of God. I questioned the students and was satisfied with their answers. In the evening I celebrated the Lesser Vespers.

November 8. Thursday. I celebrated the Vigil Service, the Liturgy, and a prayer service with a proclamation of the "Many Years" for the imperial family and for the Right Reverend Mikhail, Bishop of Irkutsk. Before the Liturgy I baptized an infant.

November 10. Saturday. I celebrated Vespers.

November 11. Sunday. I celebrated Matins and the Liturgy.

November 15. Thursday. I gave Final Communion to an ailing person.

November 17. Saturday. I celebrated Vespers.

November 18. Sunday. I celebrated Matins and the Liturgy.

November 19. Monday. I celebrated Vespers, performed a memorial service, and celebrated the Vigil Service.

November 20. Tuesday. I celebrated the Liturgy and a prayer service.

November 21. Wednesday. I celebrated the Vigil Service and the Liturgy.

November 24. Saturday. I celebrated Vespers.

November 25. Sunday. I celebrated Matins, the Liturgy, and a Vigil Service dedicated to St. Innocent.

November 26. I celebrated the Liturgy and a prayer service to St. Innocent.

November 28. Wednesday. I anointed an ill person.

This month I read volumes 6, 7, and 8 of [Karamzin's] *A History of Russia*. I was also occupied with the construction of the belfry. I did not go to the school, since the students' lessons were cancelled because of freezing weather.

December

December 2. Sunday. I celebrated Matins and the Hours.

December 5. Wednesday. I celebrated the Lesser Vespers.

December 9. Sunday. I celebrated Matins and the Hours.

December 15. Saturday. I celebrated Vespers.

December 16. Sunday. I celebrated Matins and the Liturgy, and performed a funeral service for a deceased infant.

December 22. Saturday. I celebrated Vespers.

December 23. Sunday. I celebrated Matins, the Liturgy, and Vespers.

December 24. Monday. I celebrated Matins, the Hours, and Vespers together with the Liturgy.

December 25. Christmas. I celebrated Matins, the Hours, and a prayer service. During the Liturgy, I gave for the second time a sermon that I had written for this day, concerning the worship of Jesus Christ.

December 26. Wednesday. I celebrated Matins and the Liturgy.

December 27. Thursday. I celebrated Matins and the Hours.

December 29. Saturday. I celebrated Vespers.

December 30. Sunday. I celebrated Matins and the Liturgy.

This month I read volumes 9 and 10 of [Karamzin's] *A History of Russia*.

1829
January

January 1. Tuesday. I celebrated the Vigil Service, the Liturgy, and the customary prayer service.

January 4. Friday. I celebrated the Hours.

January 5. Saturday. I celebrated Vespers with a Blessing of the Water.

January 6. Epiphany. I celebrated Matins and the Liturgy. After the Liturgy I blessed the water at the river.

January 7. Monday. I celebrated Matins, the Hours, and a prayer service.

January 13. Sunday. I celebrated Matins and the Liturgy. I sacramentally blessed one marriage.

January 20. Sunday. I celebrated Matins and the Hours.

January 27. Sunday. I celebrated Matins and the Liturgy.

January 28. Monday. I went to the school and showed the students the letters of the Aleut alphabet.

January 30. Wednesday. I celebrated the Vigil Service and the Liturgy.

This month, besides supervising the construction of the belfry, I wrote church books and compiled records. I also read the third volume of Buffon and the second volume of the *Physics Letters*.

February

February 2. The Presentation of Our Lord in the Temple [Candlemas]. I celebrated the Vigil Service and the Liturgy.

February 3. Sunday. I celebrated the Vigil Service, the Liturgy, and a prayer service. The appointed sermon was read during the Liturgy.

February 8. Friday. I celebrated Matins and the Liturgy.

February 9. Saturday. I celebrated the Vigil Service in the evening. At its appointed time, I celebrated the Liturgy and a prayer service to St. Innocent.

February 10. Sunday. I celebrated Matins and the Liturgy. The appointed sermon was read at the Liturgy.

February 16. Saturday. I celebrated Matins and the Liturgy. I celebrated a memorial service.

February 17. Sunday. I celebrated Matins and the Liturgy. The appointed sermon was read at the Liturgy.
    Comment: There was thunder and lightening on the night of the 17th, for the first time during my residence here.

February 24. Sunday. I celebrated Matins and the Liturgy. During the Liturgy a sermon on the Last Judgement was read. After Vespers, in a public building with all of the Aleuts in attendance, I explained the practice of asking for forgiveness and then exhorted them to clear their consciences with repentance. [I taught them that] for this no offerings are needed or required by God, other than a contrite and obedient heart...and so on.
    After Matins, I read the prayers for the beginning of the forty-day fast [Lent], and services began on this day.

February 27. Wednesday. I celebrated the Liturgy of the Presanctified.

This month I read Church history and attended to the construction of the belfry.

March

March 1. Friday. After Matins I gave sufficient instruction to those preparing for the sacraments. I heard Confession from ninty-five Aleuts of both genders, doing this after the Liturgy of the Presanctified and after Vespers.

March 2. Saturday. After Matins I prayed over two infants. I celebrated the Liturgy. After the sermon I gave Communion to all those who had confessed.

March 3. Sunday. I baptized an infant. I celebrated the Liturgy, at which was read the second appointed sermon. Vespers brought the services to an end.

March 6. Wednesday. In school I began to teach about the Law of God. I taught about the natural proofs of the existence of God, and about God's properties.

March 8. Friday. In school I taught about the fact that even though a natural awareness of the existence of God has been written into the heart and soul of every man, this awareness is not enough without revelation, since our reason may err both in Faith and in matters of the Law. Therefore, by the grace of God, we have the revelation found in the books of the Holy Scriptures. I taught about the nature of the Holy Scripture...and so on.

March 10. Sunday. After baptizing three infants, I celebrated the Liturgy, at which was read the appointed sermon. I celebrated Vespers at the appointed time.

March 13. Wednesday. In school I taught the first section of the Symbol of Faith [Nicene Creed], and made the students write in Aleut.

March 15. Friday. I taught the second section of the Nicene Creed.

March 17. Sunday. I celebrated the Liturgy, including a reading of the appointed sermon, and celebrated Vespers at its appointed time. Daily services began on this day.

March 20. Wednesday. I celebrated the Liturgy of the Presanctified.

March 22. Friday. I celebrated the Liturgy of the Presanctified. After Matins I duly taught those preparing for the sacraments, and in the afternoon I heard Confession from seventy-seven Aleuts, both men and women, and two Russians.

March 23. Saturday. I celebrated the Liturgy; after a reading of the sermon, I gave Communion to all those who had confessed, with the exception of one widow, at my advice.

March 24. Sunday. I celebrated Matins, the Liturgy, and Vespers.

March 25. The Annunciation of the Mother of God. I celebrated Matins with the Akathistos, the Liturgy, and Vespers.

March 27. Wednesday. In the evening, I celebrated Vespers and Matins (from the Great Canon).

March 28. Thursday. I celebrated the Hours and the Liturgy of the Presanctified.

March 31. Sunday. I celebrated Matins, the Liturgy, and Vespers.

This month I read: (1) *Christian Philosophy*; and (2) *On the Mystery of the Cross.*

April

April 5. Friday. I celebrated Vespers.

April 6. Lazarus Saturday. I celebrated Matins, the Liturgy, and the Lesser Vespers.

April 7. The Entry of Our Lord into Jerusalem [Palm Sunday]. I celebrated the Vigil Service and the Liturgy.

April 8. Monday. I celebrated Matins and the Hours together with the Liturgy of the Presanctified and a reading of the Gospel.

April 9. Tuesday. I celebrated Matins and the Hours together with the Liturgy of the Presanctified and a reading of the Gospel.

April 10. Wednesday. I celebrated Matins and the Hours together with the Liturgy of the Presanctified and a reading of the Gospel. After Matins I instructed those preparing for the sacraments, and in the afternoon I heard Confession from thirty-six Aleut men and women and one Russian.

April 11. Thursday. I celebrated the Liturgy; after the sermon had been read, I gave Communion to all those who had confessed.

April 12. Friday. After Matins I instructed the observants and after Vespers I heard Confession from them—twenty-seven Aleuts of both genders.

April 13. Saturday. I celebrated the Liturgy, at which I gave Communion to all those who had confessed. After giving due instruction, I heard Confession from thirty-six other males—Russians, Creoles, and Aleuts.

April 14. Easter. I celebrated the Liturgy, at which I gave Communion to all those who had confessed and to numerous youngsters.

April 15. Easter Monday. I celebrated the Liturgy and gave Communion to numerous youngsters.

April 16, 17, 18, 19, 20. Easter [week]. The Liturgy was celebrated daily. On Saturday, in addition to the Liturgy, there was a Vigil Service in the evening.

April 21. Sunday. I celebrated the Liturgy and a prayer service.

April 22. Monday. I celebrated Vespers and a Vigil Service dedicated to St. George.

April 23. Tuesday. I celebrated the Liturgy and a prayer service for those traveling by sea; on this day I moved over onto the ship in order to take it to Unga.

April 25. Thursday. At nine o'clock in the morning under a partial tailwind, we weighed anchor. At six o'clock we passed through Unalga Strait and into the Southern Sea. We sailed from this date until the 1st of May.[7]

May

May 1. Wednesday. At two o'clock in the afternoon we dropped anchor in the harbor on Unga Island [Delarof Harbor], right at the village. Within the hour I had moved over onto shore, where I was met with evident joy by each and every inhabitant.

May 2. Thursday. In the morning I gathered all of the inhabitants into the tent. I then duly taught them, through an interpreter, about the Christian truths and virtues. I spoke at even greater length about the fact that each Christian should suffer and forbear with faith and refrain from boasting, since a Christian should imitate Jesus Christ, and since suffering purifies us and we shall sooner or later meet with the need for forbearance...and so on. I concluded my lesson with the words of the beloved disciple of Christ [John]: "My children, learn to love one another."

In the afternoon, I heard Confession from thirty males and celebrated the Vigil Service.

May 3. Friday. After a reading of the Rule of Prayer, I celebrated the Liturgy in the tent, on the same spot at which this sacrifice had been performed on my first journey.[8] I gave Communion to all who had confessed and to as many as twelve youngsters.

In the afternoon I chrismated six infants, sacramentally blessed three marriages, and heard Confession from forty-three females. At its appointed time I celebrated Vespers with Matins.

May 4. Saturday. After a reading of the Rule of Prayer, I celebrated the Liturgy and gave Communion to all those who had confessed but one (out of necessity) and to twenty-four young people.

At this time all of the inhabitants here, except for five who were temporarily away, had been heard in Confession and given Communion.

In the evening, I celebrated the Vigil Service.

May 5. Sunday. I celebrated the Hours in the tent. In the afternoon I instructed the Aleuts who had arrived, and then married four of them. After Vespers and the Rule, I heard Confession from them.

May 6. Monday. After a reading of the Rule of Prayer, I celebrated the Hours in a home and gave Communion from the reserved sacrament to all five people who had confessed. At four o'clock I set off on my return course to Unalaska, in amongst three three-man baidarkas. In the evening we stopped at the small uninhabited island of Nerpechii.

May 7. Tuesday. Departing at four o'clock, we reached the village of Pavlovskoe at ten o'clock. This village is located on the southern side of the Alaska Peninsula. Assembling the inhabitants in the tent within the hour, I taught them sufficiently about the dogmas of the Faith and about the essence of Christianity—that is, about the imitation of Jesus Christ. In the afternoon I chrismated four young people. After conducting Vespers and Matins together at their appointed time, I heard Confession from thirty-nine people, both men and women.

May 8. Wednesday. After a reading of the Rule of Prayer, at five o'clock I celebrated the Liturgy in the tent, which stood on a spot used previously. I gave Communion to all who had confessed except for one woman (by necessity). After the Liturgy I brought the elements to the home of a very aged woman. I heard Confession from her and then gave her Communion.

At 6:30 I left to continue on my way, and at four o'clock in the afternoon we arrived at the village of Bel'kovskoe, on the Alaska Peninsula. At the appointed time I celebrated a Vigil Service to St. Nicholas.

May 9. Thursday. After gathering all of the children over the age of reason, I celebrated the Liturgy in the tent, on the same spot as used previously. I gave Communion to the youngsters and infants—to as many as forty-five people in all.

In the morning I gathered all of the inhabitants in the tent and duly instructed them on the dogmas of the Faith and the essence of Christianity. I ended my teaching with the words "Love one another."

In the afternoon I chrismated five infants, sacramentally blessed four marriages, celebrated Vespers and Matins, and heard Confession from fifty-one people.

May 10. After a reading of the Rule of Prayer, and after I had heard Confession from one Russian, I celebrated the Liturgy in the tent and gave Communion to all of the chrismated infants and to all those who had confessed except for two women (by necessity).

In the afternoon I sacramentally blessed two marriages and gave Final Communion to a sick person.

May 11. Saturday. We set out at five o'clock. Because of a headwind, we stopped on a small island after we had traveled more than thirty versts. In the evening I celebrated Vespers and Matins.

May 12. Sunday. After singing the Hours, we set out with a tailwind and arrived at the mouth of Morzhovoi Bay at two o'clock. From there we followed the shallow, narrow, and winding bay toward the site of the old village, which had been located on the southern shore of the Alaska Peninsula. From there we were transported by stream to a large lake, on which we traveled to the very tip, which is the point closest to the present-day village. Finally, after crossing about four versts on foot, we reached Morzhevskoe village at 6:30. This village is located on the northwestern tip of the Alaska Peninsula, next to Isannakhskii Strait, the strait separating the Alaska Peninsula from Unimak.

May 13. Monday. After assembling the inhabitants in the tent, I duly taught them about the dogmas of the Faith and the essence of Christianity. At its appointed time I celebrated Vespers and Matins and heard Confession from nineteen women.

May 14. After a reading of the Rule of Prayer, I chrismated two infants. After hearing Confession from nine people, I celebrated the Liturgy in the tent, on a spot used on a previous visit, and gave Communion to all who had confessed and to all the young people.

May 15, 16, 17, and 18. Headwinds and rough seas prevented our departure.

May 19. Sunday. I celebrated the Vigil Service in the evening. I celebrated the Hours, adding a prayer service for those desiring to travel by water.

At 4:30 we set out across Isannakhskii Strait for Unimak Island. At four o'clock in the afternoon we arrived at Shishaldinskoe village [Sisaguk] on Unimak's northern shore, having traveled no less than eighty versts. After the inhabitants had assembled in the tent and I had duly taught them about the dogmas of the Faith and the essence of Christianity, I celebrated Vespers and Matins. Afterwards, I heard Confession from forty-two people.

May 20. Monday. After a reading of the Rule of Prayer, I chrismated twenty-eight people, both males and females and of various ages, celebrated the Liturgy in the tent, and gave Communion to all those who had confessed and all the youngsters (except for one Russian). In the afternoon, I sacramentally blessed seven marriages.

At this time all of the inhabitants here had been chrismated, married, heard in Confession, and given Communion.

May 21. Tuesday. A strong westerly wind made travel by sea impossible, so that, in order to hasten my return to Unalaska, I left the baidarka and paddles in this village until an opportune time for the trip; I took my necessities and at six o'clock in the morning set out on foot for a nearby village, accompanied by ten people. (Everyone went with me for over a verst as a send-off.) After covering more than forty versts of smooth and fairly level terrain, I stopped for the night in an uninhabited spot. After putting up the tent, I celebrated Vespers and the Matins Service for the remembrance of Easter.

May 22. Wednesday. After a singing of the Hours, we continued on and reached the village of Pogromskoe [Pogromni] at two o'clock. This village is located on the western side of Unimak, at a distance of over eighty-five versts from Shishaldinskoe. At its appointed time, I celebrated Vespers and the Vigil Service in a house.[9]

May 23. Once the inhabitants had assembled, I instructed them on dogma and on the essence of Christianity. After a reading of the Rule of Prayer, I heard Confession from six people. I chrismated four people, blessed the water, celebrated the Liturgy, and gave Communion to all who had confessed and to one youngster.

In the afternoon I sacramentally blessed two marriages and celebrated Vespers.

May 24. Friday. At six o'clock we continued on with our route. After going no more than twenty versts along a high area covered with burned rock, we arrived at the village of Nosovskoi. This village is located on the southwestern tip of Unimak, next to the strait that separates that island from Akun and others.

May 25. Saturday. I taught sufficiently the local inhabitants and the people who had accompanied me [from Shishaldinskoe]. I chrismated three people, and celebrated Vespers and Matins at their appointed time.[10]

Comment: Upon getting up in the morning I felt rather unwell; I had a cold and fever.

May 26. Sunday. After a reading of the Rule of Prayer, I heard Confession from four people, celebrated the Hours, and gave Communion from the reserved sacrament to all who had confessed and to one young person.

Comment: The state of my health remained unchanged.

May 27. Monday. I sacramentally blessed one marriage.

This and the previous two days were very boring, and also fairly gloomy ones for me. I could not imagine that our baidarkas would arrive on this day, or the following day, because of a strong wind from the east. This fact, my poor state of health, and the almost total lack of provisions troubled me greatly (though this was the first of any such unpleasantness in all of my travels). However, God, Who comforts everyone, showed His kindness by gladdening me on this day. First of all, the state of my health began to improve noticeably at noon; it had troubled me greatly because of the cold weather and the complete lack of any remedies. Secondly, contrary to all expectations, the baidarkas appeared at four o'clock.

May 28. Tuesday. A strong easterly wind detained us and prevented our departure.

Comment: By evening my health had completely recovered.[11]

May 29. After a prayer had been sung, we set out across Unimak Pass at 5:30 with a calm tailwind. This is one of the widest straits in the Fox chain. After passing some islands—Ugamak, Tigalda, and Avatanok—we arrived at 4:30 at Artel'novskoe village, which is located on Akun Island, right across from Akutan. We had sailed for more than eighty versts.[12]

May 30. Thursday. I chrismated two infants. A headwind prevented our departure.

May 31. Friday. A headwind again prevented our departure.

During this month I read volume five of *Christian Philosophy.*

June

June 1. Saturday. We set out at 3:30 in the morning into a quiet headwind, and we finally arrived in Harbor village [Unalaska] at eleven o'clock at night, having crossed the western [?—Z.] strait safely, but only after facing some danger. More than once along the way we had stopped to wait out unfavorable winds and currents, or a riptide. Thus ended my journey, the first of this year to Unimak and the second to Unga and the Alaska Peninsula.

At twelve o'clock midnight I celebrated the Lesser Vespers (without a ringing of the bells).

June 2. Pentecost. I celebrated the Vigil Service and the Liturgy, in accordance with custom, and at its appointed time I celebrated the Lesser Vespers. Before the Liturgy, I prayed over and baptized two infants born during my absence.

June 3. Monday. I heard Confession from, and gave Communion to, a dangerously ill Aleut. After the Matins Service, I anointed him. I celebrated the Liturgy at its appointed time.

June 8. Saturday. I celebrated the Vigil Service.

June 9. Sunday. I celebrated the Hours since we lacked the supplies [for Communion?].

At twelve o'clock I set out by baidarka for the nearby village of Imagninskoe [Imagnee], which is no more than six versts from the Harbor. Here I duly instructed a very elderly and ill woman, heard Confession from her, and gave her Communion from the reserved sacrament. I returned at five o'clock.

June 14. Friday. At 6:30 in the evening, a ship arrived from Sitka: the brig *Golovnin*. It brought word of the birth and baptism of Konstantin Nikolaevich and Ekaterina Mikhailovna, of the signing of a treaty of perpetual peace with Persia, and of the outbreak of war with the Ottoman Porte...and so on.

Comment: The same ship brought the manager of the Novo-Arkhangel'sk office, Kirill Timofeevich Khlebnikov, representing the chief manager.

June 15. Saturday. After reporting the news to the office, I celebrated Vespers and the Vigil Service.

June 16. Sunday. After a reading of the Hours, there was read the Manifesto on the outbreak of war with the [Ottoman] Porte; a prayer service was celebrated with a ringing of the bells. Upon completion of the Liturgy, the Manifesto was read on the conclusion of the war with Persia, and a prayer of thanksgiving was celebrated for all the blessings that God showers and lavishes on Russia. The ceremony contained kneeling prayers and a ringing of the bells.

Since the ship that had arrived needed to go to Nushagak, and from there to St. George Island, I decided to go with it in order to visit the inhabitants of those places. I sought the consent of Kirill Timofeevich Khlebnikov. I also asked whether it would not be possible for the ship to make a trip to St. Paul Island as well. To my delight, my request was granted, and so I began to prepare for the trip.

June 19. Wednesday. In school I gave the students an examination on the Divine Law, sacred history, grammar, and reading in both alphabets. They answered satisfactorily, in the presence of Kirill Timofeevich Khlebnikov, the captain of the brig *Golovnin*, and other officials.

June 20. Thursday. In church, before a gathering of the ship's officers and crew, I celebrated a prayer service for those desiring to travel by water. At 1:30, having boarded the ship, we weighed anchor and left. However, we had not gone far when we stopped for the night because of a calm. We set out on the following day.

[Signed:] Priest of the Ascension Church of Unalaska,
Ivan Veniaminov. August 3, 1829.

NOTES

1. A new chapel has been built by the locals to replace the decrepit old one. In this they had the financial assistance of the Russian-American Company. It was built from driftwood by the Creole Stefan Kriukov, using my plan and facade, with a log frame, a [one word illegible] and a little sanctuary. It is a good, solid building. The foundation was laid on September 13, 1826, and it was finished by December of 1827 (except for the church porch, which is still missing).

2. Information about them has already been given to the Right Reverend Mikhail, Bishop of Irkutsk.

3. The inhabitants were off hunting birds used in their clothing and in the preparation of their food.

4. One wave poured over the baidarka and struck against the skin of the baidarka quite forcefully. Glory be to God!—nothing bad happened, other than that the cargo became a little wet.

5. One of these people died the following day, after suffering from asthma for a long time.

6. This is the same isthmus over which General [sic] Rezanov passed, and which I myself had traversed during my return from Unga in 1827.

7. As usual, for the first three days I suffered from seasickness. I am now quite certain that I shall never grow accustomed to sea voyages, for the motion of a choppy sea nauseates me even when I am in a baidarka.

8. [Orthodoxy sometimes refers to Communion as a sacrifice at which Christ is both priest and victim—Trans.]

9. As I crossed one steep cliff my life was endangered because of my lack of familiarity with such a situation, but I crossed safely.

10. On the morning of the 26th those who had accompanied me departed, and since the baidarkas were still not available, I instructed that they be gotten quickly without fail, either by sea or by land.

11. The last five inhabitants of Nosovskoi have moved to a nearby village. It appears that a village will never exist here again, since the inhabitants have all moved. This move began with the arrival of the Russians.

12. I may note that as recompense for our long, boring stay on Unimak, we traveled quite far on this date, and our trip was quite a happy one. The reasons for its success were a rather strong favorable ocean current and the wind, which started out as a quiet tailwind and changed to a moderate partial tailwind.

JOURNAL NO. 7
June 21, 1829, to July 1, 1830, Unalaska.[1]

June

June 21. Friday. At ten o'clock in the morning we weighed anchor. After coming out of [Unalaska] Bay, we set a northeasterly course.

June 25. Tuesday. I celebrated at sea the customary prayer service for the birthday of His Majesty the Emperor.

June 28. Friday. At twelve o'clock we arrived at the mouth of the Nushagak River. We stood at anchor waiting for a high tide at sea. We weighed anchor at three o'clock, and, with a favorable current and a partial tailwind, we safely and uneventfully entered the mouth of the river.[2] This mouth is broad and long, and contains sand bars that make it fairly dangerous. At eight o'clock in the evening we dropped anchor at a distance of more than twenty versts from the fortress.

June 29. Saturday. At six o'clock in the morning, during a rising tide, I took all my necessities and set out for the fort of Novo-Aleksandrovsk [Nushagak]. I arrived there safely at 9:30. In the evening I celebrated Vespers and the Vigil Service in the barracks.

June 30. Sunday. I chrismated seven Russian children and one young Aglegmiut girl. These had been baptized by the Russians. I celebrated the Liturgy in the tent and gave Communion to those who had been chrismated. After the Liturgy, I celebrated a prayer service to the Apostles Peter and Paul. At my invitation, five nomadic men attended the Liturgy in the tent. They had come here by chance. They watched the Mystical Service very attentively.

After everything had been finished, I told them through an interpreter that in the sacrament we are making a bloodless sacrifice to the true God, the creator of heaven, earth, and man. We make this sacrifice in the spirit of humility and gratitude. They listened attentively.

Comment: Nine more nomadic people arrived in the evening.[3]

July

July 2. Tuesday. Since there was no hope of any more nomadic people coming here, I invited those here to come see me and then convinced them to listen to me for a while; they willingly agreed. After evoking the aid of Him, without Whom we are capable of nothing, I spoke to them through an interpreter. I told them that there is no God other than He Whom we and many others worship. I told them about the nature of God and His creation. I explained what serves Him and what does not. Finally, I told them that man was not created for the transient life here, but for eternal life, and [I explained] what one must do to obtain the blessed eternity. After teaching them in this fashion, I then asked them what they were thinking.[4] They answered that they were believers. One of them unexpectedly asked me the following question: "How is it that I think and do that which I do not wish to think and do?" I answered that every man is this way, and so on, and that, therefore, the more one conquers himself, the greater the reward he will receive in eternity. [I said that] this is the essential duty of Christianity, and the help of God is needed to achieve it. The help of God is received through prayer, and so on.

Finally, I asked each in turn whether he would like to enter into the ranks of the believers in the true God. They all willingly agreed, with one exception.[5] One of them said to me that he would willingly do so, but that he was a shaman. I, however, told him that he could be included among the believers if he would abandon his shamanism; he consented. After this I told them the requirements for becoming a believer. Lastly, I told them that they would receive no gifts from me. They replied that they did not require any. Although nothing forbade the carrying out of the sacrament [of baptism], I instructed them to think it over more carefully and give their viewpoints the next day. The one who had not expressed a desire to become a Christian I let depart in peace.

July 3. Since the nomads who had heard me had not changed their intentions, I pitched the tent at the river and baptized them in the river. I required each of them in turn to renounce the devil, and after that I taught them how to pray, and so on.[6]

Here was the first fruit of the seeds of God's word, sown by my unworthy hand in this wild, but fertile, land!

July 6. Saturday. After conducting the Vigil Service, I instructed the Russians and the Creoles together with those newly enlightened, and heard Confession from five Russians, ten Creoles, and their wives.

July 7. Sunday. After a reading of the Rule of Prayer, I taught the nomadic women who are here in the service of the company; they had been baptized by the Russians. I chrismated them, and at the same time baptized five infants—nomadic children who had been born to pagan mothers. After this, I celebrated the Liturgy in the tent and gave Communion to all those who had confessed, except for two Russians (because of their own unwillingness). I also gave Communion to the newly enlightened who were still present.[7] In all, forty people received the sacrament. I gave a funeral service for Christians who had been buried here.

July 10. Wednesday. At four o'clock in the morning we weighed anchor and sailed safely out of the mouth of the Nushagak River. A calm caused us to drop anchor at eleven o'clock at the place where we had already been earlier on the trip. There I celebrated a prayer service of thanksgiving to the Lord God who had kindly allowed us safely to enter and leave a most dangerous harbor and to fulfill our desires with blessings.

At five o'clock in the evening we weighed anchor and sailed toward the Pribilof Islands.

July 14. Sunday. I celebrated the Hours at sea. Then we caught sight of St. George Island through the fog. At the same time, the wind changed.

Our voyage from Nushagak to St. George had been most fortunate; we covered more than 200 versts per day, and had excellent weather.

July 16. Tuesday. At eight o'clock in the morning we approached the island of St. Paul, and dropped anchor. I immediately went ashore, where I was met with the most animated joy by each and every inhabitant.

July 17. Wednesday. At nine o'clock, after gathering everyone in the chapel, I taught them sufficiently through an interpreter, speaking on the dogmas and the essence of Christianity. In the afternoon I chrismated nineteen infants and heard Confession from forty-five people, both men and women. For the youngsters, instruction replaced Confession. At its appointed time, I celebrated the Vigil Service.

Comment: Our ship went to St. George Island.

July 18. After a reading of the Rule of Prayer, I celebrated the Liturgy in the chapel. I gave Communion to as many as fifty young people and to all who had confessed, except for two women (by necessity).

In the afternoon, I heard Confession from fifty-two people—male and female—and I celebrated the Vigil Service.

July 19. Friday. After a reading of the Rule of Prayer, I celebrated the Liturgy in the chapel and gave Communion to four youngsters and to all those who had confessed, except for three women (by necessity).

July 21. Sunday. After hearing Confession from three people, I celebrated the Liturgy and gave Communion to all those who had confessed. At its appointed time, I celebrated the Vigil Service.

July 22. Monday. I heard Confession from two people who had been away temporarily. I then celebrated the Hours and a prayer service for the health of His Majesty the Emperor. After that, I celebrated a prayer service to Peter and Paul. During the Hours service, I gave Communion from the reserved sacrament to those who had confessed. I also sacramentally blessed three marriages.

Then I set out for the ship. We weighed anchor within the hour and went to St. George Island. We sailed against a headwind, which grew much stronger toward evening. As a result, it took three days to reach St. George; this trip can be done in less than seven hours.

Comment: In the morning our ship returned.

July 25. Thursday. At nine o'clock in the morning we dropped anchor at the island of St. George, and I immediately went ashore. In the afternoon I assembled everyone into the barracks and then taught them sufficiently about the dogmas and essence of Christianity. Then I chrismated seven infants and sacramentally blessed three marriages. Both before and after the Vigil Service, I heard Confession from a total of forty-six people of both genders.

July 26. Friday. After a reading of the Rule of Prayer, I celebrated the Liturgy in the tent and gave Communion to all those who had confessed and to the youngsters. I was ready to leave at eight o'clock. Our ship, however, had moved away from shore because of a driving wind, and stayed out of sight all day long.[8]

July 27. Saturday. In the morning our ship approached the island. We boarded at nine o'clock and immediately set out for Unalaska with a quiet tailwind.

July 28. Sunday. I celebrated the Hours at sea.

July 29. Monday. In the morning, at daybreak, we caught sight of the coast of Unalaska fifty versts in the distance. At 12:00 we dropped anchor in Unalaska Harbor. Thus ended my trip to the north.

August

August 1. Thursday. I celebrated Matins with the Veneration of the Cross, and celebrated the Liturgy with a Blessing of the Water at the river. After this there was a procession with the cross around the village.

August 4. Sunday. I celebrated the Liturgy.

August 6. Feast of the Transfiguration. I celebrated the Liturgy and a prayer service. Before the prayer service I baptized one infant[9] and chrismated two.

August 9. Friday. I finished all my dispatches and sent them off through the local office.

August 10. [Saturday.] *Comment*: Our ship left for Sitka.

August 11. I celebrated the Liturgy.

August 12. I gave Final Communion to an ill woman.

August 15. Feast of the Dormition. I celebrated the Liturgy.

August 16. Friday. I celebrated the Hours and sacramentally blessed three marriages.

August 17. Saturday. I gave Final Communion to an ill person and celebrated the Vigil Service. On this day I had planned to go to Akun, and I even set out. After passing beyond Amakhnak, however, I met some people coming from Akun and found out from them that Pan'kov is now busy with a great deal of work. In consequence, I returned to Unalaska. My intention had been to translate the Gospel of Matthew into Aleut with Pan'kov's help.

August 18. Sunday. I celebrated the Liturgy and sacramentally blessed two marriages.

August 22. Thursday. I celebrated the Liturgy and a prayer service with an all-day ringing of the bells.
  Comment: With a cannon salute.

August 25. Thursday. I celebrated the Vigil Service and the Hours and sacramentally blessed one marriage.

August 27. Tuesday. I performed a memorial service for the woman, now deceased, to whom I had given Final Communion on the 12th.

August 29. Thursday. I celebrated the Liturgy after a funeral service.

August 30. [Friday.] I celebrated the Liturgy and a prayer service.

September

September 1. Sunday. I celebrated the Liturgy and celebrated a funeral service for the person to whom I had given Final Communion on August 17th, now deceased. I gave Final Communion to an ill person.

September 2. Monday. I celebrated the Liturgy of Thanksgiving on this, my name day.

September 5. Thursday. I celebrated the Hours and a prayer service.

I celebrated a funeral service for the person to whom I had given Final Communion on the 1st, now deceased.

September 7. Saturday. I set off at seven o'clock in the morning for Akun; I was one among seven people in baidarkas. We successfully steered through Akutan Pass and could have reached Akun, but a southerly wind began to blow and everything portended a storm.[10] We put in, therefore, at the village of Golovskoe, on the northern side of Akutan. There we set up the tent and celebrated the Vigil Service.

Comment: That night the wind grew extremely strong, and there was a heavy rain, so that, despite all our efforts, we could not keep the tent standing. At midnight, in terrible darkness, we were forced to move into a deserted iurt.

September 8. Sunday. After hearing Confession from the inhabitants of this village,[11] I celebrated the Hours and gave Communion from the reserved sacrament to those who had confessed.

At five o'clock the wind began to lessen and change direction. Therefore, since we did not want to lose time and were apprehensive about the very poor landing here, we set out and landed again very late at night at an uninhabited spot, having gone about twenty versts.

September 9. Monday. We departed at noon. We safely crossed Akun Pass and arrived at Akun.

September 10. Tuesday. After evoking the help of God the Word, we began to translate the Gospel of Matthew and finished the first two chapters on this date.

In the evening I chrismated an infant.

September 14. Saturday. I celebrated Matins and the Hours.

September 15. Sunday. I celebrated Matins and the Hours.

September 16. Monday. I set out with Pan'kov to visit an ailing Aleut who lived about 15 versts distant, going at the latter's request. At first we traveled by baidarka, and then on foot, and thus we came to the village of Recheshnoe on the northern side of Akun. I gave Final Communion to him and turned back immediately. After returning at four o'clock, we got down to our task.

September 22. Sunday. I celebrated the Hours.

September 24. Tuesday. At nine o'clock in the morning,[12] with the help of God and the prayers of the Holy Apostle and Evangelist Matthew, we finished our translation of the entire Gospel of St. Matthew, except for two lines, namely Chapter 7, Verse 17 [VII:17] and Chapter 9, Verse 17 [IX: 17]. The first was not done because the local language has no words for a single thing mentioned therein; the second, because of its content, which is incomprehensible to many people. Instead, however, we supplemented the account of the Passion of Christ with passages from the other Gospels.

We translated in the following fashion: we would work on the translation from morning until evening, and then in the evening we would read that which we had translated that day to an assembly of the most learned Aleuts and many others who wished to be there.[13] Then we made corrections.

September 25. Wednesday. Since there were neither baidaras nor baidarkas from the Harbor, and since I did not want my presence to divert the local inhabitants from the approaching fox hunting season, I decided to leave in local baidarkas.

I set out at 6:30 and crossed Akun Pass safely. However, after getting as far as the northeastern promontory of Akutan Island, we encountered a westerly headwind, and in two attempts we could not sail around the promontory. As a result, we turned around and arrived back at Akun at two o'clock.

September 26. Thursday. The weather was the same. At 12:00 the baidarkas arrived from the Harbor.

September 27. Friday. At five o'clock in the morning, during a calm, we set out along the southern side of Akutan Island. In the middle of crossing Akutan Strait, we encountered a strong crosswind, which caused a riptide to form along the small islands in this strait.[14] Since there was no possibility of our turning around, we had to cross this hazard. We faced danger in crossing it; twice my baidarka—the heaviest of the group—was covered by a wave. But— Glory be to the All-Good!—we passed through it safely and put in at one of those small islands to wait for the riptide to pass.

We continued on in the afternoon. As we were approaching a village located on the island of Unalga, my baidarka suddenly encountered an underwater disturbance [?*podvodnik*], which very nearly covered me with a breaker wave. Just the foam from this wave rolled over us, and that alone covered us up halfway. While we might not have perished if the breaker itself had hit us, there is no question that the baidarka would have overturned. After arriving at the village we discovered that our baidarka had been torn along the keel; as a result, it was almost half-filled with water. We no doubt tore it when either landing at or pulling out from the little island. Fortunately, the distance had not been great, or else everything would have gotten wet, not to mention that something worse could have happened during such a high wind and unfavorable current. And so, I faced three clear dangers on this day, but passed through safely—Glory be to God!

September 28. Saturday. I celebrated Vespers in the evening.

September 29. Sunday. After reading Matins and the Hours, we set out across Unalga Pass with a slight tailwind. After crossing the strait, we sailed for a time with the current, toward the northeastern promontory of Unalaska. Having reached this point, however, we recognized the impossibility of going around it because of a riptide and a strong *zvodnia* [?]. We turned, therefore, and went to Sechkinskoe settlement, in Bobrovskii [Beaver] Inlet on Unalaska. There I heard Confession from an ailing woman, but did not give her Communion (for good reason). Then, I set out toward the neck of land, and leaving the baidarka, proceeded on foot. We arrived in the Harbor at five o'clock.

September 30. Monday. I chrismated an infant.

October

October 3. Thursday. I gave Final Communion to an ill person.

October 6. Sunday. I celebrated Matins and the Liturgy, at which was read the appointed sermon. After the Liturgy, I celebrated a prayer service of thanksgiving to the Lord God, who had kindly allowed me to fulfill with blessings my own desires and those of many others by finishing the translation of the Holy Gospel.

October 13. Sunday. I celebrated Matins and the Liturgy.

October 20. Sunday. I celebrated Matins and the Liturgy. Before the Liturgy, I baptized three infants.

October 22. Tuesday. I celebrated a prayer service to the Virgin Mary, with a ringing of the bells.

October 27. Sunday. I celebrated Matins and the Liturgy.

This month I was busy with copying over the Gospel.

November

November 3. Sunday. I celebrated Matins and the Liturgy.

November 8. Friday. I celebrated the Vigil Service and a prayer service with a proclamation of the "Many Years" for the imperial family and for the Right Reverend Mikhail, Bishop of Irkutsk.

November 10. Sunday. I celebrated Matins and the Liturgy.

November 17. Sunday. I celebrated Matins and the Liturgy.

November 19. Tuesday. I celebrated the Vigil Service and a memorial service for the Tsar.

November 20. Wednesday. I celebrated the Liturgy and the appropriate prayer service, with a cannon salute.

November 21. Thursday. I celebrated the Vigil Service and the Liturgy.

November 24. Sunday. I celebrated the Vigil Service, the Liturgy, and a prayer service.

November 25. Monday. I celebrated the Vigil Service. In the evening, I celebrated a prayer service to St. Innocent.

November 26. Tuesday. I celebrated the Liturgy and a prayer service to St. Innocent.

This month I again copied over the Gospel.

December

December 1. Sunday. I celebrated Vespers, Matins, and the Hours.

December 2. Monday. I gave Final Communion to an ill person.

On this day I finished copying over the Gospel, and handed a copy of it over to the Aleut interpreter Daniil Kuziakin, so that he could read it.[15]

December 6. Friday. I celebrated the Vigil Service, the Liturgy, and a prayer service.

December 8. Sunday. I celebrated Vespers and Matins. I celebrated the Hours [and not the Liturgy] because of the freezing weather.

December 15. Sunday. I celebrated Vespers and Matins. I celebrated the Hours [and not the Liturgy] because of the freezing weather.

December 22. Sunday. I celebrated Vespers and Matins. I celebrated the Hours [and not the Liturgy] because of the freezing weather.

December 24. Tuesday. I celebrated Matins, the Hours, and Vespers with the Liturgy.

December 25. Christmas. I celebrated Matins, the Liturgy, and a prayer service.

Comment: With a cannon salute.

During the Liturgy I gave a sermon that I had written for this day based on the following scriptural text: "And hearing this, King Herod was troubled, and all Jerusalem with him." I spoke about what it was that produced Herod's confusion, and even more so that of Jerusalem, which had expected the arrival of the Messiah; I asked whether there is not something in us resembling such blasphemous confusion.

December 26. Thursday. I celebrated the Liturgy, at which I led a discussion of the Adoration of the Magi, as I had done in the two previous years.

December 27. Friday. I celebrated the Hours [and not the Liturgy] because of the freezing weather.

December 29. Sunday. I celebrated the Hours [and not the Liturgy] because of the freezing weather.

1830
January

January 1. Wednesday. I celebrated Matins with a midnight service, and the Liturgy with a prayer service.

January 3. Friday. I celebrated the Hours for Epiphany.

January 5. Sunday. I celebrated Vespers, Matins, the Hours, and the Vigil Service with a Blessing of the Water.

January 6. Epiphany. I celebrated Matins and the Liturgy of St. Basil the Great. Afterwards, I blessed the water at the river.

January 7. Tuesday. I celebrated Matins and the Liturgy with a prayer service.

January 8. Wednesday. I sacramentally blessed two marriages.

January 12. Sunday. I celebrated Vespers, Matins, and the Hours.

January 15. Wednesday. I sacramentally blessed one marriage.

January 19. Sunday. I celebrated Vespers, Matins, and the Hours.

January 26. Sunday. I celebrated Vespers, Matins, and the Liturgy.

January 30. Thursday. I celebrated the Hours.

This month I wrote church records and made new church books.

February

February 2. Sunday. I celebrated the Vigil Service and the Liturgy.

February 3. Monday. I celebrated Matins, the Hours, and a prayer service.

February 8. Saturday. In the evening I celebrated a Vigil Service dedicated to St. Innocent.

February 9. Sunday. I celebrated the Liturgy and a prayer service to St. Innocent.

February 16. Sunday. I celebrated Vespers, Matins, and the Liturgy. Before the Liturgy, I baptized two infants. After Vespers, I explained the practice of asking for forgiveness and the value of the fast. I then exhorted the Aleuts to undergo a yearly self-purification through Confession, for there is nothing that should cause a person to decline to make Confession.

February 17. Monday. Lent. Services began with Matins.

February 18. Tuesday. I performed a funeral service for someone who had died.

February 19. Wednesday. I celebrated the Liturgy of the Presanctified.

February 21. Friday. I celebrated the Liturgy of the Presanctified. After Matins I taught those preparing for the sacraments about what is needed for justification before God. I also taught them about Christian duty.

In the afternoon and after Vespers I heard Confession from 120 people, male and female, of various positions and ages.

February 22. Saturday. I celebrated the Liturgy and gave Communion to all those who had confessed. The appointed sermon was read during the Liturgy.

February 23. Sunday. I celebrated the Liturgy and Vespers at its appointed time. The appointed sermon was read during the Liturgy.

I read one book: *The Voice of the Trumpet Calling Us to Judgement [Glas trubnyi zovushchii na sud]*.

March

March 1. Saturday. I celebrated Matins with a memorial service and the Liturgy.

March 2. Sunday. I celebrated Matins and the Liturgy, at which an appointed sermon was read. Before the Liturgy, I heard Confession from, and gave Communion to, an ailing woman.

March 3. *Comment*: The home for unmarried girl orphans was opened.

March 8. *Comment*: Work was begun on the new iconostasis.

March 9. Sunday. I celebrated the Liturgy. This day marked the beginning of services.

March 12. Wednesday. I celebrated the Liturgy of the Presanctified.

March 14. Friday. I celebrated the Liturgy of the Presanctified.

After Matins, I instructed those preparing for the sacraments, speaking on the essence and duties of being a Christian. In the afternoon, and after Vespers, I heard Confession from 105 people of both genders and various positions and ages.

March 15. Saturday. I celebrated Matins with a memorial service, and the Liturgy. I gave Communion to all who had confessed.

March 16. Sunday. I celebrated the Liturgy and Vespers at the appointed times.

March 19. Wednesday. In the evening I celebrated Matins with the Great Canon.

March 20. Thursday. I celebrated the Liturgy of the Presanctified and celebrated a funeral service for a deceased infant.

March 21. Friday. I celebrated Matins and the Hours.

March 22. Saturday. I celebrated Matins with the Akathistos, and the Liturgy. I performed a funeral service for a deceased infant.

March 23. Sunday. I celebrated Matins and the Liturgy.

March 24. Monday. I celebrated the Liturgy of the Presanctified.

After Matins I instructed the observants on the sacrament of Repentance and on the duties of a Christian. In the afternoon, I heard Confession from fifty-one people, both men and women.

March 25. Feast of the Annunciation. I celebrated Matins, the Hours, and the Liturgy, and gave Communion to all those who had confessed, except for one Russian who was unwilling. The services concluded in the evening.

Comment: On this day ice floes were carried down from the north.

March 28. Friday. Services began in the evening.

March 29. Saturday. I celebrated the Liturgy.

Comment: The ice was carried away and the ocean cleared.

March 30. Palm Sunday. I celebrated the Vigil Service and the Liturgy.

March 31. Monday. I celebrated the Liturgy of the Presanctified.

Beyond all this, I was busy with the construction of the iconostasis, which was being built according to my plan. I went to the school and taught the

Divine Law only once during these three months because of the severe freezing weather.

April

April 1. Tuesday. I celebrated the Liturgy of the Presanctified.

April 2. Wednesday. I celebrated the Liturgy of the Presanctified.

After Vespers, I instructed the observants and heard Confession from twenty-one people.

April 3. Thursday. I celebrated the Liturgy and gave Communion to all those who had confessed.

April 4. Friday. I celebrated Matins, the Hours, and Vespers with the Burial Service. In the evening I taught, and heard Confession from fourteen people, both men and women.

April 5. Saturday. I celebrated Matins and the Hours. At two o'clock I celebrated the Liturgy and gave Communion to all those who had confessed. In the evening, I taught, and heard Confession from twelve people.

April 6. Easter. I celebrated Matins at twelve o'clock. I celebrated the Liturgy at six o'clock. I celebrated Vespers at eight o'clock.

April 7. Monday. I celebrated Matins, the Liturgy, and Vespers.

April 8. Tuesday. I celebrated Matins and the Liturgy, and sacramentally blessed one marriage between Aleuts who are leaving.

April 9. Wednesday. I celebrated Matins, the Liturgy, and Vespers.

April 10. I celebrated Matins, the Liturgy, and Vespers.

April 11. Friday. I celebrated Matins, the Liturgy and Vespers.

Before the Liturgy I baptized an infant. After the Liturgy, I celebrated a prayer service for those traveling by sea, and began my preparations for a journey to the western region.

April 12. Saturday. Aftr celebrating Matins and the Hours, and hearing Confession from an ailing woman, I set out at seven o'clock.

We had two three-man baidarkas and two one-seaters. The wind was calm and southerly. At 8:30 in the evening we arrived at Makushin village, after traveling around 100 versts in safety and without mishap.

April 13. Sunday. I celebrated the Hours.

In the afternoon, after the inhabitants had assembled at my invitation, I duly instructed them on the sacrament of Repentance and the duties of being a Christian. I spoke through an interpreter.[16] I celebrated the Vigil Service and heard Confession from twenty-two people of both genders.

April 14. Monday. After a reading of the Rule of Prayer, I chrismated two infants, celebrated the Liturgy in a tent pitched at a site used on a previous visit, and gave Communion to all who had confessed, except for one woman (by necessity).

April 14 and 15. *Comment*: A strong headwind detained us.

April 16. Wednesday. We set out at seven o'clock in the morning, with a slight partial tailwind. At two o'clock we arrived at the village of Koshiga.

Once the inhabitants had assembled, I gave them due instruction, chrismated one infant, celebrated Vespers, and heard Confession from thirty-eight people, both men and women.

April 17. Thursday. The tent was pitched on a site used previously. After a reading of the Rule of Prayer, I celebrated the Liturgy and gave Communion to the youngsters and to all those who had confessed, except for one woman (by necessity).

We set out at nine o'clock. The weather was calm and clear, and at one o'clock we arrived at the village of Chernovskoe. After the inhabitants had assembled, I duly instructed them, celebrated the Vigil Service, and then heard Confession from twenty-three people, both men and women.

April 18. Friday. After a reading of the Rule of Prayer, I celebrated the Liturgy in the tent, but not on the site used previously, because of a fierce wind. I gave Communion to all those who had confessed and to the young people.

April 18, 19, and 20. *Comment*: A high wind prevented our departure.

April 19. Saturday. I celebrated the Vigil Service.

April 20. Sunday. I celebrated the Hours, adding a prayer service for those traveling by sea.

April 21. Monday. After conducting a prayer service for the health of His Majesty the Emperor and his family, we set out at twelve o'clock into a mild headwind. We safely made our way across Umnak Pass and arrived at the village of Tulik on Umnak at 3:30.

After the inhabitants had assembled, I gave them due instruction, celebrated the Vigil Service, and heard Confession from fifteen people of both genders.

April 22. Tuesday. After a reading of the Rule of Prayer, I celebrated the Liturgy in a tent pitched on a site used during a previous visit. I gave Communion to all the young people an to those who had confessed. After the Liturgy, I sacramentally blessed one marriage.

April 22, 23, and 24. *Comment*: A high wind detained us.

April 25. Friday. We set out shortly after four o'clock, with a slight partial tailwind. After we emerged from Umnak Pass this wind increased, and we were forced to put in at Cape Kotel'novskii [Kettle Cape]. At ten o'clock the wind began to lessen noticeably; we set out and arrived with some difficulty at Egorkovskoi village at two o'clock in the afternoon.

After the inhabitants had assembled, I duly instructed the group. Then I chrismated one infant, celebrated Vespers, and heard Confession from ten people, both men and women.

April 26. Saturday. After a reading of the Rule of Prayer, I celebrated the Liturgy and gave Communion to all those who had confessed, and to all the youngsters. The Liturgy took place in the tent, which was pitched on a site used previously.

After the Liturgy, I sacramentally blessed three marriages.

We left at 6:30, and arrived at two o'clock in the afternoon at a neck of land. Leaving the baidarkas, we continued on foot, and arrived at the village of Recheshnoe [Nikolski] at 4:30.

I celebrated the Vigil Service in the chapel.

April 27. Sunday. After conducting the Hours, I duly instructed the inhabitants of the village there, together with those from many other villages—these last had assembled for the occasion.

After Vespers I chrismated three infants, celebrated the Vigil Service, and heard Confession from twelve youngsters whom I had instructed.

April 28. Monday. After a reading of the Rule of Prayer, I celebrated the Liturgy in the chapel, and gave Communion to thirty-two young people and to all who had confessed.

I celebrated the Vigil Service at its appointed time. I heard Confession both before and after this service, from forty-six people, both men and women.

April 29. Tuesday. In the chapel, I celebrated the Liturgy and gave Communion to all those who had confessed except for two women (by necessity). After the Liturgy, I celebrated a prayer service to St. Nicholas and sacramentally blessed four marriages.

After Vespers, I read the last three chapters of the Gospel of Matthew, in my translation. All listened attentively and expressed their agreement [with the translation], their gratitude, and their fervent desire to own such a booklet.

April 30. Wednesday. I celebrated Matins and the Hours, adding a prayer service for those traveling by sea.

All of the inhabitants of these six villages have been heard in Confession and have received Holy Communion.

May

May 1. Thursday. The wind became favorable enough for us to set out on our return course, so we crossed back over the neck of land. When we arrived [at the baidarkas], however, we saw that departure was impossible because of terrible turbulence. I returned to the village.

May 2. Friday. Since the wind would permit us to set out along the northern side of Umnak, we left in the baidarkas, which had been carried over on this day.[17] We left at ten o'clock, with a slight tailwind. This wind grew stronger toward evening, so that we put in at the first convenient landing spot. We had covered more than fifty versts.

May 3. Saturday. I celebrated the Vigil Service. A strong wind prevented us from continuing on our route.

May 4. Sunday. I celebrated the Hours. A strong wind prevented us from continuing on our route.

May 5. Monday. Starting at noon the wind began to grow calm, and we continued on. After going around thirty versts we stopped because of very rough seas.

May 6. Tuesday. We left at four o'clock in the morning, having calm and clear weather. We arrived at the village of Tulik at five o'clock in the evening.

May 7. Wednesday. After waiting for a favorable current, we set out across Umnak Strait at twelve o'clock, into a headwind. At seven o'clock, we arrived at the village of Koshiga.

May 8. Thursday. We set out at seven o'clock in calm and clear weather. At the halfway point on our route, however, a partial headwind began to blow. After we had turned into Makushin Bay, the wind grew much stronger. We crossed this bay with great difficulty and reached the village of Makushin at 4:30.

In the evening, I celebrated a Vigil Service in honor of St. Nicholas.

May 9. Friday. I celebrated the Hours and a prayer service to St. Nicholas.

May 10. Saturday. Since the wind changed to permit us to set out across the neck of land, I left my baidarkas in this village and sailed into Makushin Bay at four o'clock in the morning. At eight o'clock I arrived at the neck of land, and from there I went on foot to the Harbor, being accompanied by two people. After eight hours of extremely uncomfortable travel, we arrived in Captain's Harbor [Unalaska Bay]. From there we went by baidarka, and we arrived in Harbor Village [Unalaska] at six o'clock. And so, I ended my journey safely and in good health. In the evening, I celebrated the Vigil Service.

May 11. I celebrated the Liturgy.

Comment: My baidarkas arrived in the evening.

May 14. Wednesday. I celebrated Matins, the Liturgy, Vespers, and the Vigil Service at its appointed time. Before the Liturgy, I baptized two infants.

May 15. Ascension Day. Upon completion of a Blessing of the Water, I celebrated the Liturgy and Vespers at its appointed time.

May 18. Sunday. After baptizing an infant, I celebrated the Liturgy and a prayer service to the Lord God, who had found me worthy of the priestly rank on this very day nine years ago, through ordination by the Right Reverend Mikhail, Bishop of Irkutsk.

May 24. Saturday. I celebrated Matins with a memorial service, and then celebrated the Liturgy and —at its appointed time—Vespers and the Vigil Service.

May 25. Pentecost. I celebrated the Liturgy with Vespers.

May 26. Monday. I celebrated Matins and the Liturgy.

Beyond all this, I was occupied with writing and reading commentary on the Book of Genesis.

June

June 1. Sunday. Having celebrated the Vigil Service in the evening, I celebrated the Hours.[18]

June 8. Sunday. Having celebrated the Vigil Service in the evening, I celebrated the Hours at its appointed time.

June 15. Sunday. Having celebrated the Vigil Service in the evening, I celebrated the Hours at its appointed time.

June 22. Having first instructed her duly, I chrismated a Kolosh woman, and then celebrated the Liturgy and gave her Communion.

June 24. Tuesday. I celebrated the Vigil Service and the Hours.

After that I celebrated a prayer service to the Holy Mother of God of Vladimir.

June 25. Wednesday. I celebrated the Liturgy and a prayer service for the health of His Majesty the Emperor.

Comment: With a cannon salute.

June 29. Sunday. I celebrated the Liturgy and a prayer service, the latter instead of one on the 27th.

On Wednesdays and Fridays I taught in the school, reviewing the Law of God and instilling the rules of decent conduct. In my remaining time I read commentary on the Book of Genesis.

[Signed:] Priest Ivan Veniaminov
of the Ascension Church of Unalaska.

NOTES

1. [A later note is scrawled over the title page.]

2. Almost no ships ever enter or leave this mouth, not only because they fear running up on sand bars, but also because of its shallowness and the rapid current of the tides, which have heights of up to 3 sazhens [1 sazhen=7 feet].

3. There is no village of these nomadic people near the fortress, and they come here for short times, and never in large numbers. In May and last August, a large number of them were seen, but even that was no more than 100 or 150 people. However, this [dispersion] is not because they have been forbidden to gather, or because they fear the Russians, but because of local circumstances.

4. I dared not, and could not, tell them more than this because my interpreter was not very reliable.

5. There were fourteen of them.

6. I should mention that, in fact, I did not give a single one of them anything, even a shirt, except for the crosses that I placed on them during chrismation.

7. By necessity, four of them had left on the 4th.

8. When it had done this, it had been greatly endangered, so that it had been necessary to cut loose the anchor and turn out to sea to a distance of no more than 200 sazhens from the shore.

9. My daughter, who had been born on June 27.

10. While sailing alongside Akutan we met a number of whales, and faced danger in passing among them; one whale caught sight of our baidarka when he was about to surface, grew frightened, as usual, and turned suddenly. This turning created a terrible wake.

11. There are only five inhabitants, and two of them can barely move.

12. It is not boasting for me to say that this translation was carried out through unremitting labor.

13. Having heard of our occupation, many came for this from other settlements. Everyone always listened with deep attention and with the greatest satisfaction.

14. One might call this a miniature riptide [*suloichik*], since one cannot hope to survive a true riptide, especially a strong one.

15. On every evening that he read it, many people would assemble at his home to listen. He read through the entire Gospel five times. He found a mistake in one

place only, and that was not so much an error as a matter of weak and unsuitable phrasing. He corrected it well.

16. The Creole Stefan Kriukov, who resides on Umnak and has now set out for that place.

17. The interpreter Stefan Kriukov remained there, since he manages that island and was almost unnecessary to me.

18. Due to a lack of supplies [for Communion].

JOURNAL NO. 8
July 1, 1830, to July 1, 1831

July

July 1. Tuesday. I celebrated the Liturgy and a prayer service.

July 6. Sunday. I celebrated the Vigil Service and the Hours.

July 8. Tuesday. I celebrated the Vigil Service and the Hours.

July 13. Sunday. I celebrated the Vigil Service and the Hours.

July 16. Wednesday. A Russian-American Company ship, the brig *Riurik*, arrived with dispatches on board.

July 20. Sunday. After performing a memorial service for the late dowager empress Maria Fedorovna, I celebrated the Liturgy and a prayer service for victory over the Turks.

July 27. Sunday. I celebrated the Liturgy after baptizing an infant. I also prepared responses to the papers that I had received.

August

August 1. Friday. I celebrated Matins with the Veneration of the Cross, and the Liturgy with a Blessing of the Water at the river. Afterwards, there was a procession around the village with the cross, accompanied by a ringing of the bells. Upon returning to the church, I celebrated a prayer service of thanksgiving.

August 3. Sunday. I celebrated the Liturgy.

August 6. Wednesday. I celebrated the Liturgy and a prayer service.

August 7. Thursday. The ship *Riurik* left for Sitka, carrying all of my dispatches.

August 8. Friday. At seven o'clock in the morning I left for Akun in a company of three baidarkas. We set out with a calm southerly wind. After safely crossing Unalga, Akutan, and Akun passes, we arrived at eight o'clock at the main village of Akun Island, Artel'novskoe.

August 9. Saturday. I celebrated Vespers and the Vigil Service.

August 10. Sunday. After hearing Confession from twenty-five people, both the very old and the very young, I celebrated the Liturgy and gave Communion to all those who had confessed and to as many as thirty young people. The Liturgy took place in a tent pitched at the site used on a previous visit.

August 11. Monday. At five o'clock in the morning we set out from Akun to continue on. After safely crossing Avatanak Strait and Derbin Strait, we arrived at the village of Tigalda, on the island of Tigalda. Since almost none of the inhabitants was home, we sent a baidarka out for them, and almost all gathered by evening.

In the evening, I celebrated Vespers and Matins in the common building, and gave sufficient instruction.

August 12. Tuesday. After a reading of the Rule of Prayer, I heard Confession from all. Then, in a tent pitched on a site used before, I celebrated the Liturgy and gave Communion to all those who had confessed and to the youngsters. I sacramentally blessed one marriage.

Since the wind was unfavorable for the start of our return journey, I was concerned not to waste time and began to translate the Catechism into Aleut. I worked together with the interpreter Ivan Pan'kov, toion of that locale. We finished six pages, and read them aloud in the evening, before all who could be found.

August 13. Wednesday. The wind was unfavorable in the morning, so I occupied myself with translation and finished three pages.

At eleven o'clock the wind had improved, and we set out on our return course, arriving at two o'clock at the village of Avatanak, on the island of Avatanak.

I duly instructed the assembled inhabitants. After chrismating four people, I celebrated Vespers and Matins, and heard Confession from all of the adults.

August 14. Thursday. After a reading of the Rule of Prayer, I celebrated the Liturgy and gave Communion to all those who had confessed and to the youngsters—a total of thirty-seven people. The Liturgy took place in a tent pitched on a site used previously. After the Liturgy, I visited a very aged woman and gave Final Communion to her.

We set off across Avatanak Strait at nine o'clock, and arrived at Artel'novskoe village on Akun at two o'clock. From 4:00 to 10:00, I celebrated Vespers and the Vigil Service with the Akathistos to the Virgin Mary, and heard Confession from thirty-five people.

August 15. Feast of the Dormition. After a reading of the Rule of Prayer, I chrismated three people, celebrated the Liturgy, and gave Communion to all those who had confessed, except for one woman (by necessity).

August 16. Saturday. I celebrated the Hours, Vespers, and the Vigil Service, and heard Confession from all remaining who had not attended Confession.

August 17. Sunday. After a reading of the Rule of Prayer, I chrismated one woman. Then, I celebrated the Liturgy and gave Communion to all those who had confessed.

And so all of the inhabitants of the islands of Akun, Tigalda, and Avatanak had been heard in Confession and given Holy Communion.

While in Akun, beginning on the 15th, I worked uninterruptedly on translating the Catechism, and finished the entire text on the 21st. From the 22nd to the 25th we checked our translations of the Catechism and the Book of Matthew by reading them before a group of strangers who would critique them. They found no errors in the Gospel other than problems of orthography.

August 22. Friday. After the Hours, I celebrated a prayer service to mark the anniversary of the coronation of His Majesty the Emperor.

August 24. Sunday. I celebrated the Hours. Then, at four o'clock we left to return to Unalaska, and at eight o'clock we arrived at the village of Golovskoe on the island of Akutan.

August 25. Monday. After giving sufficient instruction, I heard Confession from all of the local inhabitants—seven adults.

We continued on at seven o'clock, but the wind became very strong, so that we landed at a deserted spot where there had once been a village.

August 26. Tuesday. In the morning the weather was calm and clear, and we set out across Akutan and Unalga passes, and arrived safely at the Harbor at twelve o'clock.

August 27. Wednesday. I gave Final Communion to an ill person.

August 29. Friday. I celebrated a memorial service and the Liturgy.

August 30. Saturday. After baptizing three infants, I celebrated the Liturgy and a prayer service.

August 31. I celebrated the Liturgy.

September

September 2. Tuesday. This being my name day, I celebrated the Liturgy and a prayer service of thanksgiving to the Lord God for all of the blessings that he has showered upon me.

September 5. Friday. I celebrated a memorial service, the Hours, and a prayer service.

September 7. Sunday. I celebrated the Liturgy, before which I baptized three infants. After the Liturgy, I performed a funeral service for one who had died suddenly and gave Final Communion to two ill people.

September 9. Tuesday. I celebrated a funeral service and gave Final Communion to two ill people.

September 11. Thursday. I celebrated a funeral service for a deceased person, and then I gave Final Communion to an ill person.

September 14. I celebrated Matins with the Veneration of the Cross. Then, I celebrated the Liturgy.

September 21. Sunday. I celebrated the Liturgy after baptizing an infant.

September 25. Thursday. I gave Final Communion to an ill person.

September 26. Friday. I celebrated Matins and the Hours together.

September 28. I celebrated Matins and the Liturgy, and I performed a funeral service for a deceased person.

This month I copied over the Catechism and read periodicals.

October

October 5. Sunday. I celebrated the Liturgy after baptizing an infant.

October 9. Thursday. I celebrated a prayer service in the newly built school.

October 12. Sunday. I celebrated Matins and the Liturgy.

October 15. Wednesday. I went to the school for the first time, and began to teach the Catechism and the Aleut language.

October 17. Friday. At school I taught the opening of the Catechism.

October 19. Sunday. I celebrated Matins and the Liturgy.

October 22. Wednesday. I celebrated a prayer service to the Virgin Mary and taught in school the first section of the Symbol of Faith [Nicene Creed]. I gave particular stress to the word "Almighty." Nothing in the world is done without the will of God, and therefore one must be obedient and place hope in God the Creator and the Almighty. From the 24th until the 5th of November I was unable to leave my home because I was ill with an infection.

This month I finished writing out the Catechism and gave it to the interpreter Daniil Kuziakin to read.

November

November 2. Sunday. I celebrated the Hours.

November 8. Saturday. I celebrated the Vigil Service, the Liturgy, and a prayer service with a proclamation of "Many Years" for the imperial family and for the Right Reverend Mikhail, Bishop of Irkutsk, Nerchinsk, and Yakutsk.

November 9. Sunday. I celebrated Matins and the Hours.

November 12. Wednesday. In school I went over the opening lesson and then taught the second section of the Nicene Creed.

November 16. Sunday. I celebrated Matins and the Liturgy.

November 19. Wednesday. In school, I taught the Aleut alphabet.

November 20. Thursday. I celebrated the Vigil Service, the Liturgy, and a prayer service.

November 21. Friday. I celebrated the Vigil Service and the Liturgy and a prayer service.

November 23. Sunday. I celebrated Matins and the Hours [but not the Liturgy] because of the freezing weather.

November 25. Wednesday. In school, I taught the third section of the Nicene Creed, the moral lesson of which is that there is not a single man who can be without sin, even if he has lived for but one day, except for Jesus Christ, both Man and God.

November 28. Friday. I taught the fourth section of the Nicene Creed, the moral lesson of which is that there is no other path to the Heavenly Kingdom than that taken by Jesus, and therefore we must imitate him in all things...and so on.

November 30. Sunday. I celebrated Matins, the Liturgy, and a prayer service.

Besides visiting the school this month, I read the following books: (1) *On the Mystery of the Cross*; and (2) the first volume of *Christian Philosophy.*

December

December 3. Wednesday. In school, I taught the fifth section of the Nicene Creed.

December 6. Saturday. I celebrated the Vigil Service, the Liturgy, and a prayer service.

December 7. Sunday. I celebrated Matins and the Liturgy.

December 14. Sunday. I celebrated Matins and the Hours [but not the Liturgy] because of the freezing weather.

December 21. Sunday. I celebrated Matins and the Liturgy.

December 22. Monday. In school, I instructed the students on the subjects of Russian history, Russian grammar, arithmetic, and mathematical geography.

December 24. Wednesday. I celebrated Matins, the Hours, and Vespers with the Liturgy.

December 25. Christmas. I celebrated Matins, the Liturgy, and a prayer service. During the Liturgy I gave a sermon that I had written for this day, the same as that given the year before.

December 26. I celebrated Matins and the Liturgy.

December 27. Saturday. I celebrated Matins and the Hours [but not the Liturgy] because of the freezing weather.

December 28. Sunday. I celebrated Matins and the Hours [but not the Liturgy] because of the freezing weather.

This month I read *Christian Philosophy*, volumes 1 and 2.

1831
January

January 1. Thursday. I celebrated Matins and the Liturgy with a prayer service.

January 4. Sunday. I celebrated Matins and the Liturgy.

January 5. Monday. I celebrated Matins, the Hours, and Vespers, with the Liturgy and a Blessing of the Water.

January 6. Epiphany. I celebrated Matins, the Liturgy, and Vespers.

January 7. Wednesday. I celebrated Matins, the Liturgy, and a prayer service.

January 9. Friday. In school, I taught the first three lessons from the Catechism.

January 11. Sunday. I celebrated Matins and the Liturgy.

January 13. Tuesday. I gave Final Communion to an ill person.

January 14. Wednesday. In school, after going over everything that had been read previously, I taught the sixth and seventh sections of the Nicene Creed which express the idea that distance means nothing to God.

January 15. Thursday. I conducted a funeral service.

January 16. Friday. In school I taught the eighth and ninth statements of the Nicene Creed and provided some idea of other Christian faiths; I spoke mostly about the Roman Catholics, but also discussed our schismatics and Old Believers.

January 18. Sunday. I celebrated Matins and the Liturgy.

January 21. Wednesday. In school, I taught about the sacraments of Baptism, Chrismation, and Communion.

January 23. In school, I went over the previous lesson, and then I taught about the other sacraments.

January 25. Sunday. I celebrated Matins and the Liturgy.

January 28. Wednesday. I school, I taught the eleventh section of the Nicene Creed.

January 30. Friday. I celebrated the Hours and taught in school the final section of the Nicene Creed.

In addition, this month I read the third volume of *Christian Philosophy* and compiled church reports.

February

February 1. Sunday. I celebrated Matins, the Liturgy, and Vespers.

February 2. The Presentation of Our Lord in the Temple [Candlemas]. I celebrated the Vigil Service and the Liturgy.

February 3. Tuesday. I celebrated Matins, the Hours, and a prayer service.

February 4. Wednesday. In school, I went over all of the lessons on the Nicene Creed.

February 6. Friday. In school, I began to teach about the Lord's Prayer, and about prayer in general.

February 8. Sunday. I celebrated Matins, the Liturgy, and, in the evening, the Vigil Service.

February 9. Monday. I celebrated the Liturgy and a prayer service to St. Innocent.

February 11. Wednesday. In school, I taught the preface to the Lord's Prayer.

February 13. Friday. In school, I taught the first petition of the Lord's Prayer.

February 15. Sunday. I celebrated the Hours. Matins did not take place because of a terrible storm.

February 18. Wednesday. In school, I taught the second petition of the Lord's Prayer.

February 20. Friday. In school, I taught the third petition of the Lord's Prayer.

February 21. Saturday. I celebrated Matins, the Liturgy, and Vespers.

February 22. Sunday. I celebrated Matins and the Liturgy, and performed a funeral service for a Russian who had died suddenly.

In addition, this month I read the fourth volume of *Christian Philosophy* and oversaw the making of the iconostasis.

March

March 1. Sunday. I celebrated Matins, the Liturgy, and Vespers.

March 2. The First Monday in Lent. I celebrated Matins, the Hours, and Vespers.
Daily [Lenten] services began on this date.

March 4. Wednesday. I celebrated the Liturgy of the Presanctified.

March 6. Friday. After Matins I instructed those preparing for the sacraments about what is needed for purification from sin. After celebrating the Liturgy of the Presanctified, I heard Confession from sixty-five people, mostly women.

March 7. Saturday. I celebrated Matins and the Liturgy, and gave Communion to all those who had confessed. The appointed sermon was read.

March 8. Sunday. I celebrated Matins and the Liturgy, at which was read the appointed sermon. The services concluded with Vespers.

March 15. Sunday. I celebrated Matins and the Liturgy, at which the appointed sermon was read.

March 21. Sunday. Same as on the 15th, and services continued.

March 23. Tuesday. I celebrated the Liturgy of the Presanctified.

March 24. Wednesday. I celebrated the Liturgy of the Presanctified. After Matins, I taught them sufficiently, and in the afternoon I heard Confession from as many as forty-five people, both men and women.

March 25. Annunciation. I celebrated the Liturgy and gave Communion to all those who had confessed.

March 26. Friday. I celebrated the Liturgy of the Presanctified and heard Confession from the remaining twenty-six people in the afternoon.

March 27. Saturday. I celebrated the Liturgy and gave Communion to all those who had confessed.

March 28. Sunday. I celebrated the Liturgy, and the services concluded with Vespers.

This month I read the last volume of *Christian Philosophy* and oversaw the making of the iconostasis.

April

April 1. Wednesday. In the evening, I celebrated the Matins Service with the Great Canon.

April 2. Thursday. I celebrated the Hours, and then I celebrated the Liturgy of the Presanctified.

April 4. Saturday. I celebrated Matins with the Akathistos, and the Liturgy of the Presanctified.

April 5. Sunday. I celebrated Matins, the Liturgy and Vespers.

April 10. Friday. The services began with Vespers and continued until the next Sunday

April 11. Saturday. I celebrated the Liturgy.

April 12. Palm Sunday. I celebrated the Vigil Service and the Liturgy.

April 13. Monday. I celebrated the Hours with a reading of the Gospel, and then I celebrated the Liturgy of the Presanctified.

April 14. Tuesday. I celebrated the Hours with a reading of the Gospel, and then I celebrated the Liturgy of the Presanctified.

April 15. Wednesday. The same services. Also, after Matins I instructed those preparing for the sacraments, and in the afternoon I heard Confession from twenty-six people.

April 16. Thursday. I celebrated the Liturgy and gave Communion to all those who had confessed.

April 17. Friday. I celebrated Matins, the Hours, and Vespers, together with the Burial Service. Before the Veneration of the Shroud, I read a sermon that I had written for this day using the following scriptural text: "Thus it behooved Christ to suffer and to enter into His glory." I spoke about the fact that there is no other path to the Heavenly Kingdom besides that taken by Jesus Christ.

April 18. Saturday. After the Hours, I taught and heard Confession from those preparing for the sacraments—as many as thirty of them. During the Liturgy, I gave Communion to all of them. In the evening, I heard Confession from thirty-four people.

April 19. Easter. I celebrated Matins at twelve o'clock [midnight]. At six o'clock I celebrated the Liturgy, during which the Gospel was read in Slavonic, Russian, and Fox-Aleut. There was a cannon salute. The texts were read by the priest, the cantor, and the Creole Zakh. Chichinev.

Comment: There was a cannon salute.

April 20. Monday. I celebrated Matins and the Liturgy.

April 21. Tuesday. After the Liturgy and a prayer service for the health of His Majesty the Emperor and the imperial family, I celebrated a prayer service for those traveling by sea, with kneeling prayers.

I was ready to depart for Unga.

After Vespers I swore in an interpreter who had just been provided me.

April 22. Wednesday. I celebrated Matins and the Liturgy. During the Liturgy, I gave Communion to an ill person, the former interpreter Daniil Kuziakin.

April 23-6. The wind prevented our departure.

April 23. Thursday. I celebrated Matins and the Hours.

April 24. Friday. I celebrated Matins and the Liturgy.

April 25. Saturday. I celebrated Matins and the Liturgy.

April 26. Sunday. I celebrated Matins and the Liturgy.

April 27. Monday. We set out from [Unalaska] Harbor at 5:30 in the morning in three baidarkas and safely crossed the straits of Unalga, Akutan, and Akun to arrive at Akun at 6:30 in the evening.

April 28. Tuesday. We set out against the current at seven o'clock and arrived at the island of Tigalda at five o'clock, after safely crossing Avatanak and Derbin straits.

April 29, Wednesday, and April 30, Thursday. The wind prevented our sailing across Unimak Pass.

In the early part of this month I was busy with copying over the Aleut Catechism. I had not been to school for either of the preceding two months: lessons were not being held because of freezing weather, which continued almost until June.

May

May 2 and May 3. Headwinds prevented us from continuing our trip.

May 2. Saturday. I celebrated Matins in the common building.

May 3. Sunday. I celebrated the Hours, adding a prayer service for those traveling by sea.

May 4. Monday. We set out across Unimak Pass at ten o'clock, with a calm wind. We crossed the strait safely and without mishap and landed at half past 5:00 at the former site of the village of Nosovskoi. We left there at 6:30 and arrived at the village of Pogromskoe at nine o'clock.

May 5. Tuesday. Since there were only eight inhabitants here, and three were infants and two of the adults were to come with me, I found it unnecessary to celebrate the Liturgy. I duly instructed them and heard Confession from them. Then, after a reading of the usual Rule of Prayer and the Hours, I gave Communion from the reserved sacrament to two women and one youngster. Before the Hours, I chrismated two infants.

At seven o'clock we continued on, and at 7:30 in the evening we arrived at Shishaldinskoe village on Unimak.

After the inhabitants had assembled, I gave them sufficient instruction about the essence of Christianity. After teaching, I celebrated the Vigil Service, and then heard Confession from forty people, both males and females, of various ages.

May 6. Wednesday. After a reading of the Rule of Prayer, I chrismated five people and baptized one infant. Then, in the tent, I celebrated the Liturgy and gave Communion to all those who had confessed, except for three women (by necessity).

We set out at eight o'clock, but since a headwind developed, we put in at Cape Lanin [Lapin] after going about twenty-five versts.

May 7. Thursday. We set out at four o'clock in the morning, but a growing easterly wind caused us to put in at a deserted place after traveling about thirty versts.

At nine o'clock in the evening the wind grew quieter. We did not wish to miss the opportunity, and so set out.

May 8. Friday. At 6:30 in the morning we arrived at the village of Morzhovoi, located on the strait that runs between Unimak and the Alaska Peninsula. We had traveled around sixty versts.

At its appointed time, I celebrated Vespers and a Vigil Service dedicated to St. Nicholas. The Rule of Prayer was also read.

May 9. Saturday. After a reading of the Rule of Prayer, I duly instructed them and then heard Confession from all, except for one woman. After chrismating two infants, I celebrated the Liturgy and gave Communion to all those who had confessed, except for one woman (by necessity). After the Liturgy, I celebrated a prayer service to St. John the Theologian and to St. Nicholas. I sacramentally blessed one marriage.

In the evening, I celebrated Vespers and Matins.

May 10. Sunday. I celebrated the Hours, adding a prayer service for those traveling by sea. The wind prevented our departure.

May 11. Monday. We set out on foot across the neck of land. There was a strong northerly wind. Carrying our baidarkas, we set out with the wind at nine o'clock. At four o'clock we stopped, not far from Cape Tochil'nyi [Tachilni] on the southern side of the Alaska Peninsula.

May 12. Tuesday. The wind remained the same, and so we changed our location only slightly because of the difficulty of landing. We landed on the right-hand promontory of Morozovskaia Bay [Cold Bay].

May 13. Wednesday. The same wind prevented us from sailing across the bay.

Comment: It was as cold as five degrees below zero.

May 14. Thursday. The wind grew quieter at noon, and at two o'clock we set out. We arrived at Bel'kovskoe village at 7:30.

At nine o'clock I celebrated Vespers.

May 15. Friday. I celebrated Matins and the Liturgy in a tent pitched on a site used previously, and gave Communion to all the youngsters. Before the Liturgy I chrismated seven people, and afterwards I duly instructed the inhabitants.

May 16. Saturday. After a reading of the Rule of Prayer, I celebrated the Liturgy and gave Communion to all those who had confessed, except for three women (by necessity). In the evening, I celebrated Vespers and Matins.

May 17. Sunday. I celebrated the Hours and sacramentally blessed six marriages. Then I invited all the men there at the time [to assemble], and I read before them the preface to the translated Catechism and [selections] from the Sacred History about the Creation, the State of Bliss and the Fall of the First Man; the Flood and the Scattering of Mankind after the Flood; Abraham; and John the Baptist ; the birth, teaching, and Passion of Jesus Christ; the Lord's Prayer; and the Symbol of Faith [Nicene Creed]. I read the beginning of the Catechism and the Ten Commandments. Then I read the last three chapters of my translation of the Gospel.

Those who heard were unanimous in their approval and confirmation of the text, and they unanimously expressed their fervent desire to have these books; they signed a petition [to that effect] intended for the Bishop. This petition had also been read to them by the interpreter.

May 18, 19, and 20. Monday, Tuesday, and Wednesday. Since the wind prevented us from continuing on, I read the Catechism over together with the interpreter, and we checked it against the original. Any errors found were completely corrected.

May 21. After the Hours and a prayer service, we continued on our way, but we encountered strong winds after traveling about sixty versts; we were forced to land on the western side of Pavlovskaia Bay, opposite the village itself.

May 22. The wind remained the same, and so we once again proceeded along the inside of the bay with the intention of setting out before the wind rose. However, seeing the utter impossibility of doing this, and meeting up with even stronger winds, we stopped, landing at an extremely ill-suited and sandy place.

By nine o'clock the wind had changed directions and become less strong, and so we set out across the bay with a tailwind. We arrived safely at the village of Pavlovskoe at five o'clock.

After conducting Vespers and Matins, I instructed the inhabitants sufficiently and heard Confession from as many as forty-five people.

May 23. After a reading of the Rule of Prayer, I chrismated two infants, celebrated the Liturgy in the tent on a site used previously, and gave Communion to all, except for two women (by necessity). After the Liturgy, I sacramentally blessed four marriages. I then visited and gave Final Communion to an ill person. Then, in the home of the toion, I read the same passages as before from the Catechism and the Gospel. Also as before, all listeners approved and signed the petition.

At 11:30 we continued farther, but unfavorable winds caused us to stop on a small deserted island at five o'clock.

In the evening, I celebrated Vespers and Matins.

May 24. Sunday. I celebrated the Hours, adding a prayer service.

May 24-26. [Sunday, Monday and Tuesday.] A strong headwind hindered us from continuing our course.

May 26. Tuesday. In the evening, Vespers and the Easter Matins were sung.

May 27. Wednesday. We set out at four o'clock in the morning, with good weather. At nine o'clock we landed on the northwestern tip of Unga Island. There we sang the Hours for the Leave-taking of Paskha [Easter].

We left at 10:30 and arrived at the village of Unga at five o'clock. At the appointed time, I celebrated Vespers and the Vigil Service for the Feast of the Dormition. I also taught the young people.

May 28. Feast of the Assumption. I heard Confession from the young people and chrismated fourteen infants. Then, after blessing the water, I celebrated the Liturgy and gave Communion to all the young people—as many as sixty of them. After the Liturgy, I visited all of the inhabitants, bringing the cross and holy water.

After dinner, I invited all of the men into the home of the manager and read them the same selections from the Catechism and Gospel that I had read elsewhere. Once again, all present approved unanimously, confirming the text and signing the petition.

After Vespers, I taught the inhabitants for a sufficient time, and then after Matins I heard Confession from all—from as many as fifty-eight people.

May 29. Friday. After a reading of the Rule of Prayer, I celebrated the Liturgy and gave Communion to all those who had confessed, except for three women (by necessity). After the Liturgy, I visited and gave Final Communion to an ill person, and then sacramentally blessed one marriage.

Since the wind was quite favorable for us to begin our return trip to Unalaska, we lost no time, setting out along the southern side of Unga, in the fog. At nine o'clock in the evening we stopped at a small deserted island, the first off Unga.

May 30. We set out again at four o'clock. The heavy fog, however, caused us to lose one another. As a result, we in the first two baidarkas arrived at Bel'kovskoe village at twelve o'clock, while the third, carrying my traveling companions, arrived at one o'clock, and the last boat, which carried the interpreter, arrived at six o'clock in the evening. In the evening I celebrated Vespers and Matins in the home of the manager.

May 31. Sunday. After celebrating the Hours with an added prayer service, we set out at 4:30, under calm weather conditions. During the passage across Morozovskaia Bay [Cold Bay] the wind began to blow from the north, but then grew quiet. At two o'clock it began to blow very strongly from the southwest, and so at four o'clock we were forced to land at a very ill-suited landing place.[1]

June

June 1. Monday. Because of the poor landing place, we could barely get away at ten o'clock, under calm and clear conditions. We safely crossed Morzhovskii Bay and landed at half past one at the village of Morzhovoi, where all the inhabitants were on hand. We landed in order to take on food. There I heard Confession from one woman who had not been there during my previous visit.

At five o'clock we set out into Isannakhskii Strait, [2] and we stopped in the middle of it at eight o'clock, at the site of a former village.

June 2. Tuesday. We left Issanakh, on the southern side of Unimak Island[3] at four o'clock in the morning. At six o'clock we passed through the small pass between Unimak and Ikatak,[4] and at ten o'clock we landed on the laida [intertidal zone] because of a leak that had opened up in one of the baidarkas.[5]

June 3. We set out at three o'clock in the morning. At five o'clock in the evening, we stopped at Krata [or Kresta?], which is located on the southern tip of Unimak Island. While en route, we stopped for one-half hour to examine the wind, which had begun to blow quite strongly halfway through the trip.

June 4, 5. The wind would not permit us to sail through [Unimak] Pass.

June 6. Saturday. Although the wind once more made it impossible to travel through the pass, it did permit us to move to a more convenient spot. We set out at eight o'clock and landed right at the pass itself at ten o'clock. I celebrated the Vigil Service at its appointed time.

June 7. Pentecost. At eleven o'clock I celebrated the Hours with Vespers and kneeling prayers.

I read Matins in the evening.

June 8. Monday. In the morning, I celebrated the Hours, adding a prayer service for those traveling by sea.

The wind grew quieter at three o'clock in the afternoon, and we set out for the pass. After safely going through it, and after passing safely by a riptide alongside Ugamak Island, we landed on the southern tip of Ugamak Island at nine o'clock.

June 9. Tuesday. After waiting for a favorable tide, at 6:30 we set out across Ugamak Pass, into a headwind. We arrived at Tigalda Island at nine o'clock. We stood at anchor there for two hours, and took guides on board. Then we continued on to cross, safely and without mishap, two other passes and arrived at Akun Island at 6:30.

June 10. Wednesday. We left Akun at 4:30 and successfully crossed Akun Strait. When we reached Akutan Pass, however, we encountered a strong headwind from the north and were forced to stop at 10:30 in Basinskaia Bay on Akutan Island.

At six o'clock the wind died down and the tide became favorable, and so we crossed Akutan Pass and stopped for the night at eight o'clock on a small, deserted island next to Unalga.

June 11. Thursday. At four o'clock we set out for Unalga. There we waited for a favorable tide and then set out into a rather strong headwind. We successfully crossed Unalga Strait,[6] and stopped at eleven o'clock at Kalekhtinskaia [Kalekta] Bay on Unalaska. The wind prevented us from traveling around Cape Kalekhta, and so we carried our load across the neck of land and arrived in Harbor Village [Unalaska] at five o'clock in the evening.

Thus concluded my trip to Unga, the third during my stay on Unalaska, and the first during this year.

It is with Christian joy that I saw, and now report, that my previous [two] visits had certainly not been in vain.

June 13. Saturday. I celebrated the Vigil Service in a tent: they had begun to put up the new iconostasis during my absence, and this work had not yet been completed on this date.

June 14. Sunday. I celebrated the Hours in the tent, and chrismated and baptized two infants.

June 18. Thursday. A Russian-American Company ship arrived from Sitka. It brought news. The first report was a sad one: the Right Reverend Mikhail, Bishop of Irkutsk, had passed away last June 5 (1830). The second was joyful: Russia had defeated the Turks and signed with them a treaty of Eternal Peace. I also received dispatches.

June 20. Saturday. I celebrated the Vigil Service in the church.

June 21. Sunday. Before the Hours, I celebrated a memorial service for the Bishop. After the Hours, [which was held in place of the Liturgy] because the iconostasis was still not completed, I celebrated a prayer service of thanksgiving, in accordance with this decree [*ukaz*], with kneeling prayers and a three-day ringing of the bells.

Comment: With a cannon salute.

June 22. Monday. I celebrated a memorial service and the Hours.

June 23. Tuesday. I celebrated a memorial service and the Hours.

June 24. Wednesday. I celebrated a memorial service and the Vigil Service.

June 25. Thursday. I celebrated the Hours and a prayer service for the health of His Majesty the Emperor.

June 27. Saturday. I celebrated the Vigil Service.

June 28. Sunday. I celebrated the Hours, Vespers, and a Vigil Service dedicated to St. Peter and St. Paul.

June 29. Monday. The iconostasis had been put in place and all the icons set on it, and the curtains and Royal doors had being built (although the latter had not been completely decorated). Nothing, therefore, prevented the celebration of the Liturgy, and so on this day the iconostasis was consecrated. Incidentally, the Communion table had not been touched or moved in the course of the work. We consecrated the iconostasis with the ceremony described below.

At eight o'clock the bells rang the usual call to worship. At nine o'clock water was blessed in the middle of the church with the Lesser Blessing, and it was used to sprinkle the Communion table, the sanctuary, all new icons, and the entire church. While this was happening, singers sang Psalm 25. After this sprinkling and singing had been completed, and after a special litany, "Many Years" was proclaimed for His Majesty the Emperor and for the imperial family, accompanied by a ringing of the bells. Then the Hours were read and the Liturgy performed, with added prayers of thanksgiving.

After arriving in Unalaska, I became particularly busy with setting up and making the iconostasis. On Wednesdays and Fridays I went to the school, where I reviewed the entire Catechism from the beginning. By the end of June, I had reviewed up through the fourth statement of the Nicene Creed. The students had begun to study [only] on June 5th, because the weather had been freezing.

[Signed:] Priest of the Unalaska Ascension Church,
Ivan Veniaminov, July 2, 1831.

NOTES

1. At this site one can see traces of a very large village.

2. Between Unimak and the Alaska Peninsula.

3. We were taking a new route. Actually, one might call it an old route, since no one had gone this way since 1811. It is quite good in comparison to taking the northern side of Unimak.

4. [Formerly charted as an island, today known as the Ikatan Peninsula—Ed.]

5. At this spot, too, there were vestiges of a very large village.

6. [Note missing in text.]

JOURNAL NO. 9
July 1, 1831, to September 1, 1832

July

July 1. Wednesday. I celebrated the Liturgy and a prayer service for the health of His Majesty the Emperor and his family.

Comment: [July] 4. The brig *Okhotsk* arrived and brought the new chief manager of the colonies, Baron Wrangel. The chief manager left on the 8th.

July 5. Sunday. I celebrated the Liturgy.

July 7. Tuesday. At the school, an examination was given in the presence of the chief manager. He remained satisfied with the pupils' success.

[July 8. *Comment*: See July 4.]

July 12. Sunday. I celebrated the Liturgy.

July 19. Sunday. I celebrated the Liturgy.

July 22. Wednesday. I celebrated the Vigil Service, the Hours, and a prayer service for the health of His Majesty.

July 26. Sunday. I celebrated the Liturgy. In addition, I prepared papers to be sent to Russia and Sitka.

August

August 1. Saturday. I celebrated Matins and the Liturgy, at the conclusion of which I blessed the water at the river. Then, there was a procession around the village with the cross, accompanied by a ringing of the bells.

August 2. Sunday. I celebrated the Liturgy.

August 6. Feast of the Transfiguration. I celebrated the Vigil Service, the Liturgy, and a prayer service.

August 9. I celebrated a memorial service and the Liturgy.

August 15. Feast of the Assumption. I celebrated the Liturgy.

149

August 16. Sunday. I celebrated the Liturgy.

August 22. Saturday. I celebrated the Liturgy and a prayer service for the health of His Majesty the Emperor.

August 23. Sunday. I celebrated the Liturgy.

August 29. Saturday. I celebrated a memorial service and the Liturgy.

August 30. Sunday. I celebrated the Liturgy and a prayer service.

In addition, I readied papers and sent them off together with the Aleut translation of the Catechism.

September

September 2. Wednesday. My name day. I celebrated Matins and the Liturgy, adding a song of thanksgiving to the Lord God who has blessed me.

September 6. Sunday. I celebrated the Liturgy.

September 8. Tuesday. I celebrated the Liturgy.

September 12. Saturday. I celebrated the Vigil Service.

September 13. Sunday. I celebrated the Hours.

September 14. Monday. I celebrated the Vigil Service and the Liturgy.

September 20. Sunday. I celebrated Matins and the Liturgy.

September 22. Tuesday. I gave Final Communion to an ill person and prayed over two infants.

September 24. Thursday. At eight o'clock I set out in a baidarka to visit the sick and elderly inhabitants of the nearby villages.

At eleven o'clock we arrived at the village of Kalekhta. There were no sick or newborn there, and so we continued on, arriving at 3:30 at the village of Unalga (on Unalga Island). There were no ill or newborn there, either, and so, in order not to waste time, we sailed on. At 6:30 we arrived at Borkinskoe village. The Rule of Prayer was read to those on hand to take Communion.

September 25. Friday. After hearing Confession from four elderly and ill women, I gave Communion from the reserved sacrament. I baptized one infant and chrismated two. We departed at six o'clock, and at ten o'clock we arrived at Bobrovskoe village [Beaver]. Because there were no ill persons or newborns there, either, we continued on, arriving at Sechkinskoe settlement at two o'clock. Here I heard Confession from, and gave Communion to, two ill women. Then, we set off for the isthmus. We crossed it on foot, and arrived at [Unalaska] Harbor at seven o'clock in the evening.

September 27. Sunday. I celebrated Matins and the Liturgies of the Resurrection and of St. John the Theologian. I gave Final Communion to an ill person.

September 30. Wednesday. I celebrated a funeral service for the person, now deceased, to whom I had given Final Communion on the 27th.

In addition, from September 10th on, I copied over my Aleut translation of the Gospel [of St. Matthew], checking it for errors.

October

October 4. Sunday. I celebrated Matins. After baptizing two infants, I celebrated the Liturgy, sacramentally blessed a marriage, and gave Final Communion to an ill person.

October 8. Thursday. I gave Final Communion to an ill person. On this day I finished copying over the Gospel and gave it to the local translator to read.

October 11. Sunday. I celebrated Matins and the Hours.

October 18. Sunday. I celebrated Matins and the Liturgy and baptized an infant.

October 22. Thursday. I celebrated the Hours and a prayer service to the Virgin Mary.

October 25. Sunday. I celebrated Matins and the Liturgy.

Because of the cold, it was impossible to conduct studies in the school, and so I worked on making my own clock.

November

November 1. Sunday. I celebrated Matins and the Liturgy.

November 8. Sunday. I celebrated the Vigil Service, a memorial service, the Liturgy, and a prayer service.

November 15. Sunday. I celebrated Matins and the Liturgy.

November 18. Wednesday. I went to the school and began to teach the Aleut language. I also demonstrated the letters of the Aleut alphabet.

November 19. Thursday [original erroneously states "Friday"]. I celebrated a memorial service and, in the evening, the Vigil Service.

November 20. Friday. I celebrated the Liturgy and a prayer service.

November 21. Feast of the Presentation of the Blessed Virgin. I celebrated the Vigil Service and the Liturgy.

November 22. Sunday. I celebrated Matins and the Hours.

November 25. Wednesday. In school I demonstrated how to use the letters of the Aleut alphabet; in the evening I celebrated a Vigil Service to St. Innocent.

November 26. Thursday. After baptizing an infant, I celebrated the Liturgy and a prayer service to St. Innocent accompanied by a ringing of the bells.

November 27. Friday. In school, the students began to take dictation in the Aleut language.

November 29. Sunday. I celebrated Matins and the Hours.

I read periodical publications for 1829. My free time was spent working on my clock, which I finished.

December

December 2 and 4. Wednesday and Friday. In school, I continued to demonstrate Aleut spelling.

December 6. Sunday. I celebrated the Vigil Service, the Liturgy, and a prayer service.

December 7. I gave Final Communion to an ill person.

December 9 and 11. Wednesday and Friday. In school, we worked on the same material as that covered in the previous two classes.

December 13. Sunday. I celebrated Matins and the Liturgy.

December 16 and 18. Wednesday and Friday. In school, I demonstrated how to translate from Russian into Aleut, and the other way around.

December 20. Sunday. I celebrated Matins and the Liturgy.

December 23. Wednesday. In school, I worked on the same material as in previous lessons. Then, the students were dismissed until January 3.

December 24. Thursday. I celebrated Matins, the Hours, and Vespers, with the Liturgy of St. Basil the Great.

December 25. Christmas. I celebrated Matins, the Liturgy, a prayer service, and, at its appointed time, Vespers.

December 26. Saturday. I celebrated Matins and the Liturgy.

December 27. Sunday. I celebrated Matins and the Liturgy.

This month I read Church and biblical history.

1832
January

January 1. Friday. I celebrated Matins, the Liturgy, and a prayer service.

January 3. Sunday. I celebrated Matins, the Liturgy, and a prayer service.

January 5. Tuesday. I celebrated Matins, the Hours, and Vespers, with the Liturgy of St. Basil the Great, and with the customary Blessing of the Water.

January 6. Epiphany. I celebrated Matins, the Liturgy, and a Blessing of the Water at the river. At its appointed time, I celebrated Matins.

January 7. Thursday. I celebrated Matins, the Hours, and a prayer service.

January 11. Sunday. I celebrated Matins and the Liturgy.

January 13. Wednesday. In school, I began to work on teaching the Law of God. Today I listened to the Catechism lessons set for this holiday.

January 15. Friday. In school, I taught that Christian learning is the most necessary learning, for only it can lead to true bliss, and so on.

January 17. Sunday. I celebrated Matins and the Liturgy.

January 20 and 22. Wednesday and Friday. In school, I taught the first and second statements of the Nicene Creed, explaining each word separately as to its meaning, its background, and so on.

January 24. Sunday. I celebrated Matins and the Liturgy.

January 27 and 29. Wednesday and Friday. In school, I went over the previous lesson, and then taught the third and fourth statements of the Nicene Creed.

January 30. Saturday. I celebrated the Vigil Service and the Hours.

January 31. Sunday. I celebrated Matins and the Liturgy.

In addition, I compiled church accounts and reports (and worked on making my own organ).

February

February 2. The Presentation of Our Lord in the Temple [Candlemas]. I celebrated the Vigil Service and the Liturgy.

February 3. Wednesday. I celebrated the Vigil Service, the Liturgy, and a prayer service.

February 5. Friday. In school, I taught the fifth statement of the Nicene Creed.

February 7. Sunday. I celebrated Matins and the Liturgy.

February 8. Monday. I celebrated Matins, the Liturgy, and an evening prayer service to St. Innocent.

February 9. Tuesday. I celebrated the Liturgy and a prayer service to St. Innocent.

February 10 and 12. Wednesday and Friday. In school, I taught about the sixth and seventh statements of the Nicene Creed, and there was a reading from the Gospel of Matthew concerning the Last Judgement.

February 13. Saturday. I celebrated Matins and a Memorial Liturgy.

February 14. Sunday. I celebrated Matins and the Liturgy.

February 17. Wednesday. In school, I reviewed briefly all of the lessons and then taught the eighth statement of the Nicene Creed.

February 21. Sunday. I celebrated Matins, the Liturgy, and Vespers.

February 22. Monday. I celebrated Matins and the Hours. Beginning with this day, services were continuous until the 29th.

February 24. Wednesday. I celebrated the Liturgy of the Presanctified.

February 26. Friday. The same service. After Matins, I gave instruction for some time to those preparing for the sacraments, speaking on the essence of Christianity.[1] In the afternoon, I heard Confession from ninty people, both males and females, of various ages.

February 27. Saturday. I celebrated the Liturgy and gave Communion to all those who had confessed; the standard lesson was read.

February 28. Sunday. I celebrated the Liturgy at which was read the standard lesson. The services were concluded with Vespers.

The Holy Gospel, which I had given to the translator to read, was returned to me with written comments. I gave it once more to the toion Pan'kov, so that he could read it.

March

March 2 and 4. Wednesday and Friday. In school, I taught about the sacraments of the Church.

March 6. Sunday. I celebrated Matins and the Liturgy, at which was read the standard lesson. I also celebrated Vespers.

March 9 and 11. Wednesday and Friday. In school, I taught about the resurrection of the dead and the life to come.

March 13. Sunday. I celebrated Matins and the Liturgy, at which was read a condensed version of a sermon written by Bishop Filaret. Services began on this day.

March 16. Wednesday. I celebrated the Liturgy of the Presanctified.

March 18. Friday. I celebrated the Liturgy of the Presanctified, and after Matins I taught those preparing for the sacraments. In the afternoon, I heard Confession from 120 persons, both males and females, of various ages.

March 19. Saturday. I celebrated the Liturgy and gave Communion to all those who had confessed. The appointed sermon was read.

March 20. Sunday. I celebrated Matins and the Liturgy, at which was read the appointed sermon, in abbreviated form, written by Bishop Filaret.

March 23. Wednesday. I celebrated the Liturgy of the Presanctified, and, in the evening, Matins with the Great Canon.

March 24. Thursday. After Matins, I taught those preparing for the sacraments, I celebrated the Liturgy of the Presanctified, and, in the afternoon, I heard Confession from ninty people.

March 25. Feast of the Annunciation. I celebrated Matins and the Liturgy, and gave Communion to all those who had confessed. At the Liturgy, another sermon by the Right Reverend Filaret was read in abbreviated form.

March 26. Saturday. I celebrated Matins with the Akathistos and the Liturgy.

March 27. Sunday. I celebrated Matins and the Liturgy. The services concluded with Vespers.

March 30. Wednesday. In school, I reviewed the first four lessons, with an added explanation of the moral of the words "Almighty Creator." For example, if God is almighty, then nothing happens to us without His having willed it; this extends down to a single hair on our heads, and so on.

Besides carrying out these duties, I read the first volume of *Christian Philosophy*.

April

April 1. Friday. In school, I reviewed the previous lesson, and then finished my teaching. The services began with Vespers.

April 2. Saturday. I celebrated Matins and the Liturgy.

April 3. Palm Sunday. I celebrated the Vigil Service and the Liturgy.

April 4, 5, and 6. Monday, Tuesday, and Wednesday. On each day, I celebrated the Liturgy of the Presanctified with readings from the four Gospels, as is customary. After Matins, I instructed those preparing for the sacraments. In the afternoons I heard Confession from thirty-six people.

April 7. Thursday. During the Liturgy, I gave Communion to all those who had confessed.

April 8. Friday. At Vespers, I gave a sermon that I had composed on the theme that there is no path to the Heavenly Kingdom other than that which Jesus Christ traveled. This was the same sermon as was delivered the previous year, but this time it had been supplemented and revised. After Vespers, I heard Confession from forty-two people.

April 9. Saturday. Starting at two o'clock, I celebrated the Liturgy and gave Communion to all those who had confessed. In the evening, I heard Confession from thirty-eight people.

April 10. Easter. Matins began at twelve o'clock, and the Liturgy took place at six o'clock. At the Liturgy, the Gospel was read in Slavonic, by the priest; in Russian, by the cantor; and also in Aleut, read by the same man as last year, Chichinev. Communion was given to all those who had confessed and to the youngsters—to as many as thirty people.

April 11 through April 16. During all of Holy Week, there were the usual services and the Liturgy was performed every day. After the Liturgy on Saturday, I celebrated a prayer service for those desiring to travel by water and found myself ready to depart on a journey to the western regions. I celebrated Vespers in the evening.

April 17. Sunday. I celebrated the Liturgy and a prayer service.

April 19. Tuesday. I celebrated a Memorial Liturgy.

At one o'clock, I set out in a party of three three-man baidarkas, and at seven o'clock in the evening we arrived at the village of Makushin. After celebrating Vespers with Matins, I taught the inhabitants about what is necessary in order to obtain remission of our sins, and about what is needed for true repentance. I gave special attention to the young people.

April 20. Wednesday. After a reading of the Rule of Prayer, I heard Confession from all of the adult local inhabitants. I chrismated three infants, celebrated the Liturgy on a site used previously, and gave Communion to all those who had confessed and to the young people. After the Liturgy, I taught about the mystery and essence of Christianity, that is, about how we must imitate Jesus Christ to the extent of our powers. I spoke briefly about the life of Christ. I also spoke about prayer: how, when, and about what we should pray. Finally, I spoke about how we should not look at the bad examples in our brethren, or anyone else, and about how we should never boast in front of anyone, even ourselves, about our forbearance of injury or our good deeds.

I gave Final Communion to an ill person and to a very elderly woman. Then, at ten o'clock, we continued farther on our course, arriving at six o'clock at the village of Koshiga. After conducting Vespers together with Matins, I taught the locals about the nature of repentance, and so on.

April 21. Thursday. After a reading of the Rule of Prayer, I heard Confession from all of the adults, chrismated two infants, celebrated the Liturgy, and held a prayer service for the health of His Majesty. I gave Communion to all those who had confessed and to the young people. After the Liturgy I taught about the same topics that I had discussed in the first village and sacramentally blessed two marriages.

At 3:30 I set out, and we arrived at the village of Chernovskoe at 7:30. After celebrating Vespers together with Matins, I taught the inhabitants about repentance, as I had in the first few villages.

April 22. Friday. After a reading of the Rule of Prayer, I heard Confession from all and chrismated two infants. Then, I celebrated the Liturgy and gave Communion to those who had confessed and to the youngsters. I taught about the essence of Christianity, and so forth. I sacramentally blessed two marriages. In the evening I celebrated a Vigil Service to St. George.

April 23. Saturday. I celebrated the Hours and, at its appointed time, a Vigil Service.

April 24. Sunday. I celebrated the Hours and, at its appointed time, the Vigil Service. Because of severe wind, it was impossible to leave between the 22nd and the 26th of April.

April 26. Tuesday. At six o'clock in the evening we set out. After safely crossing Umnak Strait, we arrived at the village of Tulik, on the island of Umnak, at ten o'clock. After chrismating three infants, I celebrated the Vigil Service and, after the usual teaching, I heard Confession from all of the adults.

April 27. Wednesday. After a reading of the Rule of Prayer, I celebrated the Liturgy and a prayer service for the health of His Majesty. I gave Communion to all of the inhabitants there. After the Liturgy, I taught about the essence of Christianity and so forth, just as I had in the first village.

Because of severe turbulence it was impossible to leave before the 30th.

April 30. We set out at 5:30. At 7:30 we arrived at the neck of land near Recheshnoe village. Within the hour, we sent word to this village. I celebrated Vespers there.

During this journey, I used my free time to read over the Aleut Gospel, together with the translator Semen Pan'kov. I corrected the orthographic markings.

May

May 1. Sunday. I celebrated Matins, and then went on foot to the village. We arrived there at 8:30. I celebrated the Hours in the chapel and chrismated ten infants. I baptized one newborn. After Vespers I gave instruction about what is needed for repentance, and then heard Confession from all those living here—from as many as forty people.

May 2. Monday. I celebrated Matins and the Liturgy in the chapel and gave Communion to all those who had confessed and to the young people. After the Liturgy, I celebrated a prayer service to St. Nicholas (to whom this chapel is dedicated), and taught the same subjects as in previous villages.

After Vespers, I taught about how the magnificence of God's House will not save us if we do not pray diligently and do not fulfill the commandments of Him Who lives in that House.

May 3. Tuesday. At five o'clock in the morning, we went back to the neck of land in the company of almost all of the inhabitants, and at seven o'clock we set out in the baidarkas on our return voyage. At seven o'clock in the evening, we arrived at Kotel'nyi Cape, and because of both the wind that had developed and the roughness of the sea, our pulling in to the coast was very dangerous.

May 4. Wednesday. We were prevented from traveling by the wind and roughness.

May 5. Thursday. At eleven o'clock we set out. At nine o'clock in the evening, we arrived at the village of Koshiga, after passing by Tulik and Chernovskoe.

May 6. Friday. A strong wind prevented us from departing, and on that evening we finished checking over the Aleut Gospel.

May 7. Saturday. Although there was a great deal of roughness, which made traveling somewhat dangerous, the wind was calm, and so we set out at seven o'clock in the morning. We arrived at the village of Makushin at one o'clock in the afternoon. I celebrated Vespers together with Matins.

May 8. Sunday. Upon a reading of the Hours, I set out in a baidarka for Makushin Bay, heading for the neck of land. We arrived there at 10:30. At twelve o'clock, we set out on foot across the neck of land, and we arrived at Harbor Village [Unalaska] at seven o'clock. Our baidarkas remained at Makushin, because the wind made it impossible to travel by sea. I celebrated the Vigil Service.

May 9. Monday. I celebrated the Liturgy.

May 13. Sunday. I celebrated the Vigil Service and the Hours.

May 18. Wednesday. I celebrated Matins, the Liturgy, and Vespers, and a Vigil Service for the parish feast day.

May 19. Ascension Day. After a purification of the waters, I celebrated the Liturgy and then Vespers at its appointed time.

May 22. Sunday. I celebrated the Vigil Service, the Hours, and a prayer service to St. Constantine and St. Helen, for the health of His Majesty and of the imperial family.

May 28. Saturday. I celebrated Matins and a Memorial Liturgy.

May 29. Sunday. I celebrated the Vigil Service and the Liturgy together with Vespers.

May 30. [Monday.] I celebrated Matins and the Liturgy.

After returning from my travels, I worked continuously on rewriting the Gospel in Aleut; by the end of the month, it had been rewritten and checked.

June

June 1. Wednesday. At four o'clock in the afternoon, a ship arrived, bringing dispatches from the Irkutsk Consistory and from the chief manager.

June 5. Sunday. The Liturgy was preceded by the customary memorial service for the Right Reverend Mikhail, who had been appointed on this day. After the Liturgy, I celebrated a prayer service of thanksgiving for the birth of the Grand Princess Alexandra Mikhailovna, in accordance with the instructions of the Bishop of Irkutsk, the Right Reverend Irinii. The service contained kneeling prayers and a proclamation of the "Many Years" for the imperial family and the Most Reverend.

June 9. Thursday. My household departed for Okhotsk, taking papers for the Bishop.

June 12. Sunday. I celebrated the Liturgy.

June 15 and 17. Wednesday and Friday. In school, I taught the fifth chapter of the Gospel of Matthew, beginning with the thirteenth verse. We read both in Russian and in Aleut.

June 19. Sunday. I celebrated the Liturgy.

June 22. Wednesday. In school, I taught the sixth chapter of Matthew.

June 24. Friday. I celebrated the Vigil Service and the Liturgy.

June 25. Saturday. I celebrated the Vigil Service and the Liturgy, following the service appointed for the 27th of this month. After the Liturgy, I celebrated a prayer service for the health of His Majesty the Emperor.
Comment: This service was accompanied by a cannon salute.

June 26. Sunday. I celebrated the Liturgy.

June 28. Tuesday. The Russian-American Company ship *Chichagov* arrived, and on it came the chief manager of the colonies, Captain of the First Rank and Cavalier, Baron Wrangel.

June 29. Wednesday. I celebrated the Liturgy.
Comment: On June 29th, the ship *Chichagov* departed, but the chief manager remained here.

Having sent off the dispatches on the first ship, I prepared replies to all of the papers that I had received.

July

July 1. Friday. I celebrated the Liturgy and a prayer service for the health of His Majesty and the imperial family. On this day a vessel, the galiot *Morekhod*, arrived.

July 2. Saturday. I had not visited the inhabitants of the Pribilof Islands for three entire years, and so I asked the chief manager to provide me with the means to go to these islands. He permitted me to set out together with him on the galiot, which was first going to Nushagak, and then to these islands. So, on this day I moved over to the ship. We weighed anchor at two o'clock.[2]

July 8. Friday. At six o'clock in the evening, we dropped anchor at the mouth of the Nushagak River, at the Aglegmiut settlement.

July 9. Saturday. Starting at midnight with the onset of an unfavorable current, the chief manager and I set out for the redoubt located approximately twenty versts from this village. My assistant, the cantor, arrived with the religious items late that night.

July 10. Sunday. I celebrated the Hours in the barracks. After the Hours, I assembled all of the nomadic people who had been baptized and taught them through a translator about the existence of Almighty God the Creator, who sees all, is beneficent, and cares about everything, and so on. In the evening, I celebrated Matins, and taught once more, speaking about the Divine Law.

July 11. Monday. I chrismated with Holy Oil all of those nomads and Creoles who had been christened.

July 12. Tuesday. I celebrated the Vigil Service and heard Confession from all the Russian and Creole men living here and from their wives.

July 13. Wednesday. I celebrated the Liturgy in a tent, on a site used previously. I gave Communion without Confession to all those who had been chrismated, and to all who had confessed, except for several Russians who did not desire the sacrament. After completing the Liturgy, I taught the nomadic people once again, exhorting them to be good and sincere toward God and their fellow men. At eleven o'clock, we set out in a baidara for the ship, and at two o'clock we put in at the Aglegmiut settlement because of headwinds and unfavorable currents. Our ship had gone to the mouth of the river.

July 14. Thursday. In the morning, I visited the baptized inhabitants in their huts. At ten o'clock, we set out across the Nushagak River. At four o'clock we stopped at Cape Konstantin, in order to wait for a favorable current. We set out at eleven o'clock at night, and arrived at the ship at one o'clock in the morning.

July 15. Friday. We weighed anchor at nine o'clock in the morning and sailed for the Pribilof Islands.

Comment: We faced headwinds for this entire voyage.

July 17. Sunday. I celebrated the Hours at sea.

July 24. Sunday. I celebrated the Hours at sea, and soon afterwards we dropped anchor at St. George Island. Within the hour, I went ashore and chrismated fifteen infants. I immediately returned to the ship. At ten o'clock in the evening, we weighed anchor and went to the island of St. Paul.

July 25. Monday. At eleven o'clock, we dropped anchor at the island, and at seven o'clock I moved onto shore, having bid farewell to the chief manager. During my entire time with him, I had been honored by the favorable disposition that he displayed toward me, and by the attention that he paid me.

July 30. Saturday. I celebrated the Vigil Service and taught the local inhabitants about Confession.

July 31. Sunday. After conducting the Hours, I taught about Christian Duty. In the evening, I heard Confession from forty persons, both men and women.

August

August 1. Monday. I celebrated Matins with kneeling prayers and the Liturgy in the chapel. I gave Communion to all those who had confessed and to the young people—to as many as twenty people. After the Liturgy, I blessed the water at a new well[3] that had been especially prepared for this, and blessed with a cross the inhabitants in their homes.

August 5. Friday. After the Vigil Service, I heard Confession from all those remaining except for four women.

August 6. Saturday. I celebrated the Liturgy and gave Communion to all those who had confessed.

August 7. Sunday. I celebrated the Liturgy and gave Communion to all the young people.

August 14. Sunday. I celebrated the Hours. In the evening, I celebrated the Vigil Service with the Akathistos and heard Confession from the four remaining women.

August 15. Monday. I celebrated the Liturgy and gave Communion to all those who had confessed. I barely finished the Liturgy Service because of my poor health. I had begun to feel unwell that morning, but I recovered completely by the 20th.

August 19. Friday. I sacramentally blessed two marriages.

August 21. Sunday. I celebrated the Hours. At four o'clock I caught sight of the ship *Chichagov*, which was arriving from the north. It dropped anchor at the island at seven o'clock.

August 22. Monday. I heard Confession from two local men who had been on the ship. Then, I celebrated the Hours, and a prayer service for the health of His Majesty. Then, I gave Communion from the reserved sacrament to all those who had confessed. At nine o'clock I moved over onto the ship and immediately left for St. George Island.

August 23. Tuesday. In the morning, we approached St. George Island in order to take on cargo. In the meantime, I went ashore and heard Confession from all the local inhabitants, after reading the usual prayers. The lack of a harbor here made it impossible for me to stay until morning to celebrate the Liturgy, and so I followed the wishes of the local inhabitants by leaving several portions of the reserved sacrament for the ill. I gave suitable instruction to the local manager concerning the keeping and use of these elements in cases of extreme need.

At three o'clock I went to the ship, and at four o'clock we weighed anchor and sailed for Unalaska.

August 28. Sunday. We entered Unalaska Harbor at seven o'clock, and I went ashore at eight o'clock.

August 29. Monday. I celebrated the Hours.

August 30. Tuesday. I celebrated the Liturgy and the appointed prayer service.

I have the honor of bearing witness before you, my Bishop, that the fruits of my earlier teaching are visible if I only know how to see them. I think it superfluous, however, to speak here of the manner in which I was received and in which my teaching was attended—to do so would be to repeat an account that has already been given many times, for their zeal is always constant. I will relate only that in any village, upon my arrival, each and every person leaves off with his affairs—even if that be the preparation of food—and sits around me, prepared to listen for as long as it suits me to speak. In a word, in this regard they are sheep of Christ's flock such as are very hard to find nowadays. Glory be to God the Word, Who gives the Word to me, and Who comforts them and us with the Word!

[Signed:] Priest Ioann Veniaminov
of the Unalaska Church of the Ascension.
August 30, 1832, Unalaska.

NOTES

1. I teach the adults separately from the youngsters, and sometimes I also teach the groups of young boys and girls separately; I give appropriate instruction to each group.

2. For the first three days after I board a ship, I always suffer from the usual seasickness.

3. There is not one stream on the entire island.

JOURNAL NO. 10
September 1, 1832, to September 1, 1833

September

September 2. Friday. I celebrated Matins and the Liturgy, adding a prayer service of thanksgiving to the Lord God, who had blessed me with a successful and safe completion of my journey and allowed me to reach this point in time.

September 4. Sunday. I celebrated the Liturgy after baptizing an infant.

September 5. Monday. I celebrated the Hours and a prayer service.

September 8. The Nativity of the Mother of God. I celebrated the Liturgy and gave Final Communion to the head of the office, who was ill.

September 11. Sunday. I celebrated the Liturgy.

September 14. The Exaltation of the Honorable and Life-Giving Cross. I celebrated the Vigil Service and a Blessing of the Water at the river in place of the service I would have performed on August 1. There was a procession with the cross around the village.

September 18. Sunday. I celebrated Matins and the Liturgy.

September 23. Friday. I celebrated Matins and the Liturgy. I performed a funeral service for the late office manager, Iakov Dorofeev.

September 25. Sunday. I celebrated Matins and the Liturgy.

September 26. Monday. I celebrated Matins and the Hours.

Soon after my return from my journey, namely on September 10, an exercise book was set up for recording the tasks that I require of the two pupils who are carrying out the duties of church servitors. This was done in accordance with the Bishop's instructions concerning the instruction of priests and unordained clergy [servitors]. Because they have learned here at the school, they know to perfection four of the subjects named in the instructions: the Short Catechism, the abbreviated Sacred History, calligraphy, and the entire first part and half the second part of the arithmetic course. They are also partly able to sing from notes and, having learned grammar, can read sufficiently well. They still must be instructed, then, on the following: (1) the authorized court chant for the Divine Liturgy; and (2) the typicon. The above-mentioned chant is not available here (as I reported to the Irkutsk Consistory on July 13, 1832).[1]

This month they learned thoroughly the plain Sunday Service from the Short Typicon. As for recording in a notebook those words that they stress incorrectly when reading, I considered this to be not entirely necessary for two reasons. Firstly, the local unordained clergy are locals and knew no Russian at all before entering the school. I believe, therefore, that occasional errors in stress on their part are excusable; such errors, moreover, are rather infrequent. Secondly, since they are not yet confirmed in their offices, they may or may not end up serving in those offices.

This month I read the first volume of *Christian Philosophy* and the Psalter in verse.

October

October 2. Sunday. I celebrated Matins and the Liturgy.

October 9. Sunday. I celebrated Matins and the Liturgy.

October 16. Sunday. I celebrated Matins and the Liturgy.

October 22. Saturday. I celebrated the Hours and a prayer service to the Mother of God.

October 23. Sunday. I celebrated Matins and the Liturgy.

October 30. Sunday. I celebrated Matins and the Liturgy. Before the Liturgy, I performed a memorial service for the imperial family.

Out of necessity, on the 12th I took upon myself the duty of doing all of the teaching in the local school. I was occupied with this task until Easter.

This month the unordained clergy learned the typicon instructions concerning the combining of the Resurrectional Service with services to saints who warrant the Vigil and the polyeleion, or combining the Resurrectional Service with the pre- and post-feast services.[2]

November

November 6. Sunday. I celebrated Matins and the Liturgy.

November 8. Tuesday. I celebrated the Vigil Service, the Liturgy, and a prayer service. Before the Liturgy, I celebrated the customary memorial service for His Most Reverend Mikhail.

November 13. Sunday. I celebrated Matins and the Liturgy.

November 19. Saturday. I celebrated a memorial service and a Vigil Service beginning in the evening.

November 20. Sunday. I celebrated the Liturgy and a prayer service with an all-day ringing of the bells.
   Comment: Accompanied by a cannon salute.

November 21. The Presentation of the Mother of God in the Temple. I celebrated the Vigil Service and the Liturgy.

November 26. St. Innocent's Day. I celebrated the Vigil Service beginning in the evening, and the Liturgy. I also celebrated a prayer service to St. Innocent.

November 27. Sunday. I celebrated Matins and the Liturgy. Before the Liturgy, I celebrated a memorial service.

The unordained clergy learned the daily service, and, beyond that, they took turns helping me in the school, teaching reading and writing to the pupils of the third form.
   In addition to fulfilling my tasks connected with the school, I read *The Mystery of the Cross*.

December

December 1. Sunday. I celebrated the Hours [and not the Liturgy] because of a high wind and severe cold.

December 6. The Festival of St. Nicholas the Wonderworker. I celebrated the Vigil Service, the Liturgy, and a prayer service for the health of His Majesty the Emperor.
   Comment: Accompanied by a cannon salute.

December 11. Sunday. I celebrated Matins and the Liturgy.

December 18. Sunday. I celebrated Matins and the Liturgy.

December 23. Friday. I celebrated the Royal Hours.

December 25. Christmas. I celebrated Matins, the Liturgy, and the customary prayer service with an all-day ringing of the bells.
   Comment: Accompanied by a cannon salute.

December 26. Monday. I celebrated Matins and the Liturgy.

December 27. Tuesday. I celebrated Matins and the Liturgy. Before the Liturgy, I celebrated a memorial service for the imperial family.

Because of high winds, rather few people assembled for the holiday of Christmas. Therefore, no sermon was read. The unordained clergy learned by rote the Saturday service. They worked at memorizing, together with the other pupils, the concert piece "Today Christ..." [*Dnes' Khristos*].
   I worked at the school through the 20th. (In the period between the time I began teaching there and the time I stopped, I taught the following: grammar up to verbs, and arithmetic up through decimal fractions.)

1833
January

January 1. Sunday. I celebrated the Vigil Service, the Liturgy, and the customary prayer service.

January 5. Thursday. I celebrated Matins, the Hours, and Vespers with the Liturgy, and a Blessing of the Water.

January 6. Epiphany. I celebrated the Vigil Service and the Liturgy, with a Blessing of the Water at the river.

January 7. Saturday. I celebrated Matins and the Liturgy with a prayer service.

January 8. Sunday. I celebrated Matins and the Liturgy.

January 15. Sunday. I celebrated Matins and the Liturgy.

January 22. Sunday. I celebrated Matins and the Liturgy.

January 28. Saturday. I celebrated Matins, the Hours, and a prayer service.

January 29. Sunday. I celebrated Matins and the Liturgy. Before the Liturgy, I celebrated a memorial service for the imperial family.

January 30. Monday. I celebrated the Vigil Service and the Liturgy.

The unordained clergy finished the entire abbreviated typicon and reviewed it. I began working at the school on the 9th, and composed church records. I also read the third volume of *Christian Philosophy.*

February

February 2. The Presentation of Our Lord in the Temple [Candlemas]. I celebrated the Vigil Service and the Liturgy.

February 3. Friday. I celebrated the Vigil Service, the Hours, and a prayer service.

February 4. Saturday. I celebrated Matins and a Memorial Liturgy.

February 5. Sunday. I celebrated the Vigil Service and the Liturgy.

February 12. Sunday. I celebrated the Vigil Service, adding a service for St. Innocent. Then, I celebrated the Liturgy and a prayer service. Services continued from this date up until the 20th.

February 15. Wednesday. I celebrated the Liturgy of the Presanctified.

February 17. Friday. After Matins, I taught those preparing for the sacraments about that which is necessary for the remission of sins, and about the imitation of Jesus Christ. I heard Confession before and after the Liturgy from 125 people.

February 18. Saturday. I celebrated the Liturgy and gave Communion to all those who had confessed.

February 19. Sunday. I celebrated Matins and the Liturgy, and services concluded with the Vesper Service.

February 26. Sunday. I celebrated Matins and the Liturgy.

The unordained clergy learned the following songs from the music book: "Behold the Bridegroom," "Thy Bridal Chamber," and "When the Glorious Disciples...." They began to learn the hymns of the Passion.

Besides working at the school, I read the fourth volume of *Christian Philosophy.*

March

March 4. Saturday. Services began with Vespers and continued until the 13th of March.

March 5. Sunday. I celebrated the Liturgy.

March 8. Wednesday. I celebrated the Liturgy of the Presanctified.

March 9. Thursday. I celebrated the Liturgy of the Presanctified.

March 10. Friday. After Matins, I duly instructed those preparing for the sacraments, and in the afternoon I heard Confession from 135 people of both genders.

March 11. Saturday. I celebrated the Liturgy and gave Communion to all those who had confessed.

March 12. Sunday. I celebrated the Liturgy and Vespers at its appointed time.

March 14. Tuesday. I celebrated Vespers.

March 15. Wednesday. I celebrated Matins and the Hours. In the evening I celebrated Matins with the Great Canon.

March 16. Thursday. I celebrated the Liturgy of the Presanctified.

March 17. Friday. I taught after the Hours service. Then, I heard Confession from twenty-five women.

March 18. Saturday. I celebrated the Liturgy and gave Communion to all those who had confessed.

March 19. Sunday. I celebrated the Liturgy, and services concluded with Vespers.

March 24. Friday. I celebrated the Liturgy of the Presanctified.

March 25. Feast of the Annunciation. I celebrated Matins and the Liturgy.

March 26. Palm Sunday. I celebrated the Vigil Service and the Liturgy.

March 27. Monday. I celebrated the Hours together with a reading of the Gospel and the Liturgy of the Presanctified.

March 28. Tuesday. I celebrated the Hours together with a reading of the Gospel and the Liturgy of the Presanctified.

March 29. Wednesday. I celebrated the Hours together with a reading of the Gospel and the Liturgy of the Presanctified. After Vespers, I heard Confession from fifteen people, both men and women.

March 30. Thursday. I celebrated the Hours and Vespers with the Liturgy, and gave Communion to all.

March 31. Friday. I celebrated the Hours and Vespers with the Burial Service. In the evening I heard Confession from eight people of both genders.

The unordained clergy finished [learning] the hymns of the Passion of Christ. Accordingly, they now know everything that had been indicated in the instructions. Therefore, we have ceased assigning them problems and writing in their notebooks.

In the final days of this month, I finished a translation into Aleut of a sermon that I had written. I began this translation in January of this year. The title of this sermon is "An Indication of the Path to the Heavenly Kingdom." This text is arranged as described below.

> **Introduction.** Here it is shown that man has been created for God,[3] that there is no happiness or bliss on Earth, as the story of Solomon exemplifies, and that all of our happiness and bliss is in God. No one can draw near to God by himself, without Jesus Christ; therefore, the only road to the Heavenly Kingdom is the one road which Jesus Christ traveled while living on Earth.
>
> **Part One.** This section shows rather extensively how Christ lived on Earth and what He suffered for our salvation, based on the words of the Gospels.
>
> **Part Two.** This portion indicates what blessings Jesus Christ obtained for us by His death. Here is described the initial bliss of Adam and the evil which afflicted him and all of his descendants at the time of the Fall.
>
> After that I described the boons won for us by the teaching, life, death, resurrection, and ascension of Christ. Each topic is discussed separately. The future bliss is described, as much as this is possible.

Part Three. This part describes the very path that one must follow to obtain these blessings, namely the complete and unconditional imitation of Jesus Christ. It also shows how we should imitate Him. This portion is subdivided into three sections. The first explains the words "If anyone would come after me, let him take up his cross," and then demonstrates what is meant by renouncing oneself. The second section discusses the taking up of one's own cross. This rather lengthy section explains in detail those crosses—whether external or internal—which perfect and purify mankind. The third section explains what it means to follow after Jesus Christ. After that, a separate section demonstrates why we must, without fail, find our crosses and follow the path of the Savior.

Part Four. This portion discusses the following: (1) we cannot travel this path without the help of God, especially if we would try to place our faith in ourselves instead; (2) help comes in the form of the Holy Spirit, and it helps by giving Faith, Love, strength to bear the cross, Wisdom, Joy, Humility, and Prayer (each of these qualities is covered separately); (3) the means by which one may receive the Holy Spirit are: (a) pure living, or repentance, (b) a sensing of one's own internal poverty and a harkening to the summoning voice of God, (c) prayer, (d) constant selflessness, (e) reading of the Holy Scriptures, and (f) participation in the sacraments of the Church.

The Conclusion contains an exhortation and a statement of conviction. All of the thoughts in this composition[4] were based upon the book *Christian Philosophy*. The portion on "internal crosses" was taken from the seventh chapter of *The Mystery of the Cross*,[5] which is alluded to by the author of *Christian Philosophy*. This composition was written in such a way as to be comprehensible to everyone, or perhaps it would be better to say, as much as the impoverished Aleut language would allow.

April

April 1. Saturday. I celebrated all of the usual services. At the Liturgy, which concluded at 4:30, I gave Communion to all those who had confessed. In the evening I heard Confession from more than twenty men.

April 2. Easter. Matins began at twelve o'clock, and the Liturgy at eight o'clock. The Gospel was read in three languages during the Liturgy. The priest read it in Slavonic, the cantor read it in Russian, and the sacristan read it in Aleut. Communion was given to all those who had confessed.

April 3, 4, and 5. Monday, Tuesday, and Wednesday. There were services on all of these days, and the Liturgy was performed every day. On Wednesday, after Vespers, I performed a prayer service for those traveling by sea and prepared for a voyage.

April 6. Wednesday. I celebrated Matins and the Hours, and at a quarter to seven, I set out for the eastern region, in a company of three three-man baidarkas. At eight o'clock in the evening, we arrived at the island of Akun.

April 7. Friday. I celebrated Matins in a house, and the Hours in a tent. After the Hours, I chrismated six infants. After Vespers, I read from my sermon "An Indication of the Way to the Heavenly Kingdom," in the Aleut language. I read to the adult Aleuts who had gathered. I heard Confession from all fifty-eight inhabitants of this island.

April 8. Saturday. After Matins and a reading of the Rule of Prayer, I instructed the young people instead of hearing Confession from them, and heard Confession from ten girls. At seven o'clock, I celebrated the Liturgy (as ususal in a tent located on a site used previously). I gave Communion to all except three women (by necessity). After the Liturgy, I sacramentally blessed three marriages.

At eleven o'clock we continued on, and at 2:30 we arrived at the island of Avatanok. After a Vigil Service, I read from my sermon and heard Confession from all twenty-eight inhabitants of this island. Instead of hearing Confession from the young people, I instructed them.

April 9. Sunday. After a reading of the Rule of Prayer, I celebrated the Liturgy and gave Communion to all those who had confessed. I sacramentally blessed one marriage.

At 10:30 we set off again, and at 3:30 we arrived at the island of Tigalda. At the same time, I questioned in detail the Aleut Spiridon Smirennikov about a matter known to all. He fatally shot a nomadic[6] Aleut in self-defense. I placed upon him a penance of ten prostrations per day and he willingly accepted. After Matins, I chrismated four infants and heard Confession from all sixty-one local inhabitants. I instructed the young people.

April 10. Monday. After a reading of the Rule of Prayer, I celebrated the Liturgy and gave Communion to all, and sacramentally blessed two marriages.

At 8:45 we set out across Unimak Strait, and at 3:00 we put in at the tip of Unimak Island at the site of an old village.

April 11. Tuesday. At 4:30 in the morning we set out. We arrived at Shishaldinskoe village at 7:30 in the evening. (This village is also on Unimak.)

Before the Vigil Service I chrismated four infants, and after the Vigil Service I instructed, and then heard Confession from, twenty-eight people. I also instructed the young people.

Comment: At this location, not all of the inhabitants were at home.

April 12. Wednesday. After a reading of the Rule of Prayer, I celebrated the Liturgy and gave Communion to all. I instructed yet a few more.

We set out at six o'clock, and at twelve o'clock we stopped at Cape Vas'kin [at or near present-day Otter Point] because of the wind.

April 13. Thursday. Having set out at 4:30, we crossed Issanakh [Isanotski] Strait (the last one) at 9:00, and at 10:30 we arrived at the village of Morzhovskoe [Morzhovoi] on the Alaska Peninsula. Since the local men were gone from home, I decided to remain here until the 16th.

April 15. Saturday. I celebrated Vespers and Matins. After Matins, I gave due instruction, and then heard Confession from twenty-two adults and several male children. In the evening, all of the local men arrived here, but I left them until the next day.

April 16. Sunday. After a reading of the Rule of Prayer, I chrismated seven infants, celebrated the Liturgy, and gave Communion to all those who had confessed, and to the young people. I excepted two women (by necessity). In the afternoon, I invited all of the inhabitants and then read to them from my sermon. After Vespers and Matins, I heard Confession from nine men.

April 17. Monday. After a reading of the Rule of Prayer, I celebrated the Liturgy and gave Communion to those who had confessed. After the Lord's Prayer, I sacramentally blessed two marriages.

April 18. Tuesday. At five o'clock we set out on foot across a neck of land. At seven o'clock we seated ourselves in the baidarkas and left. At two o'clock in the afternoon, we encountered something of a headwind. At nine o'clock, while we were crossing the last bay before the village, the wind suddenly grew stronger. It grew so strong that the Communion table lying in my baidarka was blown off twice. (It weighed about twelve Russian pounds.) Therefore, we were forced to travel no small distance in the darkness, during a strong wind, moving among both submerged and exposed rocks. Furthermore, we had almost no opportunity to moor to the shore. At 10:30, we safely arrived at the village of Bel'kovskoe on the Alaska Peninsula. To our good fortune, there were no breakers, or else we would have undergone God knows what!

Comment: Not all the men were at home in this village either.

April 19. Wednesday. After celebrating Vespers and Matins, I taught the young people, and I invited all of the adults, including the inhabitants of Shishaldinskoe village who had not attended the visit to my house, and I read to them from my sermon. After that, I heard Confession from seventeen people from Unimak, and as many as twenty of the local young people.

April 20. Thursday. After a reading of the Rule of Prayer, I celebrated the Liturgy and gave Communion to all those who had confessed, and to the young people. After the celebration of the Vespers Service, I heard Confession from nine males and thirty-five females.

April 21. Friday. After a reading of the Rule of Prayer, I chrismated eight infants, celebrated the Liturgy, and gave Communion to all those who had confessed (except for three women by necessity). I gave Communion to those who had been chrismated as well.

After the Liturgy, I celebrated the customary prayer service for the health of His Majesty the Emperor.

Strong winds prevented our departure between this date and the second of May. We were going to set out on the 26th, but after covering about fifteen versts, we were forced to turn around because of a headwind.

April 22. Saturday. I celebrated the Vigil Service.

April 23. Sunday. I celebrated the Hours. The local men who had been gone arrived here on the night of the 26th.

April 27. Thursday. After the Vigil Service, I invited to my home those who had arrived. I also invited all the men who had been here. Then, I read to them from my sermon, and heard Confession from the men who had arrived.

April 28. Friday. After a reading of the Rule of Prayer, I celebrated the Liturgy and gave Communion to all those who had confessed, and to the three women who had not taken Communion previously (by necessity).

April 29. Saturday. I celebrated Vespers.

April 30. Sunday. I celebrated the Hours.

May

May 2. Tuesday. We set out at five o'clock. At 2:30 we arrived at the village of Pavlovskoe on the Alaska Peninsula. After Vespers and Matins, I instructed the young people. I invited all of the adults into a iurt, and then read to them from my sermon. After that, I heard Confession from thirty-five of the local inhabitants.

May 3. Wednesday. After a reading of the Rule of Prayer, I chrismated three infants, celebrated the Liturgy, and gave Communion to the young people. I heard Confession from everyone, except for two women (by necessity).

May 4. Thursday. At six o'clock in the morning we set out. At seven o'clock in the evening we put in at the island of Unga, without having reached a village.

May 5. Friday. We set out at 4:45. At 9:15, we arrived at the village of Unga, the farthest reach of my district.
  Comment: [apparently in another hand] N.B.
  At five o'clock I celebrated a Vigil Service. Afterwards, I instructed all of the minors, and heard Confession from twenty of them.

May 6. Saturday. I chrismated twelve infants, and then celebrated the Liturgy and gave Communion to all sixty young people. At 4:30, I celebrated Vespers and the Vigil Service. Afterwards, I invited all the adult local inhabitants who had turned up here, and read to them from my sermon, giving explanations. After this, I heard Confession from seventy-seven people, both men and women.

May 7. Sunday. After a reading of the Rule of Prayer, I celebrated the Liturgy and gave Communion to all those who had confessed and to two young people. I also sacramentally blessed five marriages. In the evening I celebrated a Vigil Service to St. John the Theologian.

May 8. Monday. I celebrated the Hours and a prayer service to St. John the Theologian. Afterwards, I sacramentally blessed two marriages using the rite for widows. In the evening I celebrated the Vigil Service to St. Nicholas.

May 9. Tuesday. I celebrated the Hours and a prayer service to St. Nicholas. In the evening, I celebrated Vespers and the Paschal Matins.

May 10. Wednesday. I celebrated the Paschal Hours and the Vigil Service in the evening.

May 11. Ascension Day. I celebrated the Liturgy with a Blessing of the Water. From the 8th through the 13th, a strong wind kept us from departing.

May 13. Saturday. At 11:30, we set out on our return course to Unalaska. At five o'clock, we put in at the tip of the island of Unga because we could not go any farther.
Comment: [in another hand, in the margin] N. B.

May 14. Sunday. In the morning, I celebrated Matins and the Hours together. It was impossible for us to continue, both on this day and the next.

May 16. Monday. Of all the inhabitants of the eastern region, from Akun to Unga, only four males had not attended Confession and Holy Communion. These four were those who had been away. Of those who had been absent, one arrived here on the previous day, among the [hunting] party Aleuts.[7] He very much wanted to take Communion. Therefore, beginning in the evening, I gave him the necessary counsel, and then in the morning I heard Confession and gave him Communion from the reserved sacrament.
Comment: [in another hand, in the margin] N. B.

After setting out at five o'clock, we put in at 7:30 at the same island, because of rough seas.

May 17. Wednesday. At 9:30, we set out, and at eleven o'clock at night we arrived at the village of Bel'kovskoe. From the 18th until the 22nd, a strong contrary wind prevented us from traveling.

May 20. Saturday. I celebrated the Vigil Service in a tent.

May 21. Trinity Sunday. I celebrated the Hours and Vespers with kneeling prayers. I celebrated a prayer service for the health of His Majesty the Emperor.

May 22. Monday. After performing the Hours, we set out at five o'clock and arrived at ten o'clock in the evening at Morzhovskoe village.

May 23. Tuesday. We set out at ten o'clock, portaging with the baidarkas and the cargo, and at 9:30 we arrived at Shishaldinskoe village (on Unimak).

May 24. Wednesday. Having set out at 6:30, we arrived at 7:45 in the evening at the tip of the island of Unimak, facing the strait. From the 25th until the 28th, the wind prevented us from traveling.

May 27. Saturday. In the evening, Vespers and Matins were sung.

May 28. Sunday. I celebrated the Hours, adding a prayer service for those traveling by sea. We set out across the strait at six o'clock, and while in fog, successfully and safely crossed four straits to arrive at the island of Akun at six o'clock in the evening.

May 29. Monday. The wind prevented us from traveling.

May 30. Tuesday. At 4:30, we set out and safely crossed three straits to arrive at eight o'clock in the evening at the harbor of Unalaska. Thus concluded my trip, the first of this year, and the fourth I had made to the eastern region. This trip lasted fifty-five days.[8]

And what can I say in conclusion? Nothing that I have not said before. First, that all the inhabitants received me with joy and even rapture, and listened to God's Word with a constant, unvarying zeal, as they always do. Second, the fruits of my teaching, or, it would be better to say, the fruits of the Word of God, are evident, even quite evident. Thirdly, I would say that no difficulty or danger in travel, even that which I experienced, could stop me from visiting the good inhabitants of these parts, people whom I would openly call exemplary sheep in the flock of Christ, such as are rare nowadays. Their virtue is proved by their zeal; their zealous and constant attention to my teachings, and their simple, heartfelt gratitude for this teaching provide the greatest satisfaction for me and are one of the greatest rewards to be found on Earth.

June

June 3. I celebrated the Vigil Service. At two o'clock, the ship *Urup* arrived from Sitka, bearing dispatches on board. To my surprise, only three decrees arrived from the Irkutsk Consistory. I received absolutely no reports of events in Russia.
　Comment: On the 1st, the vessel *Kvikhpak* arrived.

June 4. Sunday. I celebrated the Hours.

[June 6.] *Comment*: On the 6th, the *Kvikhpak* departed.

[June 7.] *Comment*: On the 7th, the *Urup* departed.

June 11. Sunday. I celebrated the Liturgy.

June 18. Sunday. I celebrated the Liturgy.

June 24. Saturday. I celebrated the Liturgy, and, in the evening, I celebrated the Vigil Service, adding a service for the 27th.

June 25. Sunday. I celebrated the Liturgy. Afterwards, I celebrated a prayer service for the health of His Majesty the Emperor.
　Comment: With a cannon salute.

June 29. Thursday. Since circumstances had prevented me from being here on Ascension Day, which is the festival of this church building, and since today was the dedication day of the church, the following celebration was held:
　After a Blessing of the Water, there was a procession of the cross around the church, accompanied by a ringing of the bells. After the Liturgy, there was a prayer service of thanksgiving with a ringing of the bells, and a proclamation of the "Many Years" for the imperial house, the Holy Synod, and Bishop Meletii, the well-remembered founder of this sanctuary, and a lover of the grandeur of God's House. During the Veneration of the Cross, I sprinkled Holy Water on the celebrants, and all the bells were rung three times. On the 15th, a large bell of 10 and 26/40 poods' weight had been raised into the belfry.

This month, I was occupied with preparing answers to the dispatches received from the Irkutsk Consistory and from the chief manager of the colonies. I also prepared other papers to be sent off.

July

July 1. Saturday. I celebrated the Liturgy and a prayer service for the health of the imperial family.

July 2. Sunday. I celebrated the Liturgy.

July 7. Friday. I traveled by baidarka to the nearby village of Imagninskoe. I gave Final Communion to two ill persons.

July 9. Sunday. I celebrated the Liturgy.

July 16. Sunday. I celebrated the Liturgy.

From the 17th through the 21st, services took place every day, but without the Liturgy, as a result of the fact that a woman who had arrived from Atka passed away.

July 22. Saturday. I celebrated the Liturgy and a prayer service, and I gave Communion to a woman who had prepared for the Sacraments, and who had taken Confession before the Liturgy.

July 23. Sunday. I celebrated the Liturgy.

July 27. Friday. I celebrated the Liturgy and a prayer service.

July 30. Sunday. I celebrated the Liturgy. Before the Liturgy, I celebrated a memorial service for the Tsar and his family.

This month, after preparing all of the papers to be sent off, I read the *Moscow Telegraph* for 1831.

August

August 1. Tuesday. I celebrated Matins with the customary kneeling prayers. After the Liturgy, I held a Blessing of the Water at the river, and there was a procession of the cross around the village, accompanied by a ringing of the bells.

[August 5.] *Comment*: Two vessels arrived on the 5th, the *Kvikhpak* and the *Aleut*.

August 6. Sunday. I celebrated the Liturgy and a prayer service.

August 13. Sunday. I celebrated the Liturgy and a prayer service.
Comment: On the 13th, the *Aleut* left for Sitka, and the sloop *Urup* arrived here.

August 15. Feast of the Dormition. I celebrated the Liturgy and a prayer service.
Comment: On the 15th, the *Urup* departed for Sitka.

August 16. Wednesday. I celebrated the Hours and a prayer service.

[Note on bottom margin, date not indicated.] *Note*: The manager of the Nushagak Redoubt in the north informed me by letter that last winter he traveled in the interior of the American continent, primarily on company business. While there, he baptized more than 150 nomadic people by their own desire, and without the inducement of presents.

August 20. Sunday. I celebrated the Liturgy.

August 22. Tuesday. I celebrated the Liturgy and a prayer service for the health of His Majesty the Emperor.
Comment: Accompanied by a cannon salute.

August 27. Sunday. I celebrated the Liturgy.

August 29. Tuesday. I celebrated the Liturgy. Before the Liturgy, I celebrated a memorial service.

August 30. Wednesday. I celebrated the Liturgy and a prayer service.

This month I read from the *Moscow Telegraph* again.

[Signed:] Priest of the Unalaska Ascension Church,
Ioann Veniaminov

NOTES

1. [Handwritten note in the left-hand margin reads: "Hasn't a book containing the court chant already been sent to him?" Right-hand margin contains "N.B." These marginal comments indicate that the manuscript copy used for the microfilm had been sent to Irkutsk. Veniaminov may have brought the documents back from Irkutsk when he returned to Russian America on one of several occasions.—Trans.]

2. [According to Paul Garret, personal communication, "Veniaminov is teaching here the minutiae of combining two liturgical layers."—Trans.]

3. [A footnote in another hand corrects the theology of this expression by stating that man was not created for God, but for his own happiness, which should coincide with God's. The note is too illegible for exact translation.—Trans.]

4. I intend to review this and finish it still more completely, and then to present it for the examination of my Bishop. Then, if it is approved, I will leave it and give it to the local inhabitants—either in handwritten form or, if possible, in printed form.

5. [In the margin, in another hand] This book has been forbidden. It is necessary to correct it in accordance with [two words illegible] by the regulations of the Holy Synod of 1825.

6. Along this chain and along the Alaska Peninsula, some nomadic Aleuts wander. They are both local Aleuts and Kodiak Aleuts. They ran off in former times, and they attack young Aleuts and try to lead them off to join the nomads as comrades.

7. The three others found it impossible to see me, and were very sorry for this fact, or so I am told.

8. Since my traveling time was about 200 hours, there and back, and assuming that I covered at least 7 $\frac{1}{2}$ versts in an hour, I covered as many as 1500 versts in total. It is very difficult to travel any great distance in a baidarka. It is necessary to sit fourteen, or sometimes sixteen hours, almost entirely without moving, and sometimes without getting out of the baidarka. Besides this discomfort, one often must spend the night in a deserted spot, and because it is cold and one cannot bring along many things, one must sometimes bear many discomforts, and even sometimes hunger.

JOURNAL NO. 11
September 1, 1833, to August 15, 1834

September

September 2. Saturday. I celebrated Matins and the Liturgy, adding a prayer service to the Lord God who has given me so many blessings.

September 3. Sunday. I celebrated the Vigil Service in the evening, and read the Hours at its appointed time.

September 5. Tuesday. I celebrated the Hours and a holy prayer service for the imperial family.

September 8. Friday. I celebrated the Vigil Service, beginning in the evening, and the Liturgy.

September 10. Sunday. I celebrated the Liturgy and a wedding service, a rite celebrated on behalf of the sacristan Ivan Balakshin, who entered into marriage with my permission.

September 14. The Exaltation of the Honorable and Life-Giving Cross. I celebrated the Vigil Service and the Liturgy.

September 17. Sunday. I celebrated Matins and the Hours.

September 24. Sunday. I celebrated Matins and the Liturgy. Before the Liturgy, I celebrated a memorial service for the imperial family.

This month I began work on composing a description of the local islands and read the newspaper *Severnaia pchela.*

October

October 1. Sunday. I celebrated Matins and the Liturgy, and I sacramentally blessed two marriages.

October 8. Sunday. I celebrated Matins and the Liturgy.

October 10. Tuesday. I celebrated Matins and the Liturgy, and a funeral service.

October 15. Sunday. I celebrated Matins and the Liturgy.

October 22. Sunday. I celebrated the Vigil Service, the Liturgy, and a prayer service in remembrance of the victories.

October 29. Sunday. I celebrated Matins, a memorial service for the Tsar, and the Liturgy.

This month, I once again worked on composing [the description of these islands]. Beginning on the 18th, I began to teach in school about the Law of God. I taught until noon on Wednesdays and Fridays.

November

November 5. Sunday. I celebrated Matins and the Liturgy.

November 8. Wednesday. I celebrated the Vigil Service, the Liturgy, and a prayer service.

November 12. Sunday. I celebrated Matins and the Liturgy.

November 19. Sunday. I celebrated Matins, a memorial service, the Liturgy, and a Vigil Service in the evening.

November 20. Monday. I celebrated the Liturgy and a prayer service.
Comment: With a cannon salute.

November 21. Tuesday. I celebrated the Vigil Service and the Liturgy.

November 25. Saturday. I celebrated the Vigil Service beginning in the evening.

November 26. Sunday. I celebrated the Liturgy and a prayer service to St. Innocent.

This month I finished composing my description of the local islands and began to compile a grammar of the Aleut langauge.
I taught about the Law of God on Wednesdays and Fridays at the school.

December

December 3. Sunday. I celebrated the Hours [and not the Liturgy] because of severely cold weather.

December 6. Wednesday. I celebrated the Vigil Service, the Liturgy, and a prayer service.
  Comment: With a cannon salute.

December 10. Sunday. I celebrated the Hours [and not the Liturgy] because of freezing weather.

December 17. Sunday. I celebrated the Hours [and not the Liturgy] because of freezing weather and high winds.

December 22. Friday. I celebrated the Hours for the pre-feast.

December 24. Sunday. I celebrated Matins and the Liturgy.

December 25. Christmas. I celebrated Matins, the Liturgy and a prayer service.
  Comment: With a cannon salute.

December 26. Christmas. I celebrated Matins and the Liturgy.

December 31. Sunday. I celebrated Matins and the Liturgy. Before the Liturgy, I celebrated a memorial service for the imperial family.

This month I continued my work on compiling the grammar and teaching the Law of God in the school.

1834
January

January 1. Monday. I celebrated Matins and the Liturgy. I also celebrated a prayer service.
  Comment: With a cannon salute.

January 5. Friday. I celebrated Matins, the Hours, and Vespers, together with the Liturgy and a Blessing of the Water.

January 6. Saturday. I celebrated Matins, the Liturgy, and a Blessing of the Water at the river.

January 7. Sunday. I celebrated Matins, the Liturgy, and a prayer service for the imperial family.

January 14. Sunday. I celebrated Matins and the Liturgy.

January 21. Sunday. I celebrated Matins and the Liturgy.

January 28. Sunday. I celebrated the Hours [and not the Liturgy] because of the extreme cold, and I celebrated a prayer service.

This month, I continued my work on the grammar and continued to teach the Law of God at the school on Wednesdays and Fridays.

February

February 2. Friday. I celebrated the Vigil Service and the Liturgy.

February 3. Saturday. I celebrated the Hours and a prayer service.

February 4. Sunday. I celebrated Matins, the Liturgy, and a prayer service.

February 8. Thursday. I celebrated a Vigil Service to St. Innocent, beginning in the evening.

February 9. Friday. I celebrated the Liturgy and a prayer service to St. Innocent.

February 11. Sunday. I celebrated Matins and the Liturgy.

February 18. Sunday. I celebrated Matins and the Liturgy.

February 24. Saturday. I celebrated Matins and the Liturgy.

February 25. Sunday. I celebrated Matins and the Liturgy. Before the Liturgy, I celebrated a memorial service for the imperial family.

This month, I finished compiling the Aleut grammar. I also taught the Law of God at the school on Wednesdays and Fridays, except on the 23rd and the 28th.

March

March 3. Saturday. Services began with Vespers and continued until the 12th of March.

March 4. Sunday. I celebrated Matins and the Liturgy.

March 7. Wednesday. I celebrated the Liturgy of the Presanctified.

March 9. Friday. After Matins, I duly instructed those preparing for the sacraments. Then, I celebrated the Liturgy of the Presanctified. Beginning at noon, I heard Confession from eighty-four Aleuts.

March 10. Saturday. I celebrated the Liturgy and gave Communion to all those who had confessed.

March 11. Sunday. I celebrated the Liturgy. Services concluded with Vespers.

March 17. Saturday. Services began with Vespers, and continued up until April 2.

March 18. Sunday. I celebrated the Liturgy.

March 23. Friday. After Matins, I duly instructed those preparing for the sacraments. Then, I celebrated the Liturgy of the Presanctified.

March 24. Saturday. I celebrated the Liturgy. In the afternoon, I heard Confession from fifty-five male Aleuts.

March 25. Annunciation Day. I celebrated the Vigil Service with kneeling prayers. Then, I celebrated the Liturgy and gave Communion to all those who had confessed.

March 28. Wednesday. I celebrated the Liturgy of the Presanctified.

March 30. Friday. After Matins, I instructed those preparing for the sacrament. Then, after the Liturgy of the Presanctified, I heard Confession from seventy-six Aleuts.

March 31. Saturday. I celebrated Matins together with a memorial service, and then I celebrated the Liturgy and gave Communion to all those who had confessed.

This month, I reviewed and expanded the sermon that I had written in Aleut entitled "An Indication of the Way to the Heavenly Kingdom," which I had mentioned in Journal No. 10 in the March section. After finishing this entirely, I began to compile a dictionary of the Aleut language with translations into Russian. I was at the school only twice, on the 13th and the 16th, and I gave general instruction on God's Commandments.

April

April 1. Sunday. I celebrated Matins, the Liturgy, and Vespers.

April 3. Wednesday. I celebrated Vespers and Matins with the Great Canon.

April 4. Thursday. I celebrated the Hours.

April 7. Saturday. I celebrated Matins with the Akathistos and the Liturgy.

April 8. Sunday. I celebrated the Liturgy and Vespers.

April 13. Friday. Services began with Vespers and continued until the trip.

April 14. Saturday. I celebrated the Liturgy.

April 15. Palm Sunday. I celebrated the Vigil Service and the Liturgy.

April 16, 17, and 18. Monday, Tuesday, and Wednesday. I celebrated with the customary readings of the Gospels and with the Liturgy of the Presanctified.

On Wednesday, after Matins, I instructed those preparing for the sacrament. After Vespers, I heard Confession from thirty Aleuts.

April 19. Thursday. I celebrated the Liturgy and gave Communion to those who had confessed.

April 20. Friday. Before the Veneration of the Shroud at Vespers, the sermon that I had composed was read. It discussed the theme that there is no path to the Heavenly Kingdom other than that which Jesus Christ himself took.

In the evening, I heard Confession from thirty-nine people, including all the pupils.

April 21. Saturday. During the Liturgy, which finished at 4:30, I gave Communion to all those who had confessed. In the evening, I heard Confession from more than twenty people of varying ranks, both male and female.

April 22. Easter Sunday. Matins began at twelve o'clock, and the Liturgy was celebrated at six o'clock. At the Liturgy, there was a Gospel reading in three languages: Slavonic, Russian, and Aleut. All those who had confessed took Holy Communion.

April 23. Easter Monday. I gave Communion to over forty people during the Liturgy.

April 24. Tuesday of Easter Week. I celebrated the Liturgy. After Vespers, I celebrated a prayer service for those traveling by water and began to prepare for the trip.

April 25. Wednesday of Easter Week. After the Liturgy, at nine o'clock, I set out from the harbor in a group of baidarkas, in order to visit the inhabitants of the western portion of my district. At four o'clock, we put in at a deserted spot because of rough seas that prevented us from traveling farther.

April 26, 27, and 28. Thursday, Friday, and Saturday of Easter Week. Remaining at the deserted spot, we celebrated Vespers together with Matins and the Hours. These days it was impossible to go on because of a westerly wind. At eleven o'clock on Saturday we set out, despite a strong and dangerous roughness in the sea. At two o'clock, we arrived at Makushin village, which has thirty-eight souls, both males and females. After Vespers, I duly instructed them and then heard Confession from twenty-nine persons.

April 29. Sunday. I chrismated two infants, celebrated the Liturgy in a tent pitched on a site used previously, and gave Communion to all those who had confessed and to the young people. After this, I taught again.

A great roughness at sea and strong winds prevented us from departing.

April 30. Monday. We set out at 5:30 in the morning and at 2:30, facing a growing headwind, we arrived at Koshiga village, which contains forty-three souls, both males and females. In the evening, Vespers and Matins were read.

At the beginning of this month, I compiled a dictionary of the Aleut language and collected as many as 1200 words from the conversational language.

May

May 1. Tuesday. After the Hours, I chrismated three infants and sacramentally blessed one marriage. After Vespers, I read from my sermon, and after the Vigil Service, I heard Confession from thirty-nine people.

May 2. Wednesday. I celebrated the Liturgy in a tent, and gave Communion to all the infants and to those who had confessed, except for two women (by necessity). At seven o'clock we set out, and at eleven o'clock we arrived at the village of Chernovskoe, which contains forty-four people of both genders. Before Vespers, I chrismated two infants and baptized a newborn baby. After the Vigil Service, I read from my sermon and heard Confession from thirty people, both men and women.

May 3. Thursday. After a reading of the Rule of Prayer, I celebrated the Liturgy and gave Communion to all those who had confessed and to all the young people.

May 4. Friday. A northerly wind prevented us from continuing our trip. Having set out at five o'clock, we arrived at nine o'clock at the village of Tulik on the island of Umnak. This village contains twenty-seven people, both males and females. After the Vigil Service, I read from my sermon and heard Confession from sixteen people.

May 6. Sunday. I celebrated the Liturgy and gave Communion to all those who had confessed and to the young people.

May 7 and 8. Monday and Tuesday. A westerly wind prevented us from traveling. In the morning on Tuesday, I celebrated a prayer service to St. John the Theologian.

May 9. Wednesday. Having set out at four o'clock in the morning, we arrived at six o'clock in the evening at the neck of land. We left the baidarkas there and proceeded on foot, arriving at 7:30 at the village of Recheshnoe. This village contains twenty-six people.

May 10. Thursday. I celebrated the Hours in the chapel. In the evening, I celebrated the Vigil Service to St. John the Theologian. After teaching the young people, I heard Confession from fourteen of them.

May 11. Friday. After chrismating six infants, I celebrated the Liturgy and gave Communion to all the young people and infants. After Vespers I read from my sermon before a gathering of all,[1] and after the Vigil Service to St. Nicholas (to whom the chapel here is dedicated), I heard Confession from forty-four people.

May 12. Saturday. After a reading of the Rule of Prayer, I celebrated the Liturgy and gave Communion to all those who had confessed (except for one woman by necessity). After the Liturgy, I celebrated a prayer service to St. Nicholas, and then, at the request of the inhabitants here, blessed the water at a stream. After the Vigil Service, in the evening, I taught some more. I taught about the means by which one may avoid sin, that is, by ceaselessly guiding one's own behavior by remembering that God is present among us, and so on.

May 13. Sunday. I celebrated the Hours and sacramentally blessed a marriage. A strong northerly wind prevented us from departing.

May 14. Monday. At four o'clock in the morning we set out on foot, and at seven o'clock we embarked in our baidarkas and began our return course to the Harbor. At three o'clock in the afternoon, a strong headwind forced us to put in at a deserted spot.

May 15. Tuesday. The same wind blew.

May 16. Wednesday. Having set out at 4:30 in the morning, we arrived at 3:30 in the afternoon at the village of Tulik.

May 17. Thursday. Having set out at 7:30, we arrived at the village of Koshiga at 5:30.

May 18. Friday. Having set out at four o'clock, at ten o'clock in the morning we arrived at the village of Makushin, but we could not go any farther because of very rough seas.

May 19. Saturday. We departed at 4:30, and we arrived at eleven o'clock at the village of Veselovskoe, which contains thirteen people of both genders. Since some of the inhabitants of this village had not attended Confession and Holy Communion because they had not been able to, I instructed them to some degree, and then heard Confession from them. I did not, however, administer the Holy Sacrament to six women because they had not prepared to receive it.

Having set out at one o'clock, we arrived at Harbor Village [Unalaska] at 4:45.

Thus concluded my journey, the fifth I had made to the western region, the first of this year. It had lasted twenty-five days.[2] It was the last that I was to make while serving in Unalaska.

May 20. Sunday. I celebrated the Liturgy, adding a prayer of thanksgiving to the Lord God who had blessed me with a joyful conclusion of my trip.

May 21. Monday. I celebrated the Liturgy and a prayer service for the imperial family.

May 27. Sunday. I celebrated the Liturgy.

Upon returning from the journey, I began to prepare papers for sending off.

June

June 3. Sunday. I celebrated the Liturgy.
  Comment: On the 3rd a ship arrived from Sitka. This ship brought the news that a new priest will be coming to Unalaska.

June 10. Sunday. I celebrated the Liturgy.

June 16. Saturday. The ship that arrived on this day brought a priest for Unalaska, Grigorii Ivanovich Golovin. It also brought papers from the Irkutsk Holy Consistory and from other places and persons.

June 17. Sunday. I celebrated the Liturgy.

June 24. Sunday. I celebrated the Liturgy.

June 25. Monday. I concelebrated the Liturgy and a prayer service.

June 29. Friday. I concelebrated the Liturgy.

During this month, I prepared my files for sending off.

July

July 1. Sunday. I concelebrated the Liturgy and a prayer service.

Beginning on the 2nd, I began to transfer to the priest Grigorii Golovin that church property which had been in my possession.

July 8. Sunday. I celebrated the Liturgy.

July 15. Sunday. The priest Grigorii celebrated the entire service and the Liturgy.

July 22. Sunday. I celebrated the Liturgy.

July 29. Sunday. I celebrated the Liturgy, adding a prayer service to the Lord God who had blessed me with a performance of a ten-year service in Unalaska that had been healthy, happy, and—if I be allowed to judge from what I see—not without its successes. On this day I gave my successor the entire church archive and written record.

August

August 1. Wednesday. At the invitation of my successor, I concelebrated the Liturgy and celebrated a Blessing of the Water at the river.

August 12. Sunday. I celebrated my last Liturgy on Unalaska.

August 14. Tuesday. During the Hours, which were celebrated by the priest Golovin, I gave a sermon composed by me for this occasion. I spoke before a gathering of all those living here. The text of the sermon was the following: "A little while and you will see me no more; again a little while, and you will see me" [John 16:16]. I spoke about the fact that we all will unquestionably meet again there in the blessed eternity. Immediately after this, I set out for the ship, accompanied by each and every Aleut. The sincere gratitude and sympathy of every Aleut were attested to by his tears. At one o'clock on the same day we weighed anchor and went to Sitka.

Thus concluded my stay on Unalaska, a stay that had lasted ten years and seventeen days: from July 29, 1824, to August 15, 1834.

NOTES

1. In the course of our trip, as many as forty men had joined themselves up with us. These men had been hunting sea otters. Every time I taught they tried to listen to my teaching.

2. The time spent on the trip out and back had been about eighty hours. If we assume a travel speed of 7 $\frac{1}{2}$ versts per hour, then the distance covered, there and back, was as many as 600 versts. In conclusion, I should state that I again could see everywhere the same zeal for hearing the Word of God as I had seen previously—the same joy, and also the same gratitude. Therefore, I fulfilled my duty with joy and counted it no hardship.

EXCERPT FROM THE JOURNAL OF THE
PRIEST IOANN VENIAMINOV
*Covering his stay in Sitka from August 23, 1834,
until May of 1836.[1]*

1. From my arrival in Sitka until recently, every Sunday and holiday had been given over to services with the Liturgy, except for the two middle days in Easter of 1835 and three Sundays in a row in June of last year. The first lapse was due to my illness, which prevented me from being in church. The second was due to a stay at the mineral springs, where I tried to cure my ailment.[2] Also, during Lent of both last year and this year, there were daily services with all of the Liturgies. Last year there were 544 people observing Lent; this year, there were 523. The latter number includes the chief manager of the colonies.

2. I baptized and said prayers over sixty-eight children. Also, six Koloshi, both men and women, were baptized. Funerals were observed for seventy-three decreased, of whom twenty-eight were given Final Communion. The others were not, for one of three reasons: they were too young, they belonged to a different denomination, or they could not.

3. Last year, I read only two sermons of my own composition.[3] This year I read ten during Lent, which is the time most suitable for instruction under local conditions.[4] Of these last sermons, the first four were written for people preparing for the sacraments, both men and women, people of various social levels; they were written using the very simplest language. These sermons were repeated more than seven times.

Comment: During Lent of last year, I instructed those who were fasting in the church after Vespers. I did this instead of giving such sermons as those listed above. I taught them extemporaneously using simple conversation. Therefore, absolutely no one took part in Holy Repentance and Communion with me without having been duly instructed.

4. From October 2, 1834, and until the present, I have taught the Catechism to the pupils of the local school. I am doing this at the suggestion of the chief manager of the colonies. I teach them twice a week, on Tuesday and Friday mornings, excluding, of course, holidays and all of Lent.

5. From May of last year until the middle of October, i.e., for the entire season of warm and suitable weather here, I taught the Divine Law to those boys who do not attend the school, and to the girls from the ages of nine to eighteen. I taught them every Sunday from 8:00 until 9:00, in the church. This group contained more than twenty-five people. I summoned them with a special ringing of the bells.

Beyond these, my immediate duties, I was occupied with the following:

A. After arriving in Sitka, I built a new clock for the belfry, working from September until the middle of November. I undertook this project at the request of the chief manager of the colonies.

B. At that time, I began to copy over the Aleut Gospel and edit the Aleut grammar which I had sent to the Academy of Sciences in the spring of 1835 through Captain (and now Vice-Admiral) Fedor Petrovich Lütke.[5]

C. I supplemented and corrected the description that I had written in Unalaska of the islands belonging to the Unalaska district.

D. I alphabetized and rewrote the Aleut-Russian glossary, which constitutes an indispensable part of the grammar which I sent at this time to the Academy of Sciences through the same Fedor Petrovich Lütke.

E. Beginning in September of 1835, in response to a written request dated August 29, 1835, from the former chief manager of the colonies, Ferdinand Petrovich Wrangel, member-correspondent of the Academy of Sciences, a request made in the name of the Academy, I took upon myself the task of keeping a meteorological journal, using the instruments provided by the Academy.

[Signed:] Priest of the Sitka Church,
Ioann Veniaminov

NOTES

1. [Note at top, apparently in a different hand, states: "Received August 1, 1836."]

2. Namely, rheumatism in my legs, a condition which I acquired specifically from traveling by baidarka in Unalaska.

3. The first was a speech of greeting upon my arrival in my present position. The second was given on Good Friday on the theme that no one can enter the Heavenly Kingdom without having suffered.

4. These sermons had the following topics:

(a) How human happiness will be obtained only in the Heavenly Kingdom. In order to obtain it, one must receive the Holy Spirit, and so on.

(b) The means for obtaining the Holy Spirit, especially repentance modeled on the Prodigal Son.

(c) The obligations of those confessing in preparation for the sacraments.

(d) What should be done both before and after Communion.

(e) For the First Sunday in Lent. How one ought to experience faith. Without fail, a believer must base everything else on faith.

(f) For the Second Sunday. The source of illness in an infirm person, and how he may be cured.

(g) For the Fourth Sunday. The name of God.

(h) For the Fifth Sunday. Natural man is not capable of understanding, desiring, or asking for that which he truly needs.

(i) For Palm Sunday. The inhabitants of Jerusalem are not the only men who have received Jesus Christ with mixed emotions; he has always been received that way everywhere.

(j) For Good Friday. What the path of Jesus Christ is, and how we must travel along it.

5. In the last year, I had the honor of receiving from him the gift of a copy of the account that he has published of the journey around the world of the ship *Seniavin*, in which, among other topics, he mentions me in an extremely flattering light.

TRAVEL JOURNAL OF THE
PRIEST IOANN VENIAMINOV
Kept during his journey to California and back,
July 1, 1836, to October 13, 1836.

Since company business required that a ship be sent to California this year and spend a considerable amount of time there, I saw this as a most suitable occasion to visit the inhabitants of Fort Ross, who belong to this church. I indicated this desire to the chief manager of the colonies and received his official permission to set out for Fort Ross on church business.

June 30. Tuesday. I celebrated the customary prayer service for those desiring to travel by sea and then moved onto the ship, taking the cantor with me. I placed Filipp Kashcvarov, the teacher of the local school, in charge of conducting services on holidays and baptizing newborn infants in cases of emergency.

July

July 1. Wednesday. We weighed anchor at five o'clock in the morning and began on a westerly course, but the lack of wind caused us to drop anchor and stand. This calm detained us until the following day.

July 2. Thursday. We weighed anchor at two o'clock. That night we left the bay, passing into the open sea. By the morning of the 3rd, we were already quite distant from any shore. Then, starting at noon, we received a tailwind, and the weather was good. This weather stayed with us all the way up until the 14th, and was so favorable that we raced across a distance of 200 to 300 versts per day. As usual, I suffered from seasickness for the first three days.

July 5. Sunday. I celebrated the Hours at sea.

July 12. Sunday. I celebrated the Hours. On this day we approached the latitude of Fort Ross, and if the wind had permitted, we would have anchored there on the 13th. The wind, however, became strong, and the weather turned cloudy, and so we stayed at sea until the 14th.

July 14. Tuesday. On this day the wind lessened, and we came within sight of Fort Ross. We contacted the people on shore.

July 15. Wednesday. We dropped anchor in Bodega Bay at three o'clock. This bay is located at thirty-eight degrees north latitude, thirty-five versts to the south of Fort Ross.

July 16. I set out on horseback and arrived at the Fort after five hours at a moderate gait.[1] Fort Ross is a rather small, but quite well-built settlement or village of twenty-four houses and some iurts for the Aleuts. It is surrounded by arable fields and forests. In the center of town, there stands a stockade with two watchtowers equipped with cannon. Within the stockade are found the chapel, the home of the office manager, the store, the barracks, and several apartments for prominent residents. Fort Ross contains 260 people: 154 male and 106 female. There are 120 Russians, 51 Creoles, 50 Kodiak Aleuts, and 39 baptized Indians. The chapel is constructed from wooden boards, as are almost all of the local houses. It has a small belfry and is rather plain; its entire interior decoration consists of two icons in silver rizas. It does not compare in wealth, then, to the chapel on the island of St. Paul, a chapel that belongs to the Unalaska church. On St. Paul, moreover, almost all of the residents are Aleut and there are no more than thirty families. The chapel at Fort Ross receives almost no income from its members or from those Russians who are occasional visitors.[2]

July 18. Saturday. Following custom, I celebrated the Vigil Service in the chapel.

July 19. Sunday. I chrismated eight infants, celebrated the Liturgy, and gave Communion to the newly chrismated.

July 22. Wednesday. I sacramentally blessed eight marriages.

July 24. Friday. I sacramentally blessed six marriages.

July 26. Sunday. I chrismated twelve young people together with two adult Indians. Then, I celebrated the Liturgy and gave Communion to the young people who had just been chrismated.

July 27. Monday. On this day, we began the daily cycle of services—Vespers, Matins, and the Hours—for those wishing to fast in preparation for the sacraments. After Vespers I instructed those preparing for the sacraments.

I came down with a cold on this day, and was so ill that I could not go out until the 29th.[3]

July 29. Wednesday. Feeling somewhat better, I went to the chapel before Vespers and instructed those preparing for the sacraments. For several days, including this one, I taught the children after Vespers, giving them an idea of the nature of God. I gathered them in the chapel and taught them the Lord's prayer with the cantor's help.

July 30. Thursday. Once again, I stayed in because of illness.

July 31. Friday. At the Hours and Vespers I instructed those preparing for the sacraments. After the Hours I heard Confession from twenty-seven people of both genders.

August

August 1. Saturday. After instructing and chrismating two adult Indians, I celebrated the Liturgy and gave Communion to all those who had confessed and to all who had been chrismated. After the Liturgy, I celebrated a Blessing of the Waters at a stream, and then there was a procession with the cross around the stockade.

After Vespers, I heard Confession from twenty-four young people of both genders.

August 2. Sunday. After instructing and chrismating the adult Indians together with seven children, I celebrated the Liturgy and gave Communion to all those who had confessed and to all those who had been chrismated.

August 3 and 4. Monday and Tuesday. During the Hours and Vespers, I instructed the people who had newly begun to prepare for the sacraments. After Vespers, I instructed the children.

August 5. Wednesday. I instructed during the Hours, and heard Confession both before and after Vespers. I heard Confession from forty-six people, both men and women.

August 6. Thursday. I celebrated the Liturgy and gave Communion to all those who had confessed.

August 7. Friday. At the Hours and Vespers I instructed those preparing for the sacraments.

August 8. Saturday. During the Hours I instructed together all those preparing for the sacraments, and then after the Hours I spoke through an interpreter to those Aleuts who did not know Russian. Before Vespers I heard Confession from thirty-seven people, both men and women.

August 9. Sunday. After the usual Rule of Prayer, I instructed and chrismated eight people. Then, I celebrated the Liturgy and gave Communion to all those who had confessed and to all those who had been chrismated.

August 10 and 11. Monday and Tuesday. At the Hours and Vespers, I instructed those preparing for the sacraments. On Monday, I instructed the children after Vespers.

August 12. Wednesday. At the Hours, I instructed everyone together, and then after the Hours I gave separate instruction to the Aleuts, using an interpreter. Before Vespers, I heard Confession from thirty-four people, both men and women.

Comment: On this date, our ship departed for the port of Monterey, from which it will continue on to the Port of San Francisco. It should sail to Sitka from there.

August 13. Thursday. I chrismated fifteen people of various ages and both genders and then celebrated the Liturgy and gave Communion to those who had confessed and to all those who had been chrismated.

August 14. Friday. I gave instruction during the Hours. Before Vespers, I heard Confession from twenty-four people.

August 15. Wednesday. I celebrated the Liturgy and gave Communion to all those who had confessed.

August 16. Sunday. I chrismated two people, one a Lutheran and the other a Catholic Indian woman. Then, I celebrated the Liturgy, gave Communion to those chrismated, and concluded services with Vespers.

August 19. Wednesday. Services begain again for those who had been away.

August 20. Thursday. I taught at the Hours and Vespers.

August 21. Friday. I taught at Matins and the Hours. After Vespers I heard Confession from three people.

August 22. Saturday. I celebrated the Liturgy and gave Communion to those who had confessed. Afterwards, I celebrated a prayer service for the Tsar.

August 23. Sunday. I celebrated the Hours. Our ship was supposed to leave for Sitka from the Port of San Francisco, which is approximately 150 versts distant from Fort Ross. In order to hasten my return to Sitka, therefore, I needed to travel to this port, and thereby cross the borders of Russia. We set out on horseback. In the evening we stopped for the night at a deserted spot already outside the borders of Russia.

August 24. Monday. At four o'clock in the afternoon we arrived at the first California mission that I was to see, San Rafael. Here, for the first time, I saw a Catholic church and met a monk of the Franciscan order. This monk—or padre, as they are usually called—had the name of Quijos. Our acquaintance was quite brief because we were hurrying to meet the ship.

August 25. Tuesday. We set out from San Rafael in a boat and traveled along San Francisco Bay, arriving at the port itself. Severe winds, however, forced us to make a dangerous landing at an abandoned island, where we spent the night.

August 26. Wednesday. We arrived at the port, but discovered that our ship had not yet returned from Monterey. We stopped at the ship of a foreigner, Bekkher [Becker], who had been at Fort Ross, and who had returned from Fort Ross together with us. He received us cordially.

August 27. Thursday. At nine o'clock our ship arrived in the harbor and I moved over onto it.

August 29 and 30. Saturday and Sunday. I celebrated the Hours on the ship.

September

September 2. Wednesday. It was clear from the circumstances that we would not be sailing until the middle of September. Therefore, I decided to visit the neighboring missions. On the evening of the 2nd the captain and I left in a launch, headed for the mission of San Jose (i.e., St. Joseph, the husband of Mary). This mission is located on the left-hand shore of southern San Francisco Bay.

September 3. Thursday. We arrived on land at four o'clock in the morning and set out for the mission on horses that belonged to that mission. At nine o'clock we reached the home of the padre, who received us very warmly. We stayed with him until Monday, or until Sunday by their calendar, and shared his table. I would say that this priest and monk, Jose Maria de Jesus Gonzalez, is the most educated and kindly of any of his brethren in all of California. At this mission I observed the rites of burial and infant baptism, attended Mass four times, and saw all of the [Roman Catholic] religious implements and how they differ from ours. The priest and I conversed about religious matters.[4]

We saw all of the public institutions of the mission, its workshops and its beautiful fruit orchards. In short, the padre, out of favorable feelings toward me, omitted almost nothing from what he showed me. This mission and the one most nearby are the only two missions that still exercise a right carried over from earlier times: they own and command the Indians as slaves. The Mexican government has taken the Indians away from the other missions and given them the rights of citizenship, in other words, the right to be idle. The San Jose mission, though, is very well run and the Indians are very satisfied with the present padre, who feeds and clothes them quite adequately.[5] The mission has a primary school which serves as many as fifty Creole and Indian boys.

September 7. Monday. We set out at three o'clock for the next mission, Santa Clara. Padre Gonzalez himself accompanied me all the way to the mission. At Santa Clara, Padre Jesus Moreno received us, again with great cordiality. We also met another priest, who was not a monk.

September 8. Tuesday. Here I saw three priests concelebrate the Liturgy at the same time, but at different altars and, of course, in a whisper; in general, these priests always whisper during the Liturgy except on certain holidays.

September 9. Wednesday. We set out to return to the ship and arrived there safely on the night of the 11th. Before doing anything else, I attended the Liturgy at the San Francisco Mission. While in California, then, I managed to visit four missions and meet five priests.

The missions are all constructed quite uniformly according to a single plan: the central building, called the mission, is a large, quadrilateral, one-story building with a door in the center. The building is constructed of unfired brick and roofed with tile. One side is designated for the church, another for the padre, and the others for storerooms and workshops. Several blockhouses made of the same material extend out next to the mission; these are for the Indians. The married and single Indians are housed separately.

September 13. Sunday. I celebrated the Hours.

September 14. Monday. I celebrated the Hours. At seven o'clock in the morning, we weighed anchor and headed for Sitka. At four o'clock on October 13th, we dropped anchor in Sitka after a voyage that we could consider fortunate, given the time of year.[6]

Upon returning to Sitka, I received papers. Among these was a notice that the Academy of Sciences, having received my Aleut Grammar (which I had sent to the Academy) had awarded it the publication portion of the Demidov Prize [an annual prize granted for outstanding work recognized and published by the Academy of Sciences].

To my great surprise, however, I received no papers whatsoever from the Irkutsk Consistory except for a decree dated August 3, 1835.

Over the course of this year, besides visiting the inhabitants of Fort Ross, I was occupied with the following:

1. The appointed services and the Liturgy were celebrated on all Sundays and holidays, and on eighteen weekdays as well. During Lent, we celebrated daily services with all the Liturgies except for on the sixth Sunday, in accordance with internal regulations of the Church. Those preparing for the Lenten sacraments numbered 550 in 1837. Of these, only four did not attend Holy Communion. In all, 745 people were heard in Confession and given Communion; this number includes the inhabitants of Fort Ross.

2. This year thirty-seven children were baptized. We also baptized three adult Koloshi and four of the nomadic American inhabitants of the shores of Bering Strait who happened to come here.[7]

During the baptism of these nomads, I acted as I had, and as I had instructed, at Nushagak, i.e., at the baptism I did not give or allow the godfathers to give clothes or anything else to the newly baptized, not even so much as a shirt. The only gift I allowed was crosses. I did this so that neither these nomads nor their countrymen would undergo Holy Baptism for any ulterior motives.

We performed twenty-two marriages and fifty funerals. Of the deceased, eleven had been given Final Communion. The others were too young, had difficulties connected with their Confessions, or could not possibly take Final Communion.

3. I delivered five sermons of my own composition[8] and four others that I had written the previous year for those preparing for the sacraments. The latter sermons I revised and delivered more than fifteen times, i.e., to every person preparing for the sacraments.

4. At the school, I continued to teach the Law of God. I taught twice per week, except during Lent and during my absence.

5. From May until June, i.e., up until my departure, I taught the Divine Law and general morals at the church before the Liturgy, just as I had done the year before. I taught the children who did not attend the school, and especially the girls from seven to seventeen years in age. As many as thirty people would gather.

Besides these, my direct duties, I worked at the following outside activities:

a. From the very first day of my return from California, i.e., from October 15, up until the 1st of April, I was continuously involved in daily work on checking my translations into Aleut: the Catechism, the Gospel of Matthew, and a sermon that I had written entitled "A Brief Indication of the Way to the Heavenly Kingdom." I checked these texts strictly, correcting them for grammar.[9] I also wrote them over. Now, I dare to say that these translations are as correct and as clear and flawless as possible, given the present state of the Aleut language.

b. I continued to keep meteorological records using instruments sent by the Academy [of Sciences]. I had received a written request to do this from Corresponding Member F. Wrangel. I sent these records to the Academy.

Signed, Hierei Ioann Veniaminov,
of the Sitka Archangel Church
April 29, 1837, Sitka.

NOTES

1. I must admit that the healthful air, the pure blue sky, the geographical position, and the native vegetation all immediately strike and captivate one who was born north of 52 degrees and has never been south of that latitude, especially one who has lived on Unalaska and Sitka.

2. I have learned that in 1823, the officers and crew of the frigate *Kreiser* donated a considerable sum toward the building of a church that was to be at Fort Ross. There can never be a church here, however, for this location is not Russian, but rather belongs to California. How has this money been used? The answer is unknown.

3. It is so easy to catch a cold here that even the native residents fall ill almost every year. This propensity is due to the quick shifts from hot to cold found here. These shifts may take the temperature from 28 to 8 degrees in approximately two hours. Sometimes the change is even greater. Other times one may encounter unbearable heat while up in the mountains and then come down out of the hills to face a fog and temperatures of as low as 7 degrees.

4. This marked the first occasion on which I have ever used the Latin language, in which I explained my ideas to the best of my abilities.

5. Soon after our visit, the Californians seceded from Mexico, and then drove out all of the Mexicans. There were so few native-born Californians, however, that there was almost no one to fill the unofficial ranks in the government and to occupy military and civilian positions, besides the Indians.

6. We saw smoke while we were at sea. At the time we were more than 800 versts from the nearest shore, which was Columbia. This smoke was carried along by the wind and was fairly thick. It continued for seven hours straight. On the next day the wind shifted, but the smell of smoke continued for twenty more hours, although it grew weaker. The smell resembled that of burning grass or tundra.

7. [Editor's note: Refers to four of the five natives from the St. Michael/Golovnin Bay area whom the Russian-American Company seized and brought to Sitka late in the summer of 1836 in retaliation for the native attack upon St. Michael redoubt in August of 1835. All five became infected with smallpox and one died of the disease, but the other four were baptized by Veniaminov in April of 1837. The company returned them to their homeland in the summer of 1837 hoping that, by their tales of what they had seen of Russian power, they would deter their countrymen from future attacks on the Russian posts. Records of the Russian-American Company, *Correspondence of the Governors General, Communications Sent*, vol. 14, no. 320, f. 363v-367, 14 June 1837.]

8. [The new sermons were:]

a. For the Sunday of Orthodoxy [First Sunday of Lent]. One should not doubt the truths of the faith, but rather be sufficiently convinced of the faith's true grounding.

b. For the Second Sunday. Faith is beneficial not only to those who have it, but also to those whom believers are moved to help.

c. For the Third Sunday. We have no other path to take but that of suffering and bearing the cross.

d. For the Fifth Sunday. Every man who has not been born again acts with the spirit of vanity.

e. For Good Friday. On Love.

9. The Aleut grammar rules which I had compiled allowed me to see new aspects of the language. I myself was surprised to see how I had sometimes pronounced words, or written them in the translation, in forms corresponding to their direct meaning, but incorrect because of my misunderstanding of their roots. Now, however, to check this work on a larger scale, I am sending the translations to the priest on Atka, Iakov Netsvetov, who knows both languages perfectly. He has stated his desire to examine these documents and to add special explanations and footnotes to make them comprehensible to the inhabitants of Atka as well; the Atkans use a different dialect of the same language. I asked him to attest to the accuracy of both my translations and his notes by signing them in his own hand.

AFTERWORD
A story about Father Veniaminov
by Father Ismail Gromoff.[1]

Did he think of his children, our father, in his great age and blindness? Did he remember us living here on our green island?

Ivan Veniaminov was born in Russia in 1797. His father died when he was young, and he was raised by his uncle. When he was nine he went to the church school where he stayed for eleven years.

In 1817 Veniaminov married. In 1821 he became a priest. Why did he come to Unalaska?

In 1823 the church asked someone to move to Alaska. No one would do it. Then Veniaminov heard about the Aleuts and how they were devoted to prayer and to the Word of God.

With his mother, his wife, his son, and his brother he left Russia in 1823. He reached Unalaska in 1824. His first work was to rebuild the church. He taught the Aleuts to build and carve and together they made a great church to the glory of the Ascension of the Lord. This church was opened 150 years ago.

He traveled in baidarkas to many villages many times. We know that he went to Akun at least four times.

He learned the Aleut language. He showed us how to write our language. He recorded our early ways so that we would remember them. After living here ten years he left us.

He went to Sitka. He became Bishop. He taught other priests; Netzvetov and Shaishnikoff were among the most important. He returned to Russia. He became Metropolitan.

He helped us when he was here and after he left us.

The last day of March 1879 was cold at Unalaska. The rain and the wind blew around the church and the town. We did not know it then but Veniaminov had fallen asleep in God that morning.

Did he think of his children, our father, in his great age and blindness? Did he remember us living here on our green island? We would never forget him.

---

1. Reprinted from *Aleut for Beginners*, Aleut Language Instruction, Unalaska City School, 1975, pp. 33-34.

INDEX

Academy of Sciences, 91, 198, 207, 208
Aglegmiut, 107, 162
Aian, xxxii
Ainus, xxxii
Aiugnin, Tukulan, toion, xxiii
Akun Island (Akun), xxiii, xxiv, xxv, xxvi, xxviii, xxx, xxxi, 74, 75, 76, 77, 78, 82, 102, 103, 111, 112, 113, 129, 130, 131, 140, 145, 175, 179, 180, 211
Akun Strait (Pass), 113, 130, 140, 145
Akutan Island (Akutan), xxiii, 75, 78, 103, 112, 113, 126, 131, 146
Akutan Pass (Strait), 112, 113, 130, 131, 140, 145, 146
Alaska Peninsula, xiv, xxviii, 51, 52, 53, 54, 62, 80, 82, 85, 99, 100, 103, 141, 148, 176, 177, 178, 184
Alaska State Historical Library, xiii
Alaska Territorial Museum, xxxi
Alaska, Alaskans, xv, xxvii, xxxi, 211
Aleksandr Nevskii Monastery, 16
Aleut Orthodox, xxiii, xxiv
Aleut(s): general, vii, x, xiv, xv, xvi, xvii, xix, xx, xxiii, xxiv, xxv, xxviii, xxix, xxxi, xxxii, 16, 18, 22, 23, 24, 25, 26, 27, 28, 30, 35, 36, 49, 50, 51, 52, 55, 56, 58, 59, 64, 66, 67, 71, 72, 73, 74, 78, 79, 82, 87, 88, 95, 96, 97, 113, 116, 118, 175, 179, 184, 189, 190, 195, 202, 204, 211; alphabet, xxviii, 152; catechism, xxix; culture, xxvii; faith, xxvi; gospel, 159, 198; grammar, 207, 210; history, vii, xii, xvi, xxvii; intellectual culture, xxvii; language(s), vii, ix, xvi, xx, xxvii, xxviii, xxix, xxx, xxxi, 18, 63, 64, 69, 73, 96, 111, 130, 133, 140, 150, 151, 152, 153, 157, 160, 161, 173, 174, 175, 186, 188, 189, 190, 191, 198, 208, 211; literature, xxvii; wars, xxv; words, 4, 7, 8
Aleut, 182, 183
Aleut-Russian glossary, 198
Aleutian Island(s) (Aleutians), vii, xiv, xv, xviii, xix, xx, xxi, xxii, xxiii, xxiv, xxv, xxvi, xxvii, xxxi, xxxii
Alexander Nikolaevich, Grand Duke, 58
Alexander Pavlovich (Alexander I), Emperor, 61, 64
Alexandra Mikhailovna, Grand Princess, 161
Algamalinaq (Mikhail), tion, xxiii
Amaknak (Amakhnak), island of, 28, 111
Amchitka, island of, xxi
America, American, 3, 49, 183, 207

Amur, xxxii
Annenkov, Mikhail Dmitrievich, 16
Arctic, xxvi, xxxi
Artel'novskoe, village of, 75, 77, 103, 131
Ascension Church, 49, 81, 104, 125, 147, 165, 183
Asia, Asians, xx, xxi, xxii, xxiii, xxiv, xxv, xxvi, xxxi, xxxii
Atka (Atkha), xv, xx, xix, xxxii, 182, 210
Atkan Aleut, xx, xxx, 210
Attu, xxi
Avatanak (Avatanok) Strait, 77, 130, 131, 140
Avatanak (Avatanok), island of, 77, 103, 130, 131, 175
Avatanak, village of, 130
Awadax, island of, xxi

Baikal, 37, 47
Balakshin, Ivan, 185
Balamutov, Iuda, 50, 56
Baranof Island, 3
Basinskaia Bay, 146
Beaver Inlet. See Bobrovskii Bay
Beaver, village of. See Bobrovskii, village of
Bekkher [Becker], 205
Belkofski, village of, xiv. See also Bel'kovskoe, village of
Bel'kovskoe, village of, 52, 53, 56, 99, 142, 144, 177, 180
Bering Island, xxi
Bering Sea, xiv, xviii, xxxii
Bering Strait, 61, 207
Berkh, 61
Billings/Sarychev expedition, xviii
Biorka. See Borkinskoe
Blagonamerennyi, xviii

Bobrovskii Bay, 55, 90, 114
Bobrovskii, village of, 90, 151
Bodega Bay, 202
Bonaparte, 11
Borkinskoe, village of, 90, 150
Bronevskii, Vladimir Bogdanovich, 23
Buffon, Comte de, 89, 94
Buldakov, 34, 37, 47
Buldir, island of, xxi
Butenin, Ivan Petrovich, 16

Calais, Jean, 11
California, xiii, xiv, xxx, 201, 205, 206, 208, 209
Californian Indians, xiv
Candillac, 13
Cape Kalekhta, 146
Cape Konstantin, 162
Cape Kovrizhka. See Ermoshak
Cape Lanin [Lapin], 141
Cape Tochil'nyi [Tachilni], 141
Cape Vas'kin [at or near Otter Point], 176
Captain's Harbor [Unalaska Bay], 89, 124
Chateaubriand, x, 20
Chernofski. See Chernovskoe
Chernovskoe, village of, 30, 33, 88, 121, 158, 159, 192
Chichagov, 161, 164
Chichinev, Creole Zakharii, xxx, 139, 157
Chistiakov, Lieutenant Peter Egorovich, 47
Christianity, xxiv, xxvi
Chukchi, xxxii
Chuloshnikov, Ivan (Saguakh), xxiii
Cold Bay. See Morozovskaia Bay
Columbia, 209

Creole(s), xxviii, xxix, 4, 16, 26, 50, 58, 59, 72, 83, 97, 108, 162, 202, 206
Cyrillic, xx

Deer Island. *See* Olenii Island
Delarof Harbor, 49, 54, 55, 98
Demidov Prize, 207
Derbin (Derbenskoi) Strait, 77, 130, 140
Dmitriev, Ivan Ivanovich, 62
Dolgoi Island, 52
Dorofeev, Iakov, 167
Douzetems, 15, 72

Eastern Orthodox(y), xvii, xix, xxii, xxiii, xxvi
Egorkovskoi, village of, 36, 87, 122
Ekaterina Mikhailovna, Grand Princess, 104
Elena Pavlovna, Grand Princess, 47
Ermoshak, 29, 30, 33
Euler (Eiler), Leonhard, 91
Eurasia, Eurasians, xv, xxvi, xxxi
Europe, European, xxiii, xxxi, 40
Evenks (Tungus), xxxii
Evens (Lamuts), xxxii

Filaret, Bishop, 155, 156
Finliandiia, 85
Fort Ross, xiii, xiv, xxx, 201, 202, 205, 207, 209
Fox Island(s), xxxiii, 16, 103
Fox-Aleut, xxx, 42, 139
Franciscan order, 205

Gamalei, 72
Garret, Paul, 184
Gideon, hieromonk, xviii, xix, xx, xxvi
Glotov, Aleut Ivan Stepanovich, toion, xxi, xxii, xxiii, xxvi

Glotov, S., xx
Golovin, Fr. Grigorii Ivanovich, xx, 194, 195
Golovnin Bay, 209
Golovnin, 80, 85, 86, 104
Golovskoe, village of, 78, 131
Gomziakov, [Stepan], 82
Gonzalez, Jose Maria de Jesus, 206
Greek, xv
Grekodeliarovskii, village of. *See* Unga
Gromoff, Father Ismail, 211

Harbor Village (Harbor), 33, 55, 77, 78, 89, 91, 103, 114, 124, 140, 146, 151, 160, 193. *See also* Unalaska

Ikatak, 145
Ikatan Peninsula, 148
Ikogmiut, xxxii
Ilarii, Father, 16
Iliuliuk. *See* Unalaska
Imagnee. *See* Imagninskoe
Imagninskoe, village of, 103, 182
Imperial National Anthem, 26
Indian(s), 202, 203, 205, 206, 207, 209
Innokentii, Biship, x, xxxii. *See also* Veniaminov, Ioann
Irinii, Right Reverend, 161
Irkutsk (Holy) Consistory, 17, 81, 160, 168, 181, 182, 194, 207
Irkutsk Theological Seminary, xx, xxvii
Irkutsk, x, xiii, xx, xxv, xxvii, xxxi, xxxii, 5, 19, 34, 41, 42, 49, 184
Isannakhskii [Isanotski] Strait, 52, 100, 101, 145, 176
Issanakh, 145
Ivanov, Fr. Mikhail, xviii

Juneau, xiii, xxxi

Kalekhta, village of, 89, 150
Kalekhtinskaia [Kalekta] Bay, 146
Kallistos, Bishop, ix, xi
Kamchadal(s), xx, xxii, xxiv, xxxii
Kamchatka, xviii, xxi, xxii, xxiii,
   xxiv, xxxii, 61, 79
Kamchatkan sea, 57
Karamzin, 7, 62, 91, 92, 93, 94
Karelia, xxiv
Kashega. *See* Koshiga
Kashevarov, Filipp, 201
Kashevarov, Fr. Andrew, xxxi
Kempis, Thomas á, x, 4
Kenai, xxxii
Kettle Cape. *See* Kotel'novskii Cape
Khlebnikov, Kirill Timofeevich, 16,
   34, 104
Khomiakov, Aleksei, x
Kiska, island of, xxi
Kodiak Aleuts, 184, 202
Kodiak Island (Kodiak), xviii, xix,
   xxi, xxiv, xxvi, xxxii, 49, 82.
Kolosh(i), 5, 12, 16, 125, 197, 207
Konevskii monastery, xxiv
Konstantin Nikolaevich, Grand Duke,
   104
Konstantin, 3, 34, 47
Koshiga, village of, 30, 33, 88, 121,
   124, 158, 159, 191, 193
Kotel'nyi (Kotel'novskii) Cape, 122,
   159
Kozhevnikova, Irina, 87
Krasheninnikov, S. P., 41
Krata [or Kresta?], 145
Kreiser, 14, 16, 209
Kriukov, Creole Stefan, 28, 105, 127
Krylov, 62
Kurile Islands, xxxii
Kuskokwim River, xv, xx

Kuziakin, Daniel (Daniil), xxix, 49,
   116, 133, 139
Kvikhpak, 181, 182

Lamuts (Evens), xxxii
Latin, xxi, 4
Lazarev, Mikhail Petrovich, 16
Leipzig, 40
Library of Congress, xiii
Little Sitkin, island of, xxi
Lukanin, Nikolai, xxiii, xxv
Lütke, Captain Lieutenant Fedor
   Pavlovich, 60, 198

Makarii, hieromonk, xviii, xxiii, xxiv,
   xxv, xxvii
Makushin Bay, 89, 124, 160
Makushin, village of, 29, 88, 120,
   124, 157, 160, 191, 193
Makuzhan, toion, xxi, xxii
Maria Fedorovna, dowager Empress,
   129
Maria Mikhailovna, Grand Princess,
   47
Mason, John, 13
Merkul'ev, Russian, 17
Metropolitan of Moscow, xxxi, xxxii
Mexico, Mexican(s), 206, 209
Mikhail, Bishop of Irkutsk,
   Nerchinsk, and Yakutsk, 5, 18, 21,
   25, 33, 39, 40, 63, 81, 86-87, 92,
   105, 115, 124, 133, 146, 160, 169
Mikhailovskii. *See* St. Michael
Moller, 61, 62, 80, 85, 86
Monterey, port of, 204
Morekhod, 161
Moreno, Padre Jesus, 206
Morozovskaia Bay, 141, 144
Morzhovoi (Morzhovskoe,
   Morzhevskoe), village of, xiv, 52,
   100, 141, 144, 176, 180

Morzhovoi (Morzhovskii, Morzhevskii) Bay, 52, 100, 144
Moscow Patriarchate, xxxii
Moscow, 62
Mousalimas, S. A., xiii, xxxii
Murav'ev, Matvei Ivanovich, 3, 16
Murav'ev, Pavel Matveevich, 16
Mushkal (Mushkalyax). *See* Glotov, Aleut Ivan Stepanovich

Native Eastern Orthodox, xix
Native Siberian, xxxi
Near Islands, xxi
Nerpechii, island of, 51, 99
Netsvetov, Fr. Iakov, xv, xix, xx, 210
Netsvetov, Vasil'evich, Egor, xix, xx
Netsvetova, Maria, nee Alekseeva, xix, xx
Neverov, 11
Nicholas Pavlovich (Nicholas I), Emperor, 58, 64, 66, 75, 79
Nikolski. *See* Recheshnoe
Nosovskoi, village of, 102, 105, 140
Novo-Aleksandrovsk. *See* Nushagak
Novo-Arkhangel'sk. *See* Sitka
Nushagak (Novo-Aleksandrovsk, Nushagak Redoubt), xiv, xxxii, 104, 107, 109, 162, 183, 207
Nushagak River, 107, 109, 162

Okhotsk, 149
Okhotsk, xiii, xviii, xix, xxiii, xxv, 3, 161
Old Believers, 136
Olenii Island, 53
Ol'ga Nikolaevna, Grand Princess, 5
Orthodox Christianity, xxiv
Orthodox(y), x, xi, xx, xxvi, xxvii, xxxi
Oxford University, xi

Pacific, xviii
Pan'kov, Aleut Sergei Dmitrievich, toion, xxii, xxiii, xxv
Pan'kov, Ivan, toion, vii, xxv, xxvi, xxviii, xxix, 44, 76, 77, 78, 111, 113, 130, 155
Pan'kov, Russian Dmitrii, xxii
Pan'kov, Semen, 159
Pavlof, village of, xiv, xxviii. *See also* Pavlovskoe, village of
Pavlovskaia Bay, 142
Pavlovskoe, village of, 51, 54, 99, 143, 178
Pembroke College, xi
Persia, 104
Pestriakovskoe, village of, 33
Petelin, S. S., 42
Petersburg Empire, xxvii
Petersburg, xx, xxiii, xxiv, xxv, xxxi. *See also* St. Petersburg
Petropavlovsk, xxii
Petrivelli, Alice, vii
Pogromni. *See* Pogromskoe
Pogromskoe, village of, 101, 140
Polutov, Izosim, xxiii
Pomo, xiv
Popachev, Yelisei, toion, xxiii
Popof Island. *See* Popovskii
Popov, Aleut Leontii Vasil'evich, xxi, xxii
Popovskii Island, 51
Pribilof Islands (Pribilofs), xiv, xx, xxxii, 35, 57, 60, 61, 85, 109, 162, 163
Prokof'ev, Mikhail Vasiliev, 16
Prokof'eva, Paraskeva Petrova, 16

Recheshnoe, village of, xiv, xxvi, xxix, 32, 33, 36, 86, 113, 122, 159, 192

Rezanov, "General," 105
Riurik, 17, 18, 19, 20, 129
Robertson, 19
Roman Catholic(s), xiv, 136, 204, 205, 206
Roman Catholicism, x
Russia: general, xiv, xxx, 47, 81, 85, 86, 104, 146, 149, 181, 205, 211; easternmost regions, xxxi; Eurasian, xxxi; Pacific regions, xxv
Russian America, 184
Russian Orthodox Church, xxiv
Russian Orthodox(y), xx, xxi, xxv, xxvi
Russian(s), general: xxiii, xxv, xxviii, xxix, xxxii, 3, 26, 58, 59, 60, 61, 80, 82, 96, 97, 100, 101, 105, 107, 108, 109, 119, 126, 134, 137, 162, 177, 202, 204, 209; language, xxiii, xxviii, xxx, 3, 12, 16, 18, 35, 45, 51, 63, 64, 69, 73, 82, 139, 153, 157, 161, 175, 189, 190
Russian-Aleut, xx, xxxi
Russian-American Company, xxvii, 16, 18, 29, 35, 51, 52, 56, 57, 80, 83, 85, 86, 105, 129, 146, 161, 209

Saguakh (Ivan Chuloshnikov), xxiii
St. Cyril, xv
St. George Island (St. George), xx, 35, 57, 59, 104, 109, 110, 163, 164
St. Methodius, xvi
St. Michael (Mikhailovskii redoubt), xxxii, 209
St. Paul Island (St. Paul), 35, 57, 58, 59, 104, 109, 163, 202
St. Petersburg, 10, 23
Salamatov, Fr. Lavrentii, xx
San Francisco Bay, xiv, xxx, 205
San Francisco Mission, 206

San Francisco, Port of, 204, 205
San Francisco, xxxi
San Jose, Mission, 205, 206
San Rafael, 205
Santa Clara, 206
Sarychev, G., xxiii
Sechkinskoe, settlement of, 90, 114, 151
Sedanka Island. *See* Spirkin Island
Segula, island of, xxi
Seniavin, 60, 61, 199
Sevidovskii Island, 33
Shaiashnikov, Fr. Innokentii, xx
Shashuk, toion, xx-xxi
Shelikhov, Grigorii, xxvii
Shelikhov-Golikov Company, xxv, xxvi
Shemya, island of, xxi
Shishaldinskoe, village of, 101, 102, 140, 176, 177, 180
Shishkov, 11
Siberia, Siberian, xxxi, xxxii
Simpson, Sir George, x
Sisaguk, village of. *See* Shishaldinskoe
Sitka Archangel Church, 208
Sitka (Novo-Arkhangel'sk), ix, xiii, xiv, xviii, xx, xxvii, xxx, xxxi, xxxii, 3, 17, 19, 34, 40, 62, 81, 85, 86, 104, 111, 129, 146, 149, 181, 183, 194, 195, 197, 198, 204, 205, 207, 209, 211
Sivtsov, Fr. Vasilii, xviii
Slava Rossii, xviii
Slavonic, xv, xvi, xxx, 45, 82, 139, 157, 175, 190
Smirennikov, Aleut Spiridon, 176
Smirennikov, Ivan, xxxi, 78
Sokolov, Aleksei, 5, 16
Southern Sea, 98

Speranskii, M. M., 4
Spirkin Island, 90
Stanikovich [Staniukovich], Captain
   Lieutenant Mikhail Nikolaevich,
   61, 80
Sungurov, Grigorii Ivanovich, 16
Suvorov, Ignatii, 87
Sv. Andreian i Natalia, xxi
Sv. Ioann Ustiuzhskii, xxi
Sv. Iulian, xxi
Svin'in, Nikifor, xxiii, xxv

Tanamykta, village of, 31, 88
Theofilakt, Bishop, 14
Tigalda Island (Tigalda), xxiv, xxv,
   xxvi, xxviii, xxix, 44, 76, 77, 103,
   130, 131, 140, 145, 176
Tigalda, village of, 130
Tlingits, xiv. *See also* Kolosh(i)
Tobol'sk, xix, xxii
Triest, 23
Tukulan Aiugnin, toion, xxiii
Tulik, village of, 31, 33, 36, 88, 122,
   124, 158, 159, 192, 193
Tungus (Evenks), xxxii

Ugamak Island, 76, 83, 103, 145
Umnak Island, xiv, xxiv, xxix, 27, 31,
   86, 158
Umnak Pass (Strait), 31, 122, 124,
   158
Umnak, xx, xxi, xxii, xxiii, xxvi, 59,
   75, 79, 87, 122, 123, 127, 192
Unalaska Bay (Captain's Harbor), 28,
   89, 107, 124
Unalaska Island, xiv xvii, xviii, xix,
   xxv, 49
Unalaska, ix, xiii, xiv, xv, xvi, xvii,
   xviii, xix, xx, xxi, xxiii, xxiv, xxv,
   xxvi, xxvii, xxviii, xxix, xxxi,
   xxxii, 3, 17, 32, 38, 49, 55, 56, 59,
   60, 75, 79, 81, 85, 86, 87, 88, 89,
   90, 91, 99, 101, 104, 110, 111,
   114, 124, 125, 131, 144, 146, 147,
   160, 164, 165, 179, 180, 183, 193,
   194, 195, 198, 199, 202, 209, 211.
   See also Harbor Village
Unalaskan Aleut, xx, xxx, 3, 4
Unalaskan Aleut-Russian dictionary,
   xxx
Unalga Island (Unalga), 75, 90, 114,
   146, 150
Unalga Pass (Strait), 49, 90, 98, 114,
   130, 131,140, 146
Unalga, village of , 90, 150
Unga (Grekodeliarovskii), xiv, 49,
   51, 53, 54, 55, 59, 60, 62, 82, 98,
   103, 105, 139, 143, 144, 146, 178,
   179
Unga Aleuts, 52
Unga Island, xiv, xxv, 49, 54, 55, 98,
   143
Unimak Island (Unimak), xxiii, xxiv,
   43, 75, 100, 101, 102, 103, 105,
   140, 141, 145, 148, 176, 177, 180
Unimak Pass (Strait), 103, 140, 145,
   176
University of Alaska Fairbanks, xiii
Urup, 181, 183

Vasil'ev/Shishmarev expedition, xviii
Veniaminov, Ioann (Ivan), vii, ix,
   xiii-xxxi, 3, 16, 17, 36, 38, 49, 56,
   81, 85, 104, 125, 147, 165, 183,
   184, 187, 198, 208, 209, 211
Veniaminov, Stefan, 28, 82
Veniaminova, Ekaterina, 16
Veselovskoe, village of, 28-29, 193
Vesovskoe [Veselovskoe?], 33
Voltaire, x, 11
Vsevidof Island. *See* Sevidovskii
   Island

Wrangel, Baron Ferdinand Petrovich, 149, 161, 198, 208

Yakutia, xxxii
Yakuts, xxxii
Yup'ik history, xiv
Yukaghirs, xxxii

Yukon River, xv, xx
Yupiit, xiv

Zavalishin, Dmitrii Irinarkovich, 16
Zimmerman, 13
Zollikofer, Georg Joachim, 15, 71